ROAD TO MANASSAS

ROAD TO MANASSAS

*The Growth of Union Command
in the Eastern Theatre from the
Fall of Fort Sumter to the
First Battle of Bull Run*

by

R. H. BEATIE, JR.

COOPER SQUARE

Publishers, Inc.

1961

To

M. E.

for

courage through adversity

FOREWORD

LACK OF PREPAREDNESS for war was a United States tradition in the nineteenth century. Without the military background of the formidable continental powers, this nation stubbornly refused to maintain a large, efficient armed force during peacetime. When conflict occurred, the government paid a stiff price for this attitude and was forced to create a military machine almost from the ground up.

In this volume, R. H. Beatie, Jr., one of the youngest of the Civil War writers, shows the effect of this policy on the Union forces during the early days of the struggle which raged from 1861 to 1865. The author tells in detail of the period between the fall of Fort Sumter and the First Battle of Bull Run. The book falls into three divisions: the first, describing command and recruiting problems, along with personality sketches, at the war's beginning; the second, setting down a careful study of the first Bull Run, seen through Northern eyes; the third, analyzing the battle and relating its result to the potentialities and actions of Union leaders.

Strategy and tactics during these first, crucial days are carefully treated. Winfield Scott's plans, Robert Patterson's misadventure in the Shenandoah Valley, and the ultimate rout of Irvin McDowell's forces make up the bulk of the book. Samuel Heintzelman, David Hunter, Daniel Tyler, Dixon Miles, Erasmus Keyes, Ambrose Burnside, Israel Richardson and other major leaders have their day in court.

Mr. Beatie has used the official sources well, and gone far beyond them to state accounts, regimental histories and manuscripts for colorful detail. His critical bibliography presents scholars with a helpful list of source materials on this important period.

Personal visits to the battlefield have given the author a good sense of the ground involved in the first big battle of the Civil War. Mr. Beatie's maps have the rough clarity of those done by commanders on the actual field of conflict. Excellent pictures of important leaders bring personal warmth to this account.

Strong opinions concerning the qualities of the Northern officers give Mr. Beatie's book vigor. Personal opinions, of course, make battles. They also help create an interesting book.

May 2, 1961   John S. Blay

TABLE OF CONTENTS

LIST OF ILLUSTRATIONS

Chapter 1

THE BASIS OF COMMAND

THE HISTORY of the United States from colonial times has been intermittently dotted with major and minor wars. Yet throughout this period, even when weapons changed and in turn altered methods, there is one thread which runs unbroken as the connecting link of all American conflicts: not once has the country been ready to go to war in any true sense of the word. In fact, most cases are characterized by a frantic build-up from nothing; unpreparedness has often bred a fear of being overrun at the outset. The Civil War is no exception.

At the fall of Fort Sumter in Charleston Harbor, the regular army of the country was the only organized, disciplined and equipped force in existence which could defend the Union; but its size and characteristics absolutely denied the possibility of using it alone to carry on the war. On April 14, 1861, the date Major Robert Anderson surrendered Sumter, there were less than 17,000 men in the army of whom only 600 were officers. Nearly half of these officers holding active commissions resigned to take up service with their states including most of the

1

higher ranking and more promising men like Robert E. Lee and Joseph E. Johnston.[1]

Many of the northern graduates of West Point in the years prior to 1861 had served their required terms in the army, then resigned their commissions to seek better opportunities in civilian life[2] so that most of the older and more experienced of them had been out of touch with military service for some time. In addition, the shortage of officers was complicated by imbalance. The artillery far surpassed both infantry and cavalry in numbers, and even those men who served in the latter two arms had undergone instruction in the use of artillery.[3]

It was obvious that more troops and officers would be needed and would have to be recruited from the civilian population. The regulars could be used in two ways with new troops: they could be kept as a military whole, compact within themselves, better disciplined than the raw recruits, and more reliable in the heat of combat. Used in this manner they would form a force somewhat comparable to Napoleon's Imperial Guard, which could brace up any part of the line that sagged or be given the pivotal point in an assault. The most difficult tasks would fall to these experienced and hardened campaigners while the remainder of the army filled out the lines about them. This was the type of army used by General Washington during the Revolution with the continentals forming a small but solid basis and the militia serving as fillers. The Mexican War was also fought in this manner, volunteers and regulars being completely divorced in organization.

As a second alternative, the regular army troops could have been used as a cadre for volunteers, being broken up and interspersed among them in order to spread proper knowledge and attitude throughout the army. The best example of such a system is the German Army of 1920 to 1935. Under the influence of von Seeckt, the guiding philosophy was that the 100,000 man Reichswehr would be corporals; corporals, sergeants; lieutenants, captains; and so on right up to the top. Every man was expected to be able to perform the duties of the next two ranks ahead of him. It was with this system that Hitler built an army by 1940 which equaled General Staff estimates of 1945. The success of the system is more than proven by the German successes in the early years of the war.[4]

The United States Army was not trained with this idea in mind as was the German Reichswehr, but such a capability is inherent in any regular army. The problem of this alternative lay in the military precedents of the country. The civil-soldier was the democratic ideal even before the time of the minute man; such troops prefer to be led by civil officers who spring from the same general background. It was only natural, therefore, that the idea of breaking up the active regular army to form the leadership of the new army should meet with widespread hostility. While all West Point graduates whose sympathies lay with union were potential leaders, especially those who held active commissions at the outbreak, the problems of tapping this source were great both inside and outside. From the point of view of a civilian enlisting in a unit, the presence of an officer known personally by the recruit was far more reassuring than that of a stereotyped, stiff-backed, imperious career soldier.[5] The regular officers themselves

resisted the breakup of proven units; and the driving of
company grade officers[6] toward higher ranks in the volunteers was resisted by older officers in the fear that it
would cause a great dearth of men capable of instructing
and indoctrinating new platoons or companies.[7] These
factors and the grass roots militia system then, united to
suppress any desire to disperse the cadre. Many officers,
too, did not want to lead volunteers because of experiences with them in Mexico which reflected their unmili-
tary attitude. To them, the basis of all organizations for
war was discipline, a quantity generally lacking in militia units.[8] It was clear that the basis of any army to put
down the rebellion would have to be the volunteers—
both enlisted man and officer. On April 15, the day after
Anderson surrendered Sumter, President Abraham Lincoln issued a call for 75,000 volunteers for three months
assigning quotas to the various states.[9] The governors in
turn summoned their militia organizations to supply the
necessary men.

The standard organization of militia units prior to
the outbreak would have warmed the heart of any good
democrat. All company, field, and non-commissioned
officers were elected by their men and could be turned
out of office if found undesirable. Approval for their
commissioning had to be granted by the governor of
the state who had the final appointive power over everything from corporal to major general. Officers could be
appointed who had no troops.[10] Attitudes toward militia service ranged from revulsion against any standing
military organization, through ridicule of the inefficiency which characterized all militia units, to enjoy-
ment of the great social and entertainment vistas which

opened every time a "drill meeting" was held.[11] With
the spirit and the officers such as they were, it goes without saying that discipline was a word little considered,
less heard, and seldom used.

The condition of the state militias varied from excellent to extinct. The Massachusetts adjutant general had
foreseen the possibility of war at the end of 1860 so he
began at once to prepare for action. During the first
two months of 1861 there ensued a series of legislative
acts which reorganized, enlarged, and made more efficient the military system of the state. All those in the
service were required to register at their HQ, and all
organizations were ordered to recruit to full strength.
Then the governor called for all those who could re-
spond in time of danger to register. Those who could
not were discharged at once and their places filled by
others who could. In the meantime clothing, arms, and
equipment were gathered for distribution while extensive and thorough drilling was begun in January and
continued incessantly. When Lincoln's telegram for
troops was received by Governor Andrew on the fifteenth, four regiments were paraded in Boston the next
day to be mustered into the service of the United States
government.[12]

In the state of Minnesota, General Order No. 2 of
October 1, 1858 gave the citizens the legal right to
organize, drill and even outfit themselves at their own
expense. Yet this militia, as it was designated, was not
mandatory; and in fact, it existed less than in any other
state. When the guns ceased firing at Charleston, there
were on the rolls 200 privates and 147 officers of all
grades. It required a hasty legislative act to enable the

state to accept the many volunteers who sprang forward in answer to the call for troops.[13]

These two states epitomize the extremes of preparedness;[14] the majority of other states lay somewhere in between and are easily characterized by the state of Pennsylvania. A few far-sighted members of its militia had built up well-disciplined and well-equipped outfits in the early months of 1861 like the Ringgold Light Artillery which was ready to march on April 16, but the major portion of the state forces were under strength and unorganized when the call went out.[15] The most important thing to realize is not that the militia of the majority of states were defunct or inactive but that they provided an excellent framework of both officers and men, particularly the former, which needed nothing more than a good impetus to fill them up completely. The fall of Sumter was just such an impetus.

The company had been the basic unit of drill and meeting; it therefore served as the basic unit for recruiting. The fever which pervaded the North in the early days after Sumter made men want to enlist as soon as possible. In fact, so great was the desire to enlist that many men who found they were unable to enter the military because the state quota was filled went to other states to take up arms. Not a few even bought their way into the "better companies," and service as a private often sold for as much as fifty dollars in many places. In a matter of a few days the quota of 75,000 had been far oversubscribed, and many still sought military service in vain.[16] In those states where the militia officers were not productive or numerous enough to fill their quotas, the governors issued authorizations to capable, trustworthy citizens of influence to raise infantry companies to be regimented by the state. These men were generally accepted by their company and elected commander. The company officers then elected the regimental commander and the field grade officers. In almost all cases, however, the effort was made to secure qualified men as officers, both by the governors in granting authorizations and by the company commanders in electing their colonels.[17] Many men of considerable prominence and influence refused to accept high commissions because they did not feel that they were qualified. Others wished to start in lower officer positions and work upward if they could.[18] The government offered yet another way to enter its service, this time bypassing the state. Simon Cameron, the Secretary of War, issued a number of authorizations for the direct enlistment of regiments. The men who recruited these regiments could do so in any state, then report direct to the federal government to be equipped, armed and mustered into service.[19]

With the 75,000 man quota filled and the federal government refusing to accept any more regiments, the states had to make a decision on the surplus regiments. New York, for example, was given a quota of seventeen regiments totaling some 13,000 men; but a few days produced thirty-eight regiments fully subscribed and eager to go. It was up to the state to keep these regiments and supply them while they hung in abeyance. The only alternatives to this were disbanding or private support. Faced with a choice of the two, the regiments always found some person or town willing to keep them housed and fed till they were called to be mustered.

In the case of New York a special representative of the
adjutant general traveled to Washington to discuss the
problem and "with some difficulty" managed to get
all the extras accepted. Andrew G. Curtin, Governor
of Pennsylvania, gradually accepted all units recruited
within his borders because he was sure they would be
needed in the very near future. A loan was subscribed
throughout the state to support this effort; and with the
encouragement which Curtin personally extended, recruiting quickly brought a large force into the service
of his state.[20]

It soon became evident that the war would last more
than the three months for which these first regiments had
been enlisted; and as April gave way to May, Lieutenant General Winfield Scott at last persuaded Lincoln
to summon troops for three years and to expand the
regular army.[21] The presidential proclamation which
was issued on the third of May called for 42,034 volunteers to serve for three years or the duration of the war
should it be shorter and 22,714 more regular troops[22]
for the standing army.[23]

This call for a longer term of service in no way dimin-
ished the enthusiasm of the populace for enlisting, and
it provided a place for the regiments already formed
but unaccepted. Many of the three-month regiments
merely took polls of their men, and those who could
not or would not enlist for three years were summarily
discharged, their places being filled by others.[24]

Meanwhile, the organization of higher commands in
the military began to run haywire. Since they had the
right to appoint general officers, the states began to brigade their regiments and appoint commanding officers

for them and the divisions which they formed. In the long run this would mean that the federal government controlled the commanding officers of the regular units and of the army as a whole. Of volunteer brigades, only those which were mixed—formed of regiments whose states did not have enough at one time to brigade them, leaving the federal government to do it—would have general officers appointed by Washington. There was much to be said against this system. Promotion of inter-state rivalry within the army would hardly be good for morale, discipline, or further recruiting; and there could never be a unified war effort if command responsibility were not centralized. With brigade and divisional officers responsible to their respective states there would be in practical, if not theoretical existence, many Secretaries of War. Officers would be responsible to the general in command of their army—and so indirectly to Lincoln's government—but they would also be answerable to their state governments. Any diversions of policy whether military or civil could result in unnecessary and certainly unwanted strife. One of the first and most necessary principles of command is centralization, which should be done at the highest headquarters possible. Under the existing system, however, with the overlapping of authority, such a principle, necessary though it may have been, was impossible.

It was to rectify this situation that the office of the adjutant general in Washington issued General Orders, No. 12 on May 22. Henceforth, all things pertaining to the organization of a regiment were standardized, from the number of officers and men to pay allotments per person. The governor of the state was authorized—

indeed, ordered—to appoint *all* officers from colonel to
lieutenant and the non-commissioned officers would be
appointed by the colonel on the recommendation of the
company captain. All brigade and divisional officers,
whether staff or line,[25] would be "Appointed by the
President, by and with the consent of the Senate."

Governor Edwin D. Morgan of New York was
highly incensed at this turn of events. The Secretary
of War had promised him he could set up two divisions
to be led by John A. Dix and James S. Wadsworth; but,
with the new orders in effect, brigading and divisioning
of the regiments plus the appointing of their commanding officers were out of his control. He decided to hold
out against the order in hopes that his desires could be
realized. The government, however, held the reins
tightly in its grasp. Cameron merely notified Morgan
that, if he refused to accept the decree, no more New
York troops would be accepted. Capitulation was necessary and hasty.[26]

State interference was removed by unilaterally stating that "the volunteers will be subject to the laws and
regulations governing the army of the United States."[27]
A unified, standardized and centralized command system had thus been set up and the major kinks removed
after little more than a month. Regiments poured into
the capital and other key cities in droves, and the armies
which would soon be called upon to defend union
against secession began to take shape. Congress did not
meet until the third of July in the special session announced by Lincoln in his call for 75,000 volunteers. It
answered the rather peremptory executive acts of the
President by authorizing on the following day a call for

500,000 troops to serve three years.[28] The basic unit of the state militias had been the company, many of which had their own names, uniforms, weapons, and social status. Regimental camps or drills were seldom held before the war. As a result, regimental evolutions and duties were unknown to almost all troops. The basic recruiting unit for volunteers and other units which did not spring from a skeletal militia existence was also the company. Governors rarely if ever gave men permission to recruit a regiment in the early months of the war; men applied and were granted permission to recruit a company. From these officers a regimental commanding officer was chosen or else, as in many cases, some other person of known military capacity was requested to head the regiment. At first these units varied in size from fifty to two hundred but the General Order of May 22 which standardized all incoming organizations denied admittance to any which had less than ten or more than 100 men on their active rolls. As all units had some raw recruits in them, some being completely composed in this manner, it was necessary to teach basic fundamentals from the bottom up. The company, as the most cohesive and easily manageable number of men, fell heir to this task when it was in its independent status; but more important, it continued to do so after it had been regimented. As a result, the unitary, coordinated feeling which characterized brigades, and even divisions, in a few months did not exist at the regimental level when Major General Robert Patterson and particularly Brigadier General Irvin McDowell set out to meet the enemy.

Tacit recognition of the company's semi-independ-

ence was given by the governors of most states who
allowed them to choose their own fellow units. Thus
there were companies which refused membership in a
regiment because it was not composed of units from
their area of the state, because they did not like the attitude of certain other units, or because of any number
of petty grievances, real and fancied.[29] To make the
situation more pronounced, there was a great deal of
ethnic enlisting. Irish, Scotch, and German companies
sprang up seeking regimentation with others of their
own nationality.[30]

The importance of this characteristic became more
evident as the time for battle drew nearer. Regimental
drill was still trying to establish the necessary coordination, leaving little or no time for other exercise. The men,
accustomed to one attitude and directive influence, had
to dilute it and become accustomed to another. Their
command relationship was reoriented, then, while they
were still trying to learn the art of soldiering, from boil-
ing coffee and eating hardtack without cracking the
teeth to marching and firing the rifle. Their accomplishment in this change left much to be desired when they
set out for combat.

Therefore, as a carryover from the militias and because any town or region could produce a company
when it could not always recruit the 800 to 1,000 men
necessary for a regiment, the company provided the
basis for recruiting. Many company officers had originally been in the militia and some had even seen service
in Mexico. Recruiters of independent new companies
were not political appointees, grafters, and friends of
the state governments who were given commissions be-

cause of the necessities caused by war. Rather, it seems that those who were allowed to raise units in the early months of the war, sought that honor with eagerness and in great number. It appears that they also were chosen because they were responsible, leading citizens and that the governors tried to be as impartial in their choice as they possibly could. The quality of leadership at the company level was, as a result, the best that could possibly be attained according to the facts then known. Without the acid test of battle it was really impossible to tell who would make a good leader and who would not; but using those qualities which appeared necessary as criteria for judgment, the people who chose the company officers, from selecting governor to electing militia, must generally be credited with a considerable amount of success. Many men who entered the scene as lieutenants and captains when war broke out exited at the heads of regiments, brigades, and even divisions in April of 1865.

While all this was in progress the government was in search of large-unit officers for the new armies, and a plan to carry on the war. Large numbers of both appeared in variegated degrees of acceptability and usefulness.

Chapter II

THE FEDERAL GOVERNMENT
ORGANIZES FOR WAR

AT THE OUTSET of war the position of Washington was precarious, to say the least. Deep in the heart of secession-prone territory, the national capital was surrounded on all sides by states which could just as easily secede as not. Virginia, just across the Potomac River and within easy shelling distance, had joined the camp of the Rebellion; and it seemed as if Maryland, despite her loyal governor, Thomas Hicks, would follow shortly, placing the nerve center of Union within the outermost lines of Confederacy.[1] It was imperative that Maryland, the crucial state which surrounded the capital on her three land borders, be held in the Union by any means necessary.

President Lincoln and General Scott saw this with equal clarity. Their first decisions were made for the protection and preservation of the capital not only by garrisoning and fortifying it but also by keeping the secessionists in Maryland suppressed. Under the leadership of General Scott the accomplishment of these aims was begun at once.

Winfield Scott was a Virginian of great military standing. When Abraham Lincoln became President, old "Fuss and Feathers" was far advanced in age and far beyond the physical fitness required for an active military campaign; yet his decision to remain loyal was one of the most important factors in the first two months of war. He was the only man capable of handling with efficiency the great problems of organization and command which immediately arose. Beginning early in life as a lawyer, young Scott had found practice slow and fraught with difficulties. The outrage of the *Chesapeake-Leopard* affair drove him into the Virginia militia as a lance corporal in command of a squad of volunteer Virginia cavalry. With the increase of martial fervor, so also did the size of the United States regular army increase and with it the rank of young Scott who succeeded in transferring from state militia to national forces. By the end of the War of 1812, Scott was a brigadier general in the regular army with a brevet for major general and a national hero throughout the country. The reduction of the regular army after the war in which five of every six officers were released found him still with his commission in command of a military department. In 1832 he had first-hand contact with secessionist sentiment when President Andrew Jackson sent him to take command in South Carolina. While there he handled the Nullifiers with a finesse and aplomb which "did much to preserve peace in a time of crises." Service against the Seminoles, Creeks and Cherokees followed. By 1841 he had succeeded the deceased Alexander Macomb as General in Chief of the Army with headquarters in Washington, his administration at once being marked by excellence and innovation.

When war with Mexico broke out Scott, now almost sixty, had first to overcome the political fears which his popularity instilled in the Democratic administration of James K. Polk before he took the field. His miraculous campaign into the Valley of Mexico resulting in the capture of Mexico City was accomplished in spite of home obstructions far surpassing any which the Mexicans could present. The attempts of the Democrats in power to discredit him and bring him to trial were foiled by the tremendous popular reception he received when he arrived home. He continued in the service of his country as General in Chief until Sumter fell in 1861—except for a brief sojourn in politics as a most unsuccessful Whig candidate for president in 1852. In the year before the war, he sought to have the United States forts and arsenals in the South reinforced to prevent seizure; but the ineffectual James Buchanan was President of the country and the disloyal John B. Floyd[2] was Secretary of War.

In his prime, Scott measured six feet five inches, weighed 230 pounds, and had the strength of an ox; but in his old age, though he remained massive and militant, gout plagued him so badly that he could not sit a horse and was unable to walk without difficulty. His bad eyesight and great idiosyncrasies only served to emphasize the fact that, when Sumter fell, he was seventy-four years old. Annoyingly demanding in respect to personal appearance and proper decorum, he was irritable in general, particularly when his aims were frustrated, his orders countermanded, or his desires bypassed. It was his plan to lead the main army in the field as he had so many times before, but such an eventuality was out of the question. In spite of all this, his ability in military affairs, in reaching the maximum goal with the minimum harshness, and in proven initiative and self-reliance made him the greatest Union asset at the outbreak.[3]

Scott set to work at once to save the capital from falling into the hands of the Confederates. Troops were needed immediately and an organization had to be set up. On April 16, the Governor of Pennsylvania had commissioned Robert Patterson Major General of Militia. When Scott heard this, he remembered the long personal friendship he and Patterson had enjoyed.

Not a native American, Patterson was born in Ireland to a family of Irish revolutionaries. In 1798, when Robert was six years old his father was sentenced to banishment for taking part in the Irish Rebellion of that year. Arriving in the United States, the family settled in Pennsylvania where young Patterson began his education in the public schools. At fifteen he entered a counting house in Philadelphia, but his incipient business career was interrupted by the War of 1812 in which he served as a lieutenant colonel, and colonel of the 2nd Regiment, Pennsylvania Militia. His commission in the regular army had risen to that of a captain when he was mustered out in June of 1815. Returning at the end of the war to a life of business, he remained in the state militia and by 1824 reached the rank of major general. In the meantime, he began to amass a sizeable personal fortune and an excellent public reputation. When the Mexican War broke out, he was commissioned a major general of volunteers to serve with Gen-

eral Scott's column; and as a well known Democrat, he
had even been considered by President Polk for command of the column before it was finally given to Scott.
At the battle of Cerro Gordo he was lifted from sickbed
to horse in order that he might lead his division into
battle, then led the pursuit to and the capture of Jalapa.
As General Scott's second in command, he fell into a
great friendship which continued after the war ended.
It was only natural, therefore, that Scott should have
Patterson, a tried and proven subordinate with combat
experience, appointed major general of volunteers in
the service of the United States Government in 1861.[4]

Accordingly, on April 19, Patterson's commission was
transferred from the Pennsylvania militia to the United
States Volunteers to serve three months.[5] General Orders, No. 3, published over Scott's signature, established
and placed him in command of the Military Department
of Washington. Under his jurisdiction now were the
entire states of Delaware, Pennsylvania, and Maryland,
plus the District of Columbia.[6] He gave up his large business at once to organize the many regiments and companies now beginning to pour into Philadelphia.[7]

That same day Fitz-John Porter, a promising graduate of the West Point Class of 1845,[8] started for Pennsylvania with orders for 5,000 stands of arms from the
Harrisburg Arsenal to be released for these new troops;
for Patterson was feeling the pinch of supplies that
plagued all commanders in the first months of the war.
He did not receive the authorization for arms until Porter arrived from Washington, and none of the arsenals
would release any material without specific federal orders, nor would the supply houses at Frankford and

WINFIELD SCOTT

ROBERT PATTERSON

Grady's Ferry do otherwise. The troops had no blankets, clothing, or cooking utensils, and very few had weapons.[9]

Of primary importance was the reinforcing of Washington and the clearing of a land route to the capital through secessionist Maryland. Scott wished the roads held which ran from Harrisburg to Wilmington and Baltimore, and from these to Washington, but Patterson notified him the day after his commissioning in the federal service that he did not have enough troops to clear them and keep up the necessary patrolling. Use of the railroads was out of the question because the Baltimore and Ohio, which controlled the only line to Washington, declined to allow the transportation of troops over what was left of its track and trestles. A study of the map revealed to Patterson that the best way to reach Washington from the northern states would be to rendezvous at Philadelphia, then entrain for Havre de Grace. There, a ship voyage could set out into Chesapeake Bay. Rather than sail around to the Potomac which would be thoroughly covered by Confederate guns, the ships would move down the bay to Annapolis, where the troops could disembark and march across to Washington. While units were entering the capital in this fashion, Patterson could build up an army and press toward Baltimore to open the land routes to Washington. The railway which crossed the peninsula between Annapolis and the capital would have to be seized and its sabotage repaired; but this would not be difficult, he was sure, as the distance was not great.

Scott approved the plan at once and ordered it put into effect as soon as possible with the hope that the roads

to Washington would shortly be clear.[10] But Patterson
began from the first moment to encounter difficulties
which he felt made it impossible to set out on his part
of the task, the opening of the land route. All the regiments which could be equipped, he complained, were
being sent posthaste to Scott, leaving none for the job
in Pennsylvania. The arms which his men received were
inferior and the cartridges did not fit them; the artillery
available amounted to one battery, hardly enough to
deal with a determined defense; the garrisoning of important fortresses in Pennsylvania added to the deple-
tion of his small forces.

Patterson greatly respected the advice and opinions
of his adjutant, Fitz-John Porter. Ahead of this young
officer was a varied, strange, and semi-tragic career filled
with unanswerable questions, but which reached its peak
when he assumed command of the newly formed Fifth
Corps in Major General George B. McClellan's Penin-
sular Campaign. It is difficult to deny that Porter later
became a fine administrator and an excellent combat
officer, but in his months under Patterson, he resisted
aggressive action at every opportunity.

Patterson had never held an independent command in
the face of an aggressive enemy. He had taken over Scott's
army in the Valley of Mexico for a brief time when the
government had relieved him but this was after the
Mexicans had been thoroughly vanquished.[11] There was
a great difference between being a good subordinate and
good independent commander. In the former position
the next higher authority was always close by if not
within hailing distance. Decisions did not arise beyond
the realm of tactics and lesser administration, but the

officer in command of an army in the field had to be able to make the major decisions which involve his units after knowing the general desires of his superiors. The impossibility of directing an army from a place far in the rear was illustrated by the disastrous attempts of Lincoln and War Secretary Edwin M. Stanton to trap Major General Thomas J. Jackson in the Valley during 1862. The good commander knows when to attack aggressively as well as when to fall back defensively. Patterson, who had fallen heir to the mammoth tasks ahead more by accident and default than by merit, had none of the necessary characteristics to exercise independent command. He did not gather all the known information then retire to sift it through before reaching a decision. Rather, he sought his course of action in the advice of his subordinates and, more particularly, his adjutant, by way of constant daily association.[12] Added to his personal lack of aggressiveness when faced with independent decision, this made an unbeatable combination for inaction, especially when the defensive attitude of Fitz-John Porter is included.

In the meantime, Patterson began the long laborious task of building up his own army. He had several regular units as a basis and a number of volunteer three-month units, but he felt that the term of enlistment for the new troops should be longer than three months. An application to that effect was submitted to Governor Curtin, plus a recommendation that 25 more regiments be enlisted by the state. All chances for having a disciplined and organized force available for long-term service disappeared, however, when the government refused Pennsylvania's request for an extension of its quota.[13]

In his service as a volunteer aide, Patterson had Senator
John Sherman of Ohio; so on April 27 he sent him to
Washington in the hopes that some personal influence
might be exerted in favor of his requests.[14]

The fact that Patterson suffered from geographic my-
opia was recognized, whether inadvertently or inten-
tionally, that same day. His department was broken up
into three departments by General Orders, No. 12. The
inability to see beyond the area that directly confronted
him was another fault which plagued Patterson from the
day he assumed command, and it was an excellent move
by Scott which removed from his control those areas
with which he was personally incapable of dealing. Under his command remained Pennsylvania, Delaware and
the northern part of Maryland. The newly created Military Department of Washington included the District of
Columbia and a portion of Maryland north of the capital,
under Colonel Joseph K. F. Mansfield; and the Department of Annapolis, under Brigadier General Benjamin
Butler of Massachusetts, covered the area about the
route between that city and the capital.[15]

Relieved of the large area beyond his own direction,
Patterson could concentrate completely on Pennsylvania problems. Despite the fact that the government
had refused his request for a larger troop quota, Governor Curtin grew more and more certain that additional regiments would be needed shortly. There were
many units in existence which had not been accepted
in the first call; and they were the ones which answered
the new legislative act for fifteen regiments of infantry
and cavalry above and beyond the federal request, which
would serve the state of Pennsylvania.[16] At last there

would be sufficient troops to begin aggressive operations.

The peculiarities which characterized the Department of Pennsylvania and its army differentiated it from all its Union counterparts during the Rebellion. The regiments which primarily composed it were recruited beyond the auspices of the federal government and thus were under the control of the state governor while its commanding officer was a United States Volunteer in the service of Lincoln's government. Because its organization was begun so early and had progressed so far, Patterson's army escaped the beneficial effects of Congressional Acts of May and continued its short-lived existence. Thus while in early days most areas had few troops, Pennsylvania had many through the foresightedness of the commanding officer and the governor. But in only seeing half as far ahead as they might have, they created a problem which was to arise later beyond all reasonable proportions: the extra troops enlisted were taken for a period of three months only. The result was that almost all three-year troops went to Washington and other places in imminent danger because Patterson had an adequate number of regiments. What would happen when the term of these three-month units, the whole of Patterson's force, expired and were discharged did not cross the mind of anyone at the time. These characteristics did not hamper the operations of June and July in any way so far as command channels between Patterson, Curtin, and Scott were concerned; nor did they create any difficulty in regard to authority; but they do account for the fact that the army in Pennsylvania was almost wholly comprised of Pennsylvania officers and three-month enlistees.

Serving as major generals under Patterson were two
native born Pennsylvanians who assumed command of
his two divisions as they began to take shape. George
Cadwalader, second in command in Pennsylvania, was
the son of a Revolutionary War general of some distinction, falling heir to a military heritage at his birth in
Philadelphia. As he was educated and raised in his birth-
place, it was only natural that he should set up his law
practice there once he had passed his bar examination.
When the Mexican War broke out, he obtained a commission as a brigadier general of volunteers, earning
a brevet for gallantry at Chapultapec. After the war
he resumed his law business, achieving a respected position in Philadelphia; and it was here that the outbreak
of war found him. The governor at once made him a
major general of Pennsylvania militia; and at the age
of 57, he entered the scene as Patterson's second in
command.[17]

When the flag of war went up over Charleston Harbor, William H. Keim[18] was one of the few men who
was ready. Educated at Mount Airy Military Academy,
Keim entered politics as a Democrat and in 1848 was
elected mayor of Reading, Pa., his home town. Following that he was elected to a vacancy in Congress during
the tempestuous fifties. By January of 1861 he was
certain that war was inevitable. Rather than wait
placidly for what he considered ultimate, he began to
drill the Ringgold Light Artillery, readying it for combat. Equipment, supplies, personnel, all were soon in complete readiness, as was Keim himself. The legislative act
which made Patterson a major general in the Pennsylvania militia elevated the foresighted Keim to the same

rank. Of the three men he was far the youngest, being more than 20 years younger than his 69-year-old commanding officer.[19]

By April 28 the war was two weeks old. General Scott, realizing that Baltimore, the key to Maryland, had to be occupied, notified the necessary people of a plan he had devised for that purpose. Four columns, each of 3,000 men, would enter the state to converge on the city. From Washington, York, and Havre de Grace, three land forces would set out on the roads to travel overland while the principal effort would be placed in boats at Annapolis to sail up the Chesapeake and strike from the bay. In Washington, General Scott found upon examination that there were not enough troops to prepare his thrust and still leave the city adequately defended.[20] Patterson, however, reported the existence of 26 regiments under his command.[21] None of them were fully equipped but all were earnestly drilling and learning the art of war. In a short time, he felt, he could place 6,000 men on the road for Baltimore from each of his cities, York and Havre de Grace. The problem of railroads had been successfully overcome by militarizing them and persuading the companies to repair the destruction wrought along the line of track.[22] Though suffering from ill health, most probably aggravated by his extreme age, Patterson seemed to have succeeded in preparing himself for combat; and Scott, pleased with this information, asked him to report the time he would be ready to advance on Baltimore.[23]

Here appeared one of the traits which most characterized Patterson's actions during his period of command: the great disparity between prophecy and actuality. He

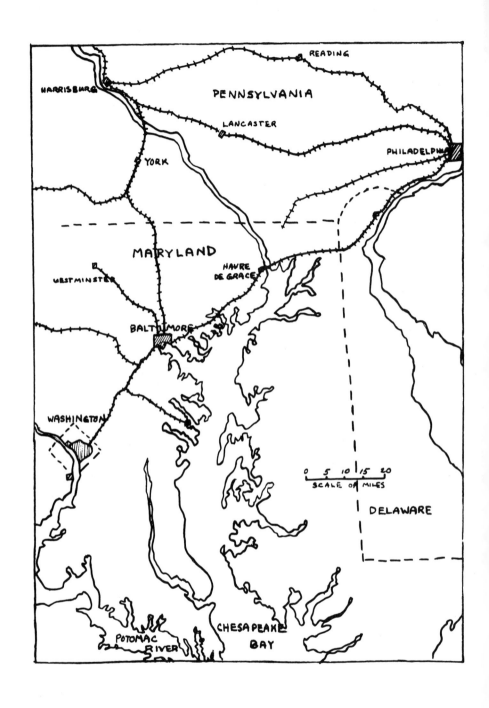

EASTERN THEATRE
April–May, 1861

had many more regiments than any other commander. His situation was far better than many because his principal area was loyal.[24] Though all these factors were evident to him and recognized by him, he managed to conjure up problems of insurmountable difficulty which blocked his way. There was always something more to be done before he could proceed with what he had said he could do; there were always some factors which seemed to stand in his way. Just a bit more time would see them cleared away, of course. Yet his inability to see any side other than the worst when faced with the actuality of action—after seeing the best side when prophesying action—ruined his effectiveness as an officer. It was upon this weakness that the association with Fitz-John Porter had its greatest effect. Such characteristics, however, do not become noticeable over such a short period of time; they merely instruct those with hindsight that they were an integral part of Patterson's personality from the outset.[25]

Over a week after the order had been issued, the two Pennsylvania columns were finally ready and under orders. With Cadwalader's division, Patterson planned to drive south from Philadelphia through Havre de Grace and on to Baltimore, while Keim, assisted by Porter, pushed his column south from York. But there were supply difficulties which had to be cleared up, rifles which had to be fixed, and other problems ad infinitum. On May 6, Patterson wrote Scott a long letter discussing all his problems, relating his plans, and promising that he would move in two days even if he were not supplied.[26] The two days passed; no large movement was made. Instead, one regiment of artillery armed as infan-

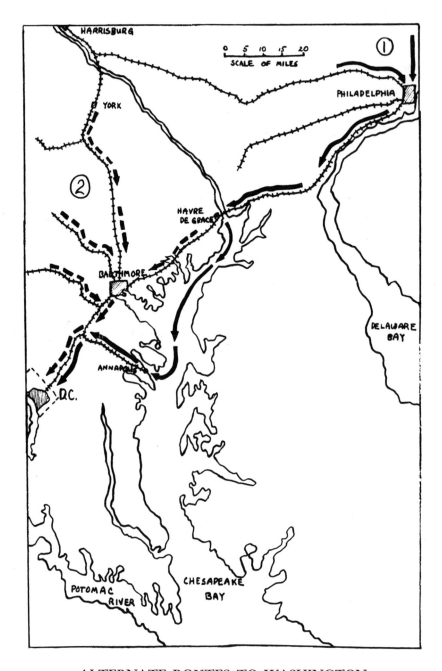

ALTERNATE ROUTES TO WASHINGTON

(1) All troops concentrate at Philadelphia, entrain to Havre de
Grace, sail to Annapolis, and by rail again to the Capitol.
(2) All troops concentrate at Baltimore and move to Washington by rail.

try, the regular battery, and the five companies of the
Third U. S. Infantry would be started toward Washington from York.[27] Porter made the necessary arrangements with the civil authorities of Baltimore to allow
the column safe passage while helping to ready the
troops. The units involved were changed. Thomas's 400
dismounted regular cavalry, a force of 3,000 volunteers
to be officered by regulars, and Sherman's old regular
battery would comprise the first attempt. But just as
the preparations neared completion a Presidential order
halted the movement before it took the road. Patterson
was to keep the troops with him and use only the sea
route to reach Washington. Days passed slowly and
nothing happened.[28] Maryland looked more and more
like a fortress.

An awkward situation was cut off in the embryo by
Benjamin Butler, who decided that the time was ripe
for the occupation of Baltimore. Fearing that General
Scott would forbid such action, Butler set out on Monday, May 13, five full days after Patterson was to have
advanced, without telling anyone. At nightfall the cov-
ering darkness, which attended the arrival of his troop
train in that city, was increased manyfold by a driving
rainstorm. Undetected, Butler pushed his drenched column up to the United States fort which overlooked the
city from a high hill, and occupied it.[29] The Commander
in Chief was not pleased to learn what had happened.
In fact, he was so displeased at the risk taken, that George
Cadwalader was ordered down from Philadelphia to
take command of Baltimore while Butler was removed
and sent to command Fortress Monroe, Va. Butler
considered this, and rightly so, a slap for his action. He

demanded approval or dismissal, not humiliation; but the government wisely avoided answering him.[30]

Although Cadwalader had permission to suspend the writ of habeas corpus, declare martial law, and exact a loyalty oath, he made efforts to mollify the populace.[31] Men caught destroying railway bridges and indulging in other acts of sabotage were turned over to civil authorities for punishment, in the hope that amicable relations could be restored.[32] Baltimore, then, the crucial focal point of secession in Maryland, had been firmly and peaceably taken by Union troops. While many of the citizens of the state were now loyal only because support for Rebel sentiment was a good distance away in Virginia, it could not be denied that the greatest crisis had passed and that the capital was now safe from immediate seizure. Yet Patterson's part in this stroke was negligible to say the least. He had exhibited traces of certain characteristics which could cause disaster at an inopportune moment if not overcome.

In the meantime, during the latter part of April and the month of May while Patterson temporized with the occupation of Baltimore, the aged Scott was directly concerned with the build-up and organization of troops in the capital itself. He and Colonel Mansfield, the commander of the Department of Washington, worked together closely to bring order out of chaos. Mansfield, a white-haired, gray-bearded, soldierly looking person, had graduated second in the West Point Class of 1822. His career had been marked with notable distinction, especially while serving as Scott's chief engineer in Mexico; and his experience in time of crisis was invaluable to the General in Chief. The friendship and esteem which these two men began in Mexico deepened considerably as they served in Washington.[33]

As the troops entered the city they were put to work immediately on the defenses. Many of the regiments were from New York and had thus been brigaded together under the command of Major General Charles Sandford, New York Militia. As an old friend and Mexican War comrade in arms, he had written to General Scott in early May asking if his services could be used in Washington. The General Orders of May 22 had not yet been published removing the power to appoint general officers from the governors, and Sandford was the quintessence of the trouble caused before its issuance. By this time Colonel Mansfield was well accustomed to his job. Many facets of its complex organization were tucked away inside his head where they were particularly unattainable by others; yet if General Sandford appeared in the city, he should by all rights supersede the present department commander. Scott solved this problem by allowing the general to assume command of all New York troops in the city, some two brigades and more, while Colonel Mansfield retained his command position because of the irreplaceability of his practical knowledge.[34]

Once Baltimore had fallen to Butler and been occupied by Cadwalader, the safety of the capital from Maryland was insured; but directly across the Potomac River from Washington was Virginia, the home of the Confederate capital and one of the seats of Confederate strength. It was necessary, if only for the safety of Washington, to gain a foothold on the west bank of the river. Without such a position future operations

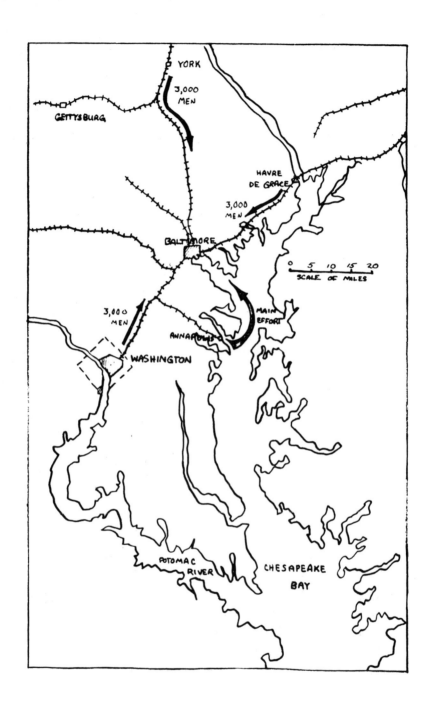

SCOTT'S PLAN
Four-pronged envelopment of Baltimore
May, 1861

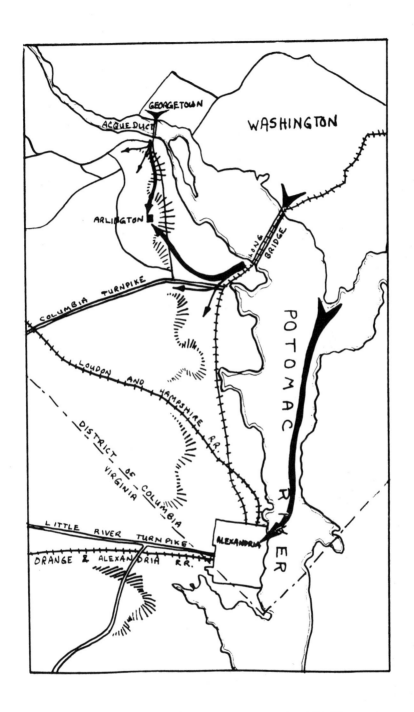

CAPTURE OF VIRGINIA SHORE UNDER
CHARLES SANDFORD
May 23-24, 1861

would be difficult or perhaps impossible. Accordingly, Scott, Mansfield, and Sandford decided on a plan to carry the Virginia shore; and Sandford was given command of the action.

On the evening of May 23, the units which were to take part began massing at their proper positions. Three columns would cross the river at the same time. The Long Bridge and the aqueduct columns, once over, would turn toward each other and converge on the Lee Mansion at Arlington, while the third force, embarked on steamers, would land at Alexandria and capture that city.[35] As dusk deepened into night the officers in command met in an old, red-brick house at the entrance to the Long Bridge to hear the final plan. The details were explained by Lieutenant Colonel S. P. Heintzelman, Assistant Inspector General of troops in Washington. He had almost finished when the rattle of a saber and the clump of boots on the stairs outside caused a pall of silence to fall over the entire room. The door opened and Mansfield entered. "Colonel Heintzelman, are you ready?" he asked. "Why don't you move, sir."

"It has not been stated who shall lead, sir."

"Why Colonel Butterfield's Twelfth Regiment, of course," was the abrupt reply as Mansfield departed.[36]

Action followed words, and at precisely 2 a.m. Butterfield's regiment[37] led the Long Bridge column across the river, while the other two started on their way, as 15,000 men set out. According to rumor, a large Confederate reinforcement had strengthened the river line that day, but the test of assault proved it false. The bridge exit was captured without opposition before the structure could be put to the torch, while the Alexandria garrison of 35 men and horses was taken quietly. Strong pickets were pushed out in all directions. Alexandria and Arlington were heavily occupied.[38] Only one event served to darken an easily successful mission. In command of a regiment of Zouaves from New York was Colonel E. E. Ellsworth. Plagued throughout his life by hard luck and failure, Ellsworth seemed to have come into his own as war drew nigh. He had begun to form companies of Zouaves which drilled and trained constantly to become excellent shots and combat troops. The nearer the war, the better he became, exhibiting his men at public functions and to paying audiences, all the while preaching preparedness and stirring the martial instincts of his viewers. At the outbreak, he recruited a regiment of New York City firemen with the aid of the fire chief and set out for the capital. He had, at last, succeeded. On May 23, just before the crossing, he wrote his family, "I am inclined to the opinion that our entrance into Virginia will be hotly contested. . . . Should that happen, my dear parents, it may be my lot to be injured in some manner. Whatever may happen, cherish the consolation that I was engaged in the performance of a sacred duty. . . ."

As his regiment entered Alexandria, he noticed atop a house a hostile flag. After giving orders for the occupation of the town he entered the house and asked the first man he met what flag it was. The reply he received was that the man was only a boarder and knew nothing about it. Ellsworth continued on up to the roof with two men and cut it down. As he came down the stairs a tenant named Jackson sprang out of the shadows with a double-barreled fowling piece. Private Francis E. Brownell, just

in front of his colonel, tried in vain to deflect the muzzle
upward as it fired. Although the private slew Jackson
instantly, it was too late. Ellsworth was dead before he
hit the floor.[39]

The next morning General Sandford and his staff
crossed over the river to inspect while the men fortified
the position. Trees were felled and built up with dirt;
trenches were dug; forts were laid out; and through it
all, the men and officers gradually began to fall into the
routine of army life. Intense heat was interspersed with
showers, teaching those regiments without tents to learn
how to live with weather.[40]

For certain reasons, General Sandford was regarded
by the government as unsatisfactory in command of the
troops in Virginia. To replace him, Scott was allowed
to choose between two men, both recently appointed
brigadier generals in the regular army: Mansfield and
McDowell.

Of Scotch-Irish descent, the McDowell family had
fled Scotland for northern Ireland because of religious
persecutions and soon left there to settle in Virginia.
From there the family again moved, this time to Ken-
tucky, and thence to Ohio where Abram McDowell,
although very often much reduced in actual fact, remained aristocratic in ancestry, spirit and thought. The
son born to him in October of 1818 was raised to have
polish and poise. In his childhood, young Irvin was
warm-hearted, affectionate and outspoken. His tutor
persuaded the family to allow him to be taken to Paris
for a year of school. This year abroad was followed by
four years at West Point where the young man was a
social standout despite his mediocre academic status at

twenty-third of forty-five graduating cadets. The total effect on his personality during these five years was one of repression. He grew more reserved and formal, albeit polished.

Upon graduation in 1838, he entered his tour of duty in the First Artillery Regiment and during the years following, held a series of staff positions. In the Mexican War where he was General John E. Wool's adjutant, he won a brevet to captain for services rendered at the Battle of Buena Vista. At the close of the war, he continued his staff positions. At the outbreak of the Civil War, he was a major on duty in Washington. General Scott had known him since his graduation and thought very highly of him so it was only natural that during the first crucial weeks McDowell should become acquainted with the inner circles of the government through Scott.

Working as an assistant adjutant general in the defenses during April, the major by his energy and intelligence began to attract the attention of important people. It was his thorough belief that there could be no reconciliation with the South and that the rebellion should be put down vigorously, views held by many of those in decision-making positions. It was in this way that McDowell met his first real backer, Salmon P. Chase. As Secretary of Treasury, Chase held great sway over the early military efforts of the war, even earning himself the epithet "General." An ex-governor of Ohio, Chase remembered young McDowell as an Ohioan in the regular army; and he early sought him out to obtain advice on all questions of military organization. The Secretary was highly impressed with the intelligence and ease of the major, determining that he should be promoted

early to a high position. In addition to the support from
this powerful source, McDowell found himself under
the aegis of Governor William Dennison of Ohio, to
whom he was related by marriage. Although home pressure forced the governor to appoint George B. McClellan to command of all Ohio troops, Dennison had
seriously considered McDowell for the post even offering it to him at one point.

With this backing plus that of Simon Cameron, the
Secretary of War, who had also seen him in action, Mc-
Dowell was assured of a sizeable promotion if the regular
army was expanded. The presidential call for 22,000
more regulars in early May provided just the opportunity. The cabinet was called to discuss the appointment
of three new major generals and several additional brigadier generals. Chase sent the major a note at the War
Department telling him to report to the White House as
soon as possible. When he arrived there, McDowell
found the meeting had already begun so he sent up his
card to notify the Secretary of his presence. In a few
moments Chase came down the stairs. After informing
him what the meeting was about, Chase stated that he
was about to propose him as one of the three major generals. McDowell was taken aback. He demurred saying
that such rapid promotion would cause jealousy among
others who were bypassed. Anyway, he had never expected to progress beyond the rank of colonel during
his military career. A brigadier generalship would be
fine. He suggested, however, that McClellan, Henry W.
Halleck, and John C. Frémont would make excellent
major generals should they be appointed. Chase acquiesced and returned to the meeting.

The subsequent promotion of McDowell to brigadier general encountered its first opposition in the massive form of General Winfield Scott. Expressing the opinion of many army men in regard to the rapid promotion of junior officers, the General in Chief, despite his liking for McDowell, was annoyed that his advice was overlooked. He was also nettled by the fact that Major Mc-Dowell, West Point Class of '38, should be suggested for promotion to brigadier general when Colonel Mansfield, West Point Class of '22 was not. Very definitely favoring the latter, Scott demanded that Mansfield be promoted to rank from the same day, May 14.[41] In this way the earlier commission would determine seniority. Whereas McDowell could only point back to a major's rank, Mansfield would show that he had been a full colonel and was thus superior.

When Scott was ordered to replace General Sandford, an old, personal friend and an esteemed officer, he was given only two men to choose between: Mansfield and McDowell.

For the same reason that he could not earlier allow General Sandford to exercise his proper rank in Washington, the old general was forced to give the command to McDowell, in spite of the fact that he was opposed to it. Scott was irate that his judgment was passed over while Mansfield was annoyed because he had to remain in the Washington defenses without a chance to win a battle.[42]

At this point in his life McDowell was six feet tall with a deep-chested, powerful build. His personal relations with friends were excellent for he was a fluent, entertaining conversationalist; but in military relations he was formal and reserved, always methodical and careful, and a strict disciplinarian. He was not a man who stirred great devotion among his subordinates, a fact which was aggravated at times by his distinct hatred for newspapermen. His personal habits were abstemious and puritanical: he drank no alcohol in any form, in fact, he did not even take tea or coffee; he never played cards; the only licenses he allowed himself was his monstrous appetite which included the ability to eat whole watermelons at one sitting. It is also to be noted that in regard to experience McDowell had seen combat but had never in his military career held any position other than that of a staff officer. Now he was to hold the overall command of an entire army. On May 27, General Orders, No. 26, set up an unnamed department to include all of Virginia east of the Alleghanies and north of the James River "under the command of Brigadier-General Irvin McDowell, U. S. A."; and late that afternoon he crossed the river to take over.[43]

Reaching Arlington, the new commander sought out General Sandford to get a statement of affairs. As it was late in the day, he decided against assuming command until the next morning. After spending the night with the New Jersey brigade he rose early next morning and at five o'clock began an inspection of the entire position. After four full days in Virginia, the troops had not yet built up suitable fortifications about Alexandria; but those at the approaches to the Long Bridge, the ferry, and the aqueduct were progressing well. Those regiments which had not been brigaded had to be taken care of and the supply situation remedied by a change of base from the capital, across the Potomac, to Alexandria, on the Virginia shore. Wagons, a constant problem in the early days of the war, were to be taken away from individual regiments and pooled for maximum efficiency.[44]

An army was beginning to take shape.

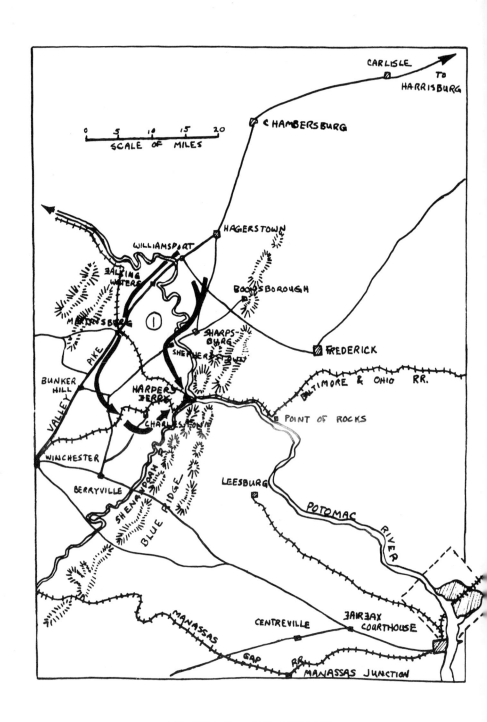

THEATRE OPERATIONS
(1) Suggested plan for the capture of Harper's Ferry
June 1, 1861

Chapter III

SCOTT AND PATTERSON
DEMONSTRATE
WHAT IS TO COME

TO UNDERSTAND the relations between Scott and Patterson it is necessary to realize what were the General in Chief's plans to win the war.

He wanted first a naval blockade of all Southern ports and a building up of the regular army without using militia or volunteers in great numbers. When an army had been thoroughly trained, it would be sent down the Mississippi, supported and supplied by a fleet of fast river steamers. The Southern states would then be cut off from their westernmost extremities and thoroughly surrounded. A gradual constriction applied from all sides would eventually cause surrender with the least loss of life and expenditure of money.[1]

While theoretically sound and reasonable, Scott's plan denied the existence of public opinion and governmental pressure which would not countenance the time necessary to build up a force required for execution. In answer to this the old man was forced to alter his plan, but it seems likely that he did it as little as possible. On May 24, after Baltimore had been thoroughly occupied

43

and Butler replaced, he ordered Patterson to stop supporting Mansfield in Washington and Cadwalader in
Baltimore. Instead, troops should be sent against Frederick, Hagerstown, and Cumberland, in Maryland.[2]

Patterson responded by ordering five regiments to
Chambersburg, Pa., shifting his headquarters from
Philadelphia to that city. In the back of his mind was
a plan to move from Chambersburg to Hagerstown,
threatening the enemy at Harper's Ferry, Va.[3] Scott
approved of this when it was submitted and added to it
himself; for in thinking of the eastern theater, his plans
included a thrust into the Shenandoah Valley. The idea
was basically the same as his Mississippi River plan: a
drive deep into Confederate territory along a natural
geographic feature, the net result of which would be the
cutting off of a large section of rebellious states from
the eastern seaboard states. If Patterson were able to
force his way up to the head of the Valley around
Lynchburg, Va.,[4] he would be behind any armies in
northern Virginia and directly behind Richmond, thus
cutting the Rebel capital off. If these thoughts did not
occur to Scott in their entirety,[5] they found subcon-
scious expression in his emphasis on Patterson's movements during the month of June and his later dealings
with the plans for an attack from Alexandria. To him
the most important movement was that of his old friend
into the Shenandoah Valley.

In adding to Patterson's plan to threaten Harper's
Ferry, Scott told him to forget about Cumberland and
prepare for a crossing at Williamsport, Md., to be
supported at the most opportune moment by a demonstration from Alexandria. With this encouragement,

Patterson proposed after crossing at Williamsport to push south, cutting the Winchester Railroad and harassing the rear of Harper's Ferry while another column advanced by way of Shepherdstown, Va. Caught in a pincers, Harper's Ferry would be captured; and the army could then march on Winchester, Va.[6]

In accordance with this plan, Patterson began concentrating his troops at Chambersburg in preparation for the movement toward Hagerstown. Brigades were set up under capable officers while supplies were gathered and wagons brought up to support the advance, under Colonel George H. Thomas. On the day of his arrival in Chambersburg, Monday, June 3, Patterson notified Scott that he planned to move out through Hagerstown with Thomas's brigade on Saturday. Part of his troops would capture and picket the Potomac ford at Williamsport, while the rest advanced on Boonsborough, Md., to block any Confederate sorties from Harper's Ferry. The remainder of the army would push on to these places as soon as possible, but by the next Monday there should be at least fourteen regiments beyond Hagerstown.[7] Information had reached him that the enemy at the Ferry could be heard felling trees and fortifying. In spite of the fact that none of his men could approach near enough to verify this fact, he feared stubborn resistance there.[8]

Scott, in the meantime, did his utmost to build up the Army of the Valley by ordering Patterson not to march until he received a regular battery of the Fourth Artillery and five companies of the Third United States Infantry. Two Ohio regiments and the first two regiments from northeastern states to pass through his area could be added to his force in order to give it more strength.[9]

By the end of the week the Pennsylvania commander figured he could march and support 8,000 troops in addition to 2,000 men on the railroad, but he deferred to Scott's orders to wait for the regular artillery and infantry. Altogether he now had 17,000 volunteers and Thomas's regulars, many of which were already closed up awaiting orders to march. Everything was ready to go except the regulars from Scott who had not yet arrived.[10] On June 8, Patterson was notified that Colonel Ambrose E. Burnside with his Rhode Island Infantry Regiment and artillery battery had been ordered from Washington to Pennsylvania and that Brigadier General Charles P. Stone with 2,500 men and two guns had been sent as a supporting expedition from the capital toward Rockville, Md., and the ferry near Leesburg, Va. "Attempt nothing," said General Scott, "without a clear prospect of success, as you will find the enemy strongly posted and not inferior to you in numbers."[11]

The state of Patterson's mind at this point was one of aggressiveness tinged with trepidation. He knew that he had forces enough to attack, that his drive was the principal effort against the enemy, and that the nation looked to him for victory. Harper's Ferry was apparently being fortified for great resistance. It would be there that the first great battle of the war would be fought. His commander had enjoined caution upon him in order that he not be over-rash in his movements. Action was a necessity, but how much? Should he set out for Harper's Ferry at once or should he move up slowly, carefully, leaving nothing to chance? Perhaps the Confederates could be maneuvered out of the Ferry as he had originally planned.

On June 10 and 11, the organization of the Army of Pennsylvania was completed and published in a general orders, for by that time all the units ordered up by Scott had arrived. Combined in two divisions under Generals Cadwalader and Keim were five brigades of four and five regiments each.[12] Two days later the plan of advance was published: Cadwalader's brigades of Thomas, Williams and Miles would march from their positions between Chambersburg and Hagerstown with three days' cooked rations in their haversacks while Keim's division of Negley and Wynkoop followed as fast as possible by rail.[13]

Two days later, the units set out according to orders, Thomas bypassing Hagerstown to the east and heading on toward the river at Williamsport while Miles followed to camp on his right rear along a stream which entered the Potomac there. The last brigade of Cadwalader's division under Williams passed through Hagerstown heading due south on the pike for Sharpsburg with a heavy picket to the front. While Keim's two brigades were brought up by rail and sent out along the pike in Williams's support, General Patterson shifted his headquarters forward from Chambersburg to Hagerstown in order to be in close touch with his army.[14]

Scott fully expected the army to cross the Potomac as soon as the ford was reached; but in the last days prior to his advance, Patterson discovered that his transportation was inadequate. He was, therefore, somewhat surprised when he heard from his commander that he was expected across the river on Monday or Tuesday

and that a demonstration would be made from the capital to draw attention away from him.[15] Scott was perfectly justified in expecting his subordinate to ford the
Potomac at Williamsport as this was the plan they had
originally agreed upon, and its aggressive execution demanded that Patterson continue to press forward beyond Williamsport. Somewhere between the plan and
the execution, however, the Pennsylvanian had conjured
up difficulties enough to force an alteration of his time-
table; and the difference of temperament in the two
men did the rest. Had another been in command, he
might have driven boldly into Virginia to continue the
campaign against Harper's Ferry. This is what Scott
naturally assumed Patterson would do, but such a commander Robert Patterson was not. He was again short
wagons and horses for his train. Despite constant reports that the Confederates were evacuating Harper's
Ferry, Porter believed that it would be strongly held;
and Patterson gladly concurred. Porter also believed
that much heavy artillery was being concentrated there
in preparation for a long siege and that the roads all
about it were well fortified and sandbagged. Siege guns
would be needed before any really active operations
could be undertaken for its capture.[16]

The day before his advance to the Potomac, Patterson had reiterated with many embellishments the plan
to cut off the Ferry—if he could mount a column strong
enough to occupy all the territory he crossed. Once into
Virginia, he did not wish to have to retreat. He would
have to be supported on all sides and must avoid bringing on a general engagement, he thought.[17]

In spite of reports from Captain John Newton, his

engineer, that Harper's Ferry had been abandoned and destroyed, Patterson continued firm in his belief that the enemy would not retreat.[18] Even the men in the marching columns could see long columns of smoke from the break in the mountains which cradled it. It must be a decoy.[19] But then again, perhaps it was not. Captain Newton must reconnoiter Martinsburg, Va., and ascertain whether or not the Rebel retreat was actual. If such turned out to be the case and the Rebels were really abandoning the line of the Potomac, General Cadwalader must cross part or all of his division to bolster the reconnaissance, harass the retreat, and occupy Harper's Ferry immediately.[20]

Every sign pointed to Rebel retreat. Camp ruins were discovered, all matériel of military value was gone or destroyed, Martinsburg was completely deserted, and the depot and iron works there had been razed by the enemy.[21] Now was the perfect opportunity to occupy the lower entrance to the Valley, seize Harper's Ferry, and set up a supply base for operations toward Winchester. The ferry at Williamsport had been destroyed, but the river was down low enough for the men to ford. They struggled over the rocky, irregular bottom in water up to their armpits and pressed unopposed into Virginia soil.[22]

Encouraged by his easy success, Patterson began to plan again. Harper's Ferry could be occupied as a headquarters, a base of operations and supply depot. The Baltimore and Ohio Railroad could be opened east and west of there. With strong forces at the Ferry, Charlestown, Va., and Martinsburg, he could set out for Winchester and Strasburg, Va. The remainder of Maryland along the Potomac would fall and the enemy would be forced to retire.[23]

Harper's Ferry occupied a peculiar position during the war, serving as an Achilles' heel to both sides. As the scene of John Brown's abortive raid in late 1859, it had particular significance to the rebellion from a historical viewpoint; but for all practical purposes it was absolutely useless and indefensible. Placed at the junction of the Potomac and Shenandoah Rivers, which happened to meet directly in the middle of the Blue Ridge Mountains, it was easily accessible by water from three directions. Lofty heights loomed directly overhead on all three sides, but its river level altitude made it a perfect place for an east-west railroad to pass through the chain, as the Baltimore and Ohio did. Despite the fact that it was easily reached by rail and water, the three disconnected heights which surrounded it made it indefensible. Should any one of the three fall into the hands of an enemy, a plunging artillery fire could destroy everything in no time—as the next year would show. It would not be until 1864, when a small man named Major General Philip Sheridan took over the Valley that the secret would be discovered. Rather than stay inside and defend vainly against all three heights, Sheridan occupied the western summits, denying the use of the Ferry to the enemy while supplying himself overland.[24] But the year was not 1864, it was 1861; and the commander was not Sheridan, it was Patterson. To him, Harper's Ferry presented the same fixation it did to others; he was drawn to it like a moth to a flame. The desire to capture the Ferry pervaded all his plans of action.

WILLIAM KEIM

IRVIN McDOWELL

In the meantime, the importance which General Scott had placed on the Valley earlier in the month had begun to wane. The very day that Patterson crossed the river into Virginia and began grandiose plans once again, the General in Chief wrote that, if there was to be no pursuit, "and I recommend none specially," all regular units should be sent to Washington along with Burnside's Rhode Island regiment.

Why the regulars were recalled to Washington is impossible to explain definitely. It may have had something to do with Scott's change of emphasis in the theatre of action. He was seventy-four years old, and the mental and physical strain consequent to his duties would have broken one much younger than he. They certainly had their effect on the old man as he grew more and more exhausted. His judgment became faulty at times, and he lost much of his discernment.[25]

But Patterson wanted to retain the regulars. Without them he felt stripped of striking power. Both his artillery batteries[26] would have to go if he obeyed. Patterson had a legitimate complaint not so much because of the loss of regular troops as the complete lack of artillery which would result. His only recourse would be to fall back across the river and entrench. The telegraph wires worked overtime as the two men each tried to defend their point of view. Scott finally replied curtly, "We are pressed here. Send the troops that I have twice called for without delay."

It could not be stated more explicitly or peremptorily; there was no discretion in that order as there had been before. The Second, Third, and Eighth Infantry, the dismounted cavalry, Burnside's regiment, and the two artillery batteries were pulled out of the line and sent to Hagerstown to entrain for Washington. Part of Cadwalader's division withdrew across the river.[27] At the same time, however, reports began to come in that General Joseph E. Johnston, the Rebel commander in the Valley, was marching on Martinsburg with an army of 15,000. Patterson was certain that the advancing Confederates would take advantage of the fact that there were no longer any regular troops with the army. It would be impossible to resist a determined attempt to cross the Potomac, without artillery, so he ordered the departure from Hagerstown halted. The units bound for Washington must be ready to march back to Williamsport at once if necessary. Negley's brigade was ordered up to reinforce; and Wynkoop, Keim's other brigade, would set out early next morning, June 18.[28]

All during the night of June 17, the remainder of Cadwalader's division, seven regiments of infantry and one troop of the Philadelphia City Cavalry, lay somewhere on the Virginia side of the river. The hours passed slowly. Unable to locate the missing units, all the officers could do was prepare for defense and wait.

Dawn of June 18 brought not only the return of the lost units but also Abner Doubleday's battery of regular artillery. Prospects appeared brighter, especially since the expected enemy attack failed to materialize. When at last there was no need to fear, the regular troops, except for Thomas's 400 dismounted cavalry, were sent on to Washington.[29] The lack of substantial regular troops in his army had a profound effect on Patterson's attitudes and plans which followed. His faith in the combat ability of his men grew smaller and his willingness to meet the enemy yet more minute. In addition to this, there arose again a great need for more regiments, always more regiments. Every time he was given discretion to call any troops to his army, he did so at once. Uneasiness ruled him more and more in his independent position, as he longed for some sort of cooperation with the forces about Washington.[30]

Two days after the regulars had left, Scott sent a note suggesting that a column of troops be placed atop Maryland Heights, Md., while the remainder of the Army of the Upper Potomac absorbed Colonel Stone, who was stretched out along the Potomac River fords from Washington to Point of Rocks, Va.; and cooperate with a thrust from the south against Leesburg.[31] This appealed to Patterson considerably.[32] Next day, he wrote back modifying and enlarging the outline of the plan as he had received it from his superior officer. The course, as he envisioned it, should be the following:

1) With a brigade of 2,100 men and Doubleday's battery of artillery, occupy and fortify Maryland Heights, laying in a store of provisions sufficient for twenty days.

2) Abandon the Williamsport line altogether, moving the supply base to Frederick; and threaten to open up Harper's Ferry.

3) Cross the Potomac River at Point of Rocks to unite with Stone at Leesburg. From there, action could be taken as discretion demanded.

The net effect of this stroke, in addition, of course, to strengthening the position of the Union armies in the East, would be to keep alive the ardor of the men.[33]

After sending his plan to Scott, Patterson detailed Captain John Newton of the engineers to reconnoiter

Maryland Heights with the idea in mind of executing the plan.[34] Ascending the western slope by a country road to Solomon's Gap, the captain turned south along the crest and headed toward the southern end. He saw at once that the roads were bad and would have to be repaired before any artillery could be brought up. The crest itself was covered with scrub timber and brush which made the going difficult. The water springs, which had been full the week before, were now dry; and there was no other supply nearer than Pleasant Valley, Md., at the eastern base of the mountain, access to which was difficult and tortuous. The only roads to the crest from the eastern flank were at Solomon's Gap, an exceptionally steep climb, and Sandy Hook. The latter had been built by the Confederates but was now choked with huge boulders. The best way to defend the ridge, thought Newton, would be to clear a 200-yard-wide swath across the crest and build a parapet at the rear of it with stockade and loopholes. The approaches from the flank could easily be blocked by felling trees, because the sides of the mountain were so steep. If 2,000 men worked ten days, they could easily fortify the crest so that they could hold out indefinitely against any frontal or flank attack.[35]

While receiving this report on June 23 and 25, Patterson was also gathering information about the enemy which clearly illustrated the complete inability of anyone in his army to collect competent intelligence. By questioning deserters from the Confederate Army of the Valley, he learned in confirmation of his fears that the enemy numbered some 25,000 men, 8,000 of whom, under Jackson, were pressing up toward Martinsburg while

the main body lay back at Winchester.[36] Other reports in
the days that followed estimated Johnston at 12,000 or
13,000 with seventeen guns and again at 15,000 infantry,
1,000 cavalry and twenty to twenty-four guns.[37] In a
personal letter near the end of the month Patterson
himself noted the enemy as 15,000 infantry, supported
by a large force of cavalry and twenty-two guns, seventeen of which were rifled. His own strength during this
time was a mere 11,000 men, 400 cavalry, and six guns
without harness.[38] In truth the total force facing him
numbered only 10,500 at the end of the month, of which
some 334 were cavalry and less than that artillery.[39]

One factor which characterized Union commanders,
and Confederate for that matter, in the early years of the
war, was a distinct tendency to overestimate the strength
and capabilities of the enemy. Most guilty of this was
George B. McClellan, but a good strong second was Robert Patterson. Nor may the claim be made that proper
and true information was unavailable to Patterson because in the most crucial decision of the succeeding
month the balance of intelligence was heavily weighted
in favor of actual truth. But Patterson himself, aided by
the fears of his subordinates who, of course, did not
have as full a picture as he, persisted in overestimating
Johnston's numbers. Logically, the Confederacy would
have difficulty in building armies and supplying them,
despite John B. Floyd's activities as Secretary of War.[40]
The major arsenals and factories were in the North. In-
dustry, railroads, and especially population figures were
heavily weighted on the side of the North. The difficulties encountered by Patterson were encountered two-
and three-fold by Jackson and Johnston. There were

many who saw these as purely natural characteristics of
the two "countries" long before actual time and conflict
had demonstrated their validity.[41] Patterson was, most
unfortunately, not one of these.

In spite of the "superiority" of the enemy, however,
he was willing to cross the Potomac again and drive them
back if permission from Washington would be granted.
It should not take more than ten days to clear up that
part of Virginia, he felt.[42] On June 25, the day Captain
Newton wrote his final report of the Maryland Heights
reconnaissance, General Scott notified Patterson that he
should continue to confront those Confederates who had
not left the area since the evacuation of Harper's Ferry.
If he felt equal or superior in numbers, he could cross
the Potomac and offer battle; and if the enemy retreated
upon Winchester, he need not follow. But if he desired
to pursue, then he must be certain of superiority. A lost
or drawn battle was considered equally disastrous by
both men. As a secondary choice, the army could unite
with Stone in a movement on Point of Rocks.[43]

This exchange of correspondence admirably illustrates
the peculiar command relationship of the two old friends.
Patterson constantly promised immediate action while
actually procrastinating. He sought the power of the
initiative and choice in all his notes; but he seemed to
place the responsibility for ultimate decision in the hands
of Scott as if, though probably not true, trying to assure
that any blame for disaster would pass over his head,
lopping off that of his superior. His request for permission to cross the river and defeat a "superior enemy" illustrates this fact; for such a decision lay well within the
latitude granted him by General Scott. In fact, it was

generally expected of him as was seen in the mix-up of June 15-16. Such a paradox naturally ruined coordination.

Scott, on the other hand, failed to realize the true fiber of his old friend. He attempted to establish the proper command relationship by giving as much authority to Patterson as was possible while still controlling the over-all coordination of forces, but in this he failed because of his inability or unwillingness to give necessary orders outright, without qualifying statements which should have been obvious to any commander in the field. Perhaps these gestures by the old General in Chief were a reaction to Patterson's lack of decision or perhaps an attempt to insure victory for all Union forces as cheaply and quickly as possible. More likely it was a combination of both which caused the strange relationship to arise. It must also be noted that the demonstration from the Alexandria-Arlington line was not forthcoming as promised when Patterson marched forward on June 15. Scott's principal function as coordinator had not, therefore, been executed well. If he were to fail in time of crisis, the result could be disastrous to Union arms and Union cause both at home and abroad.

Once he had received the reports from Captain Newton concerning Maryland Heights, Patterson began to plan his crossing of the Potomac. To clear the Williamsport Ford which was well picketed,[44] he decided to cross somewhere east and south of that place, then drive to the Shepherdstown Road junction with the Winchester Pike to cut off any Rebels in the "neck" of the river. On June 27 he sent Captain Simpson of the Engineers to join Newton and reconnoiter the crossings to be used.

It was imperative that speed and secrecy be maintained
in order to insure surprise and keep the Southerners from
reinforcing their advance lines.[45]

At midnight, Captain Newton's report indicated that
the enemy was in great strength along the river at the
intended crossing places.[46] The plan would have to be
changed. The entire army would cross at Williamsport
and push down the Valley Pike. Two days later the harness for Doubleday's battery arrived and the train was
in good enough condition to set out for combat. In spite
of the fact that the Confederates seemed to be crossing
the river below the left flank of the army during the
darkness of the 29th, Patterson was determined to cross
the river.[47]

The next day he received word from his commanding
officer that General Stone's column had been ordered to
join him with four and a half regiments in addition to
a battery of Rhode Island artillery which had entrained
for Williamsport in Washington.[48] With these excellent
additions to his command, advance was a certainty. He
telegraphed back with dramatic curtness:

Downsville, Md., June 30, 1861
Colonel Townshend,
    Asst. Adjt. Gen., U. S. Army, Washington City:
I cross at daylight tomorrow morning.
                R. Patterson
                Major-General, Commanding.[49]

Chapter IV

McDOWELL PREPARES
FOR BATTLE

McDOWELL HAD hardly assumed command of
the Alexandria-Arlington line before he began
to encounter personal difficulties. Scott was still annoyed
by his promotion and subsequent elevation to command
of the Army of North-Eastern Virginia. There was no
mention of whom he thought would be better suited to
the post, but the fact remained that he did not think
McDowell was. Two messages were sent by the old man
in an attempt to induce his young subordinate to resign of
his own volition in order that someone else might fill the
post. McDowell realized that he was young, generally
unknown beyond inner circles, and newly appointed.
It would be highly impolitic to decline a post obtained
for him through the auspices of his good works and good
friends. With these facts before him, there was no recourse but to refuse, as politely as possible, the General
in Chief's suggestion. The strain was not alleviated by
McDowell's plan of action when it was presented; and
as a result, Scott remained considerably annoyed. It became difficult to get the necessary supplies to the west
bank of the river.

Mansfield's command had been divided in half and the
active, aggressive portion given to a man far younger
and less experienced.[1] Regiment after regiment which
had been in the Washington defenses now crossed over
to come under the jurisdiction of the Army of North-
Eastern Virginia. The resultant intransigence and lack of
cooperation by Washington officers delayed everything;
for Scott and Mansfield had to approve all movements
across the river. It was not that they tried openly or
conscientiously to sabotage the war effort; they were
as loyal as any man. Rather, it should be realized that
nettled feelings reduced promptitude and coordination.
It should have been self-evident that personal feelings
had no place in war, that injured pride or balked desires
should not reduce efficiency; but such is not always the
case. It was the operational functioning of such characteristics which more often than not determined what
kind of military leader a man would make. Here, then,
was the cause of many incidents such as this: McDowell
went to Mansfield for more troops to be sent across the
river, but he was unable to obtain them.

"I have no transportation," Mansfield complained.

In charge of transportation was Brigadier General
Montgomery C. Meigs who was, logically, the next man
to see. Although there were enough wagons to go
around, Meigs did not want any released until the army
was ready to move against the enemy.

"I agree to that," replied the frustrated McDowell,
"but between you two, I get nothing."[2]

The new army itself also produced a large number of
problems which had to be overcome. Some of the regiments were committing depredations around the coun-

tryside using as their excuse the claim that the injured party was a secessionist. Since the Virginia state courts were not functioning in the area, it was necessary to set up military courts to handle the situation. All damage done by Union troops to crops, fields, trees, buildings, and even fences was to be reported by the officer in charge along with an estimated price to cover it. The owner would then be able to place a claim for reimbursement against the government.[3] True to character, McDowell was interested in the behavior not only of his men but also of his own headquarters. General Sandford had used the Robert E. Lee Mansion at Arlington, devoid of furniture as it was, for his place of command. When McDowell assumed command, the new brigadier general refused to use the house, moving out onto the grounds. He wrote a letter to Mrs. Lee assuring her that the house and grounds would be respected, and that the family could return under his protection if they so desired.[4]

The headquarters never grew very large even with the approach of battle, for the spirit of democracy resisted all military display indicative of great rank or prestige. Ostentation was not viewed favorably, but the problem was that few people realized the difference between necessity and ostentation in military matters, even General Scott. Having a command responsibility comparable to that of a major general, McDowell was a brigadier general only. It had never occurred to him at the promotion time that he should rise to such a high position in so short a period. Thus he was forced to tackle the task of organizing and leading a force far too large for the normal size staff of a brigadier general. His headquarters establishment never exceeded four small tents and a few men[5] and was a distinct handicap from the time he assumed command on May 28 until the battle itself. He was even censured by General Scott for parading eight regiments in one review as overly militant and showy.[6]

Added to this was the problem of officering the army now growing rapidly. When McDowell arrived in Virginia on the evening of May 27, he had with him a commission as colonel in the regular army for Samuel Peter Heintzelman, who was in command at Alexandria. Late that night after he had seen to his other business, he sought out Heintzelman, finding him asleep in bed at his headquarters. McDowell awoke the lieutenant colonel and presented him with his promotion.[7]

Born in Mannheim, Pennsylvania, in 1805, Heintzelman had been appointed to West Point from that state and graduated seventeenth of forty-one in the class of 1826. He saw active combat in Florida against the Seminoles, in Mexico with Scott's column, and again on the frontier against Indians and border renegades. Battle experience had been his in a goodly amount. But at the outbreak of war, he was none too happy with his situation —being a fifty-five-year-old major and then lieutenant colonel. Blunt and caustic as he was, he spoke his feeling on this and numerous other points which rankled him; and in personal appearance, he added to the vitriolic impression he created by his stern, hardy visage which was covered with a full beard, topped by long thin hair, and pierced by sharp, scowling eyes. From his youth as a cadet he had borne the sobriquet "grim old Heintzelman," and this was exactly what confronted McDowell when he presented the commission for colonel.[8]

Instead of appreciating the promotion, Heintzelman sputtered that he did not consider it a compliment; all other new colonels in the regular army dated from May 14, thus ranking him. McDowell tried to pacify his irate subordinate by saying that all regular colonels would be given brigades, but he had little effect. As the new army commander prepared to take an ungraceful departure, there was a sudden alarm on the picket lines, which saved the tension. He and Heintzelman hastened outside to the position of the Eighth New York which was turning out with alacrity, but nothing happened. When all was once again quiet, the two men took leave of each other; and McDowell moved on to the New Jersey Brigade where he spent the night.[9]

The next day dawned cold, but this failed to impede McDowell's vigor. As soon as he had assumed command from General Sandford, he issued General Orders, No. 1,[10] for the new Army of North-Eastern Virginia, his first act as commander. True to his word, he established by it several brigades placing regular colonels at their head. "Grim old Heintzelman" was given one;[11] but still smarting from his slow advancement, he wrestled with himself as to whether he should accept the new colonelcy. His wife, who was in Washington, felt he should decline; and he himself wrote the necessary letter of refusal to the War Department; but wiser counsel from his friends persuaded him not to mail it until they had interceded for him in Washington.[12] Dissatisfied as he was, he could easily cause much unpleasantness if he chose to do so. McDowell must have been aware of this.

Another of the brigades went to Colonel David Hunter, a native of the capital who had been born at the outset of the century. When he graduated from West Point in 1822, it was without particular distinction somewhat below the middle of his class. For several years thereafter, he saw service on the frontier against the Indians; but his marriage brought responsibilities which prompted resignation from the army. Military habit, however, was in his blood. The year 1842 saw him reenter the army to continue his military career. As crisis followed crisis in 1861, he began to realize that conflict was inevitable; and from his post at Fort Leavenworth, Kans., he communicated this opinion to the newly elected President. His reward was an invitation to accompany the presidential train on the inaugural trip. In trying to restrain a crowd during this journey he suffered a separated shoulder and was forced to halt, rejoining Mr. Lincoln in Washington when he had recovered. There he organized a force of 100 gentleman volunteers to guard the White House and its occupants day and night, living himself in the East Wing. Because he was constantly in the eye and service of the government, he was natural choice for promotion to full colonel on May 14 when the army was expanded. Handsome and unprepossessing, he brought to his new rank an entirely different attitude than Heintzelman in spite of his equal military longevity;[13] and as a newly appointed regular army colonel, he, too, was a natural for the command of a new brigade.

The evening of the day in which these commands were set up was signalized by a cavalry raid into Confederate lines. At 10:30 p.m. Lieutenant Tompkins of B Company, Second U. S. Cavalry, left camp with fifty men headed for Fairfax Court House, Va. The picket

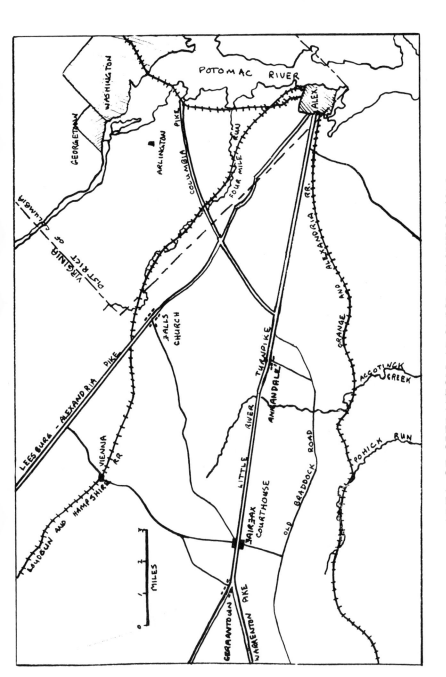

AREA OF OPERATION AROUND WASHINGTON
June–July, 1861

was surprised and captured before the unit entered the
town itself. As they rode into the street, the cavalrymen
were fired on from windows and rooftops while confronted by a mounted force at the other end of the main
street, but a quick charge drove the Rebel horsemen onto
their reinforcements. Tompkins suffered the loss of two
horses. With four men wounded, the company returned
to their own lines bearing the Southern pickets as prisoners. This aggressive little action, sent out by Colonel
Hunter, merited the pleasure and praise of General Mc-
Dowell plus the highly exalted admiration of the public.[14]

By the beginning of June, Scott was ready to plan
aggressive strokes after his troops had occupied the west
bank a week. He telegraphed McDowell to state what
numbers he would need for an advance in about five
days, so they could be readied and sent across. A movement was being contemplated in four or five days against
Manassas Junction and Gap, in Virginia, to favor Patterson's expected attack on Harper's Ferry.[15]

McDowell asserted that, in view of Confederate
strength at Fairfax Station, Fairfax Court House, Manassas Junction, and along the Manassas Gap Railroad to
the Valley, he should have 12,000 troops, supported by
two batteries of artillery and six to eight companies of
cavalry. There should also be a mobile railroad reserve
at Alexandria of 5,000 men and a heavy artillery battery. Moreover, in keeping with his typical regular army
lack of faith in volunteers, regular colonels should be in
command positions with regular subordinates to break
the troops into military trim.[16] Despite his lack of enthusiasm for having to lead volunteers in battle, however, he felt that all regiments desiring service should be

accepted in order "to overwhelm and conquer as much by the show of force as by the use of it."[17]

While Patterson continued to temporize in Pennsylvania, Scott and McDowell continued to plan in Washington. Heintzelman sent information that there were 20,000 Confederates at Manassas Junction, Fairfax Station and Fairfax Court House as of June 5.[18] Perhaps these could be bypassed by a force from Vienna, Va. Between the two commanders they decided that a force setting out from Vienna could swing down on Centreville, Va., estimated as garrisoned by only 3,000 men, leaving Fairfax Court House a few miles to the left.[19] In this way the Union column could strike Centreville and be gone before it was trapped by heavier forces. As days passed and Patterson failed to advance, it became evident that no diversion would be necessary; and on June 15 Scott confirmed this by saying that the Pennsylvania Army could not advance. McDowell could thus use his own initiative in regard to sorties against enemy positions;[20] but the plan to bypass Fairfax Court House, if laid aside, was not forgotten by McDowell.

Two days later, he decided upon a reconnaissance up the line of track toward Leesburg. Brigadier General Robert C. Schenck was to move one of his regiments by train up the Loudon and Hampshire Railroad to the point where it intersected with the wagon road from Fort Corcoran. At this junction Schenck was ordered to establish himself and patrol cautiously toward Vienna and Falls Church, paying special attention to the condition of track and bridges. No trouble was anticipated because Brigadier General Daniel Tyler had been there the day before leaving behind the Sixty-ninth New York which Schenck was to relieve.[21]

On Tuesday, June 18, Schenck, who had received his
brigade less than a week previously, set out with about
700 officers and men of the First Ohio Regiment. He
was fifty-one years old, broad chested and compactly
built; and his rugged features were an external indication
of the strong will that lay within. The Whig Party had
been his early political affiliation after admission to the
Ohio bar, but by 1860 he had become one of the most
ardent Lincoln Republicans in the nomination struggle.
On May 17, he was appointed brigadier general by the
President and immediately a great cry arose of political
favoritism. The press actively denounced the commission as an insult to the troops; one even going so far
as to say that he should be turned over to a drill sergeant
to be drilled for a month.

As a political appointee with no military experience,
Schenck was under obligation to prove himself worthy
of the high trust placed in him.[22] This may well be the
reason that he exceeded his instructions and proceeded
aboard his train with four companies[23] beyond the crossing. Without any advance guard or any attempt to dis-
cover what lay ahead, the train puffed its way toward
Vienna. On turning a blind curve, it was suddenly en-
veloped in a hail of artillery fire from unseen batteries.
Several of the cars were damaged by hits as the men
poured out to the right and left into the trees. The engineer meanwhile unhooked his engine which was in the
rear and hastened back toward Washington leaving
Schenck and his Ohioans afoot to face the enemy. Immediate withdrawal was necessary. Gathering up eight
dead and four wounded, the column moved back along
the line of track. The location of the masked Confeder-

ate batteries was never ascertained nor was the Rebel strength, submitted as 4,000 in Schenck's report;[24] and the masked battery, unseen but heartily felt, became an anathema to all commanders of advancing columns.

McDowell at once wished to attack Vienna with all of Tyler's column, but the old General in Chief recognized that the damage had been done. Only enough force to extricate the Ohioans was allowed, no more.[25] McDowell decided, after receiving his engineer reports, that Tyler's position was, itself, too far advanced and should be pulled back from Camp McDowell to Ball's Cross Roads. Tyler failed to see what advantage this would gain. In fact he saw distinct disadvantages in such a move, and was highly perturbed by the failure of the inspecting engineers to consult him or to stay for more than half an hour. A trip to army headquarters failed to produce the commander so Tyler returned to his camp to submit his objections in writing. Camp McDowell,[26] he asserted, was the best observation post in the present lines, in addition to being one of the most defensible positions. Moreover, it would, in Confederate hands, give away control of Four Mile Run Valley from Vienna to Roachs Mill and be excessively difficult to retake. With four regiments and one battery, he was certain that he could hold the position against 10,000 attackers at least two hours from the time his pickets sounded the alarm, which was ample time for reinforcement.

Here was a markedly good recognition of terrain advantages which underscored the fact that Tyler had been a good choice for brigade leadership. Born in Connecticut just prior to the turn of the century, Tyler was of distinctive lineage; for in his family there were direct

blood ties to Jonathan Edwards and Aaron Burr. Plain-
field Academy gave him his early education in preparation for Yale from which three elder brothers had graduated, but a visit to one of his brothers in the army so
swayed him toward military life that he sought and received an appointment to the United States Military
Academy. His intelligence enabled him to graduate fourteenth in the twenty-nine-man class of 1819, completing
the period of study in a full year less than usual. Artillery
was his chosen branch, and in it he soon found distinction, winning a tour of duty in Europe during the
twenties. Tyler sought successfully to award military
munitions contracts to private firms for better monetary
dealings; but in so doing he bypassed the Whitney heirs,
friends of Andrew Jackson. The artillery reorganization
of 1834 saw pressure applied which kept him from being
promoted. Incensed at such treatment, Tyler, now
thirty-five, resigned from the army to enter private life,
refusing several governmental attempts to regain his services. By the outbreak of the war he had amassed a sizeable fortune, $91,000 of which he invested in govern-
ment loans to support the Union. It was proposed that
he go to Europe to buy artillery for the North, but the
governor of Connecticut telegraphed that he might receive command, if willing, of a regiment of Connecticut
volunteers. General Scott swayed him by saying that he
could do just as much by marching in a good regiment
as by sailing to Europe. Tyler accepted the regiment,
and on June 3 was given a temporary brigade of three
regiments until more Connecticut units should arrive to
provide him a permanent brigade comparable to his commission as a brigadier general of Connecticut volun-

teers. In spite of his sixty-two years, he was fit and active, entirely unimpaired, and ready to do battle.[27]

While Tyler was thus asserting the necessity of holding his advanced position, plans for an advance on Richmond were being fomented in the heads of his superiors. Public pressure for an advance from Washington was irresistible. Lieutenant Tompkins's successful cavalry raid all the way beyond Fairfax Court House had shown what could be done by an aggressive leader. The skirmish at Vienna had already prodded the retaliatory nerve of every newspaper and person. Ben Butler, too, had added something by his defeat at Big Bethel; for although there were few men engaged and hardly enough casualties to notice, the public was incensed, and President Lincoln could not afford to ignore public opinion.[28]

In the last ten days of June, information began to arrive that the Confederates confronting the Army of North-Eastern Virginia were not as numerous or well armed as people supposed. In estimating the enemy forces confronting him at 23,000 to 25,000 men, with 2,000 cavalry and many guns, McDowell was probably over the mark;[29] for about that time a preacher who had been about the Manassas Junction area for several days, entered the Union lines near Alexandria. He reported that the Rebels were not numerous or well equipped and, more important, that they were not ready to attack while other information reported the enemy as scattered over the long line from Occoquan Creek to Leesburg.[30]

In response to a request from the capital, McDowell wrote back his opinion of the plan to thrust at Leesburg jointly with Patterson. If he were to march up the west bank of the Potomac it would leave his force completely reliant for supplies on the railroad, which would have to be repaired and maintained because of his lack of wagons. In addition, he would thus be forced to leave his rear and left flank open to attack while keeping an unfordable river to his right, unless he allowed many men to be absorbed in guarding those areas.[31]

The true line of defense, he thought, was the Rappahannock River. By placing the army along it, northeastern Virginia would be rejoined to the Union without the necessity of occupying it. To accomplish this, of course, the expulsion of the Confederates from their position centered at Manassas Junction was the first step.[32]

General Scott, reluctant though he was to abandon his Anaconda Plan for the Mississippi, realized that, if the war must be waged in the East, his young subordinate was correct.[33] He verbally called upon McDowell to submit a plan for the capture of Manassas, along with an estimate of the necessary troops.[34]

McDowell at once set out to ready a plan for presentation to the cabinet. He assumed that the maximum enemy force in the area capable of concentration in time to offer battle would not exceed 25,000 to which must be added at least 10,000 more which could be brought up by rail. Patterson and Butler must occupy their opponents long enough to keep them from joining in time for the battle. The objective would be Manassas Junction which could be reached by any of five ways:

1) Leesburg State Road, Georgetown Pike
2) The Little River Turnpike via Fairfax Court House
3) The line of track of the Orange and Alexandria Railroad

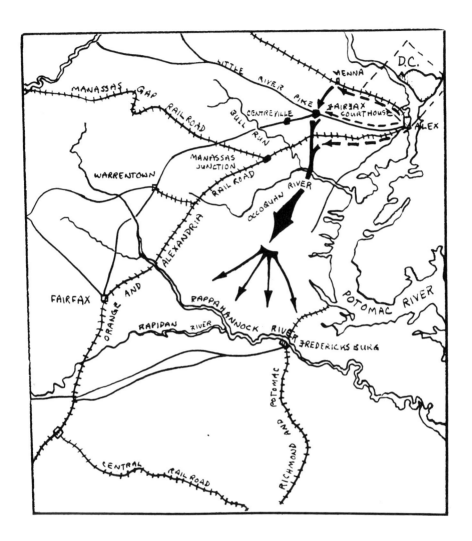

McDOWELL'S PLAN

This plan to occupy the line of the Rappahannock River and
thereby force the evacuation of Manassas Junction was submitted to Scott in late June and approved on June 29. The only
major change in execution was the addition of a fourth column
to the advance on the Court House.

4) The road which ran south of and parallel to that
line of track

5) Boat to Brentsville then cut over through Dumfries
or Evansville.

The last he ruled out because of the water trip and
the twenty-two-mile march required to reach the objective. But no single route would allow him to put
enough force forward at once. It would be better to
advance over several convergent routes. As his plan
evolved, he decided upon three columns of 10,000 each
supported by a reserve of the same number. It was important that each column be so large because each must
be able to defend itself for some time. The advance was to
be a concerted one, each division coordinating with the
others. But there were no reliable maps of the Virginia
roads in the area between the Potomac and Manassas.
Without maps it was impossible to know how service-
able the lateral roads were, so a column could conceiv-
ably be attacked in a position not readily accessible to
the other two. For safety's sake, therefore, each column
had to command power enough to be self-sufficient.

The problem of supply was great. A combination of
the recent spring rains and the amazingly poor condition
of Virginia roads had left all routes, most of which were
unsurfaced, rutted and pot-holed. There could be little
wheeled transportation to break down or delay the advance of the column, so the number of supply wagons
would have to be few. This facet of the plan already
had been arranged by Fate, through a great dearth of
wagons available to McDowell. The best supply route
open to use was the Orange and Alexandria Railroad, but
the Confederates were also aware of this fact as evi-

denced by the intermittent track and the cuts filled with boulders, dirt, and fallen trees. It would be necessary to repair the damage done this route; and as insurance a wagon train should be held ready for use if repairs failed to keep up with the advance.

In regard to his supporting arms, McDowell had little to say. He realized the inadequacy of his cavalry which numbered only a few companies of regulars, but the country through which the advance was to be made was heavily wooded. This, he thought, would offset the inferiority of his horsemen. With six batteries, three volunteer and three regular, he felt he had sufficient artillery; but any more which could be spared would be used to advantage.[35]

McDowell's outline was accepted by Scott as submitted and readied for presentation to the cabinet. On June 25, a council of war was called, Lincoln, Scott, Mansfield, Meigs, and the cabinet all reporting to hear the plan; but General McDowell, the speaker of the hour, was unavailable so the disappointed guests were all excused to meet again shortly.[36]

Early Friday morning, June 29,[37] McDowell telegraphed several of his commanders to report to Washington for a presentation of plans. Meeting Heintzelman, who arrived in the ten o'clock boat, McDowell told him of the plans in rough detail, and that he would command the left wing along the railroad.[38]

In the afternoon the cabinet reassembled with Scott, Mansfield, Meigs, and Tyler in attendance.[39] This time General McDowell appeared to present the plan for approval. Using his map,[40] the young brigadier began to explain his ideas: the largest of the three columns would

move from Vienna and bypass Fairfax Court House
leaving it to the left. If properly moved it could then
drop in behind at Germantown, cutting off the Confederates occupying the advance lines who did not
retreat at the first word of Union movement. General
Tyler had already demonstrated his grasp of terrain and
tactics; as the most respected of the brigadiers available
he would be given this column which could be the
largest of the three because it would move on the flank
exposed toward Patterson. The army would not try to
assault the Rebel positions frontally at any time if avoid-
able. Green troops faced with a frontal assault upon
dug-in artillery and infantry would not produce the
most reliable results, he was sure. Rather than attack
Manassas Junction outright he would drop down by his
left flank and cross Bull Run Creek to the south forcing
the evacuation of the Creek line and the Junction. A
move by the left would be decisive;[41] the Confederates
could do one of two things: evacuate, as he thought they
would, or give battle in an attempt to drive the army off
their flank and supply line. Any movement by the right
flank would not be decisive in itself but would place the
burden of assault on the Union troops.

McDowell had his qualms, however; he was not sure
of Patterson's cooperation in the Valley. With a functional rail line to Manassas at his disposal, Johnston,
unless constantly pressed, could desert the Valley and
join Brigadier General G. T. Beauregard without much
trouble or time. Several times McDowell emphasized
this to Scott, pointing out his disapproval of allowing
Patterson to go to Leesburg because it would end the
pressure necessary to hold Johnston in the Valley. Scott

had faith in his old Pennsylvania friend. "If Johnston joins Beauregard," he affirmed, "he shall have Patterson on his heels."[42]

The only objections to the proposed movement arose from General Sandford. It should be definitely ascertained, he felt, that Patterson was in a position to prevent the junction of Johnston and Beauregard. He also was not pleased about marching fourteen miles to win a battle. The first point had some merit. The second was ridiculous in assuming that the Army of North-Eastern Virginia could hope to take aggressive action and not have to march against the enemy. Sandford himself was in a peculiar position. Senior to McDowell not only in age but also in rank, he felt strangely out of the command picture. His objections, however, were not taken up by anyone else.[43] McDowell's plan of attack was approved and the date to move out set at one week from the next Monday. That would be July 8. There was not much time to ready an army for battle, but he would try.[44]

That evening, after his ordeal with the supreme powers, McDowell met with several of his subordinates at Colonel Hunter's house. Hunter, Heintzelman, Colonel W. T. Sherman, and Colonel William B. Franklin were there to discuss the plans which now stood approved for action. For several hours they remained together until, at last, the meeting broke up after nine o'clock, and the officers went their respective ways.[45]

William T. Sherman hardly needs an introduction. An Ohioan who graduated sixth of forty-two from West Point in 1840, he had been out of the army for some time. During the 1850's, he was a major general of

California militia and by the outbreak was privately employed in his home state. He constantly refused to seek service in the three-month troops because it would force him to resign his present job which had been difficult to attain and because he had an aversion to volunteers, second to none. Through the efforts of his younger brother, John, one of the Ohio Senators in Congress, and his brother-in-law, Thomas Ewing, he was given the colonelcy of a newly established regiment of regulars not yet recruited. He, too, had refused offers of higher rank because he felt he should rise up to them through experience. His business was reorganized so that he could leave it in capable hands, and away to Washington he went. While reporting to the White House, he met newly appointed General McDowell in a fresh brigadier general's uniform.

"Hello, Sherman. What did you ask for?" asked the officer.

"A colonelcy," was the short reply.

"What? You should have asked for a brigadier general's rank. You're just as fit for it as I am."

"I know it," snapped Sherman and took his leave.

It was this man, confident of his ability, curt in relationships, and authoritarian in his leadership, who was assigned to McDowell for any necessary duty until his regiment of regulars was recruited. Time shortly found him at the head of a volunteer brigade in the Army of North-Eastern Virginia.[46]

William B. Franklin was a Pennsylvanian, born in 1823. Graduating first in his West Point Class of 1843, he saw action in Mexico winning a brevet for gallantry at Buena Vista. After the war he remained in the army until 1857 when he resigned to accept a succession of governmental posts. In the days prior to war he was employed supervising the construction of the dome on the Capitol, and an addition to the Treasury Building. It was only natural that a brilliant young graduate of the academy, who was on the spot, should be made a colonel in the expansion of the regular army on May 14. On the first day of July he was given a brigade of two regiments, to be enlarged shortly.[47]

As June became July the plans for the advance were hastily implemented, but the date originally set for the advance, Monday, July 8, saw the first attempts at army organization, let alone aggressive action. General Orders, No. 13, from the department headquarters proclaimed brigade, divisional, and staff assignments for the campaign. There would be four divisions and one reserve division.

The organization would be as follows:

Daniel Tyler would command the largest division, which would form the right flank advancing from Vienna. The brigades of Colonel Erasmus D. Keyes, Sherman, Schenck; and Colonel Israel B. Richardson would fall under his command.

David Hunter would lead a two-brigade division of Colonels Andrew Porter[48] and Ambrose Burnside.

The vitriolic "grim old Heintzelman" had three brigades under him: Franklin, Colonel Orlando B. Willcox and Colonel Oliver O. Howard.

Reflective of McDowell's shift from his original plan was the fourth division to be led by Colonel Dixon S. Miles, which contained brigades led by Colonel Lewis Blenker and Colonel Thomas A. Davies. Instead of

three columns there would now be four advancing upon
the enemy, supported by a reserve division.[49]

The commanding officer of the fourth division was
a Marylander, fifty-seven years old, who, like all the
other division commanders, had graduated from West
Point. He, however, was almost at the bottom of his
class.[50] During his years in the army, he had seen action
in the Florida War; in Mexico, where he was brevetted
for gallantry; and in numerous campaigns against the
Indians between the end of the Mexican conflict and
the fall of Fort Sumter. In April of 1861 he was a full
colonel serving in Fort Leavenworth, Kansas, but was
immediately brought to Washington to aid in its defense. After serving briefly with Patterson in the Shenandoah, it was he who had brought the regular troops
and the Rhode Islanders to the capital after Patterson
had crossed the Potomac on June 16. A general orders
of July 6 set up a command for him to the south of
Heintzelman. An inveterate and constant drinker, he
had probably seen as much actual combat as any other
officer in McDowell's army; his experience would certainly render him valuable.[51]

July 8, therefore, passed without a move; and it appeared as if some time would elapse before any advance
might be made. The earliest day, McDowell estimated,
would probably be Saturday, July 13. In the meantime,
reconnaissances were revealing few signs of any enemy
confronting the army. Perhaps the advance would be
unresisted; perhaps it would be ambushed.[52] On Saturday, General Scott called Dan Tyler to headquarters
where he informed him that the army would set out next
day and that his division would concentrate on Vienna

the first night. "Old Fuss and Feathers" was confident of the result, pointing to McDowell's superiority in numbers and proclaiming that there was no excuse for a bad result.

"Suppose General Joe Johnston should reinforce Beauregard. What result should you expect then, General?" asked Tyler. Scott became irate. "Patterson will take care of Joe Johnston."

Tyler, thoroughly cowed by this outburst, meekly replied, "I know them both and will be agreeably surprised if we do not have to go against both."[53]

The next day dawned pleasantly, but the forward movement which General Scott had prophesied failed to materialize. McDowell collected his officers at Arlington, Va., to run over the plans, setting the move for the next day; but he, too, was presumptuous in his estimation of his ability to start the army forward.

July 15 was rather cool compared to the day before, but once again no movement was made. Units were still arriving on the west bank of the Potomac to be brigaded and supplies were not yet ready. The commander of the Army of North-Eastern Virginia called a last meeting of his officers, this time in Washington. Heintzelman would follow the track line of the Orange and Alexandria Railroad, swinging south of Sangster's Station and driving by his left for Brentsville. Miles would press forward on the Little River Turnpike but at Annandale turn off to the left and follow the Old Braddock Road which paralleled the Pike. Hunter's division, which would be directly behind Miles, would continue on along the Pike itself while Tyler on the right flank moved out to Vienna and swung down behind Fairfax

Court House toward Germantown, thus cutting off and capturing the advance Confederate brigade. Tyler, Hunter and Miles would move out at 2:00 p.m.; Heintzelman at 2:30.[54]

The meeting adjourned; the officers returned to summon their brigade commanders to lay out the plans for the following day.[55] July 16 would see action.

HARPER'S FERRY LOOKING EAST

SAMUEL HEINTZELMAN

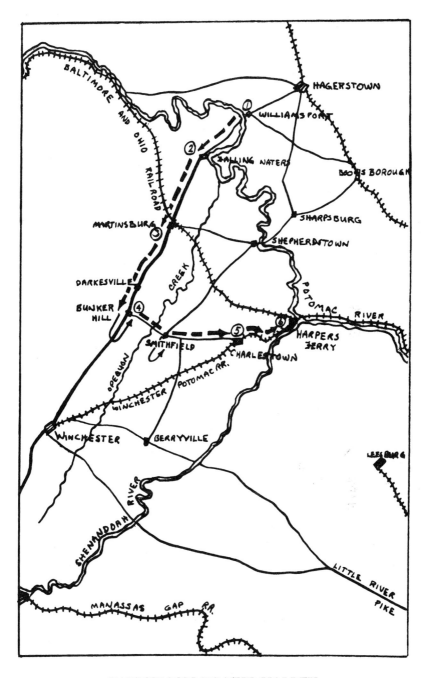

PATTERSON IN THE VALLEY
(1) Left July 2, 1861. (2) Arrived July 2, left July 3. (3) Arrived July 3, left July 15. (4) Arrived July 15, left July 18.
(5) Arrived July 18, left July 21. (6) Arrived July 21.

Chapter V

"THOUGH I WALK
THROUGH THE VALLEY . . ."
Psalm 23, Verse 4

O N THE last day of June, Patterson had written the dramatically curt note that he would cross the following day; but as usual his promise varied from actuality. When that day arrived, he merely issued his order of march for July 2. The army, tired of constant inaction and stagnant waiting, readied itself happily. New uniforms were issued to some units and supplies to all while the inevitable letter writing took place.[1]

At four in the morning the Army of the Upper Potomac started down the banks of the ford at Williamsport. Keim's division led the way with the brigade of Abercrombie supported by Hudson's section of artillery and a squadron of cavalry in front. First into the water were McMullen's Philadelphia Rangers, the cavalry unit, and 150 men of the Eleventh Pennsylvania Regiment. As they fought the swift, knee-deep water over the rocky, irregular bottom, enemy picket fire opened up with great volume and small accuracy. Scrambling up the steep opposite bank they cleared away the opposition while the main force followed.[2]

Behind Abercrombie came Thomas, followed by Negley, with Cadwalader's division bringing up the rear.[3] Many of the farms along the road ahead showed the inevitable traces of war: fences were gone, crops damaged and untended, buildings deserted.[4]

After marching one mile in single column, Patterson sent Negley, the rear brigade of his leading division, to the right to parallel the advance of the army and protect its open flank from attack.[5] Under a clear sky, the column pressed on unopposed. Enemy pickets posted in a strong natural position at a mill and along its run pulled out without offering resistance. About five miles from the crossing, the road made a turn through a series of wheat fields. Beyond the fields were enemy breastworks of fence rails and logs along a tree line.[6]

It was 9:15 when B Company of the First Wisconsin, the advance picket unit, opened fire on the enemy. The regimental commander at once sent up A Company to reinforce his forward line while Abercrombie deployed the First Wisconsin to the left and the Eleventh Pennsylvania to the right of the road. Hudson's guns swung into battery on a knoll with the Philadelphia Cavalry in support.[7] On the right, three companies[8] beat off a flanking force of Rebel cavalry while the artillery fired on the Confederate lines and the large white house on the hill behind. The Twenty-third Pennsylvania swept behind the Wisconsin regiment and onto its flank to prolong the line, but Abercrombie was in need of more striking power. He called for help from the brigade in his rear, and Thomas obliged by signaling that he would swing left to outflank the Confederate position. Twenty-five minutes from the first firing it was all over. Thomas's

men far overlapped the Rebels, causing them to withdraw precipitously.[9] Exuberantly, the Yankees pressed
across the undefended barricades, past the white house
now partially destroyed by artillery fire, and into the
Rebel camp, which was almost intact.[10]

A neat little action had been executed with skill and
finesse, which revealed a high degree of initiative and
an excellent amount of perception on the part of Keim's
brigade leaders, for neither Keim nor Patterson had
reached the field in time to exert any appreciable influence on the encounter.

George H. Thomas was a Virginian who had overcome the hostility of his fellow officers, his men, and the
government to retain his regular army commission and
even be promoted to Albert Sidney Johnston's[11] vacated
colonelcy at the outbreak of war. Gifted with a fine
martial bearing and figure, he fulfilled the military picture with his internal tenacity and coolness. In a West
Point class of forty-two he stood twelfth upon graduation in 1840. Among his classmates were "Cump" Sherman of Yankee fame and Dick Ewell, who would lead
"Stonewall" Jackson's corps after Chancellorsville. Action in Mexico, which brought him brevets for gallantry
at Monterey and Buena Vista, was followed by active
combat against the Seminoles in Florida and later against
the Kiowas in Texas. At Martinsburg he demonstrated
several of those qualities which constant campaigning
had taught: terrain perception, aggressiveness, and estimation of the enemy. As soon as he had realized that
the enemy had withdrawn from their position behind
the barricades, he ordered his men to cease fire.

"The brigade on the right seems to be hotly engaged,"

commented one of his officers noticing the rattle of musketry from Abercrombie's troops.

"I hear no return fire," snapped Thomas.[12]

Thomas's companion, John J. Abercrombie, was also a West Pointer, but of eighteen years more service and with much lower academic standing. In fact, he was almost at the bottom of his class which had also graduated David Hunter and Joseph Mansfield. By the outbreak of war, he was a full colonel who had seen action in Florida, Mexico and the far West. As a brother-in-law of General Patterson and a soldier with nearly forty years of experience, it was only natural that he should receive a brigade in the Army of the Upper Potomac.[13]

The encounter at Falling Waters exerted an inestimably good effect on the morale of the army. After weeks of boredom when the glory of war seemed as near as the farthest star, the men had begun to despair of ever seeing combat; but the exhilaration and confidence which they felt after twenty-five minutes of fire and maneuver was like a tonic. They were anxious to press on after the "fleeing" foe who had been "ignominiously routed" from prepared defenses. The fact that the Confederate troops had been under orders to give way if attacked in force was not known, nor did it cross any man's mind. Victory, present and ultimate, was in command.[14]

For the rest of the day, Patterson rested about Falling Waters on his laurels, content to allow the enemy that time as a head start in withdrawing. He had been notified that General McDowell would be on the road in less than a week to capture Fairfax Court House and Manassas Junction; he felt secure in his ability to keep Johnston

in the Valley for that length of time. The next day he set
out for Martinsburg, marching unopposed the entire
way; and soon, led by the Twenty-third Pennsylvania,
the Army of the Upper Potomac entered the town amid
cheers from the loyal population.[15] For precaution's sake
a patrol of infantry and cavalry[16] passed beyond the
town on the Pike toward Winchester. In the vicinity of
Berkeley School House, Confederates were encountered
who were more anxious to rejoin their friends than to
fight; but in spite of their haste, they managed to leave
one dead and two wounded men behind in the encounter.[17]

The enemy, then, was not aggressive and not inclined
to resist the advance of Patterson's army. They had been
"driven" from their position at Williamsport, their
scouts were reluctant to face Union patrols, and they
seemed inclined to withdraw in the face of any aggressive movement. In almost two months of singularly
wishy-washy campaigning, Patterson had not suffered
one reverse, nor had he been stoutly resisted. At Martinsburg, he had found the train depot a smouldering
ruins. The track to Harper's Ferry was destroyed, and
scattered about lay the remains of forty-eight locomo-
tives which could not be taken south.[18] Everything was
propitious for him to strike a blow, before an enemy
which feared him could be reinforced and find its courage.

The fact was that he failed to march forward, deciding that he should wait until he could bring up more supplies and build up a depot with his small train of wagons.
The country, he asserted, was short of provisions so he
could not cut himself loose from his supply lines.[19] It

seems odd that Patterson could claim this when, in 1864, after four years of war ravages, the Shenandoah Valley still served as the breadbasket of the Confederate border states causing Phil Sheridan to spend considerable time in burning the entire Valley from top to bottom. It is hard to believe that the ripe wheat and produce crops[20] could have escaped Patterson's eye. Nevertheless, he was determined to wait at Martinsburg until his trains were ready to set out again. In the meantime, he called for more troops.[21]

The dissatisfaction with Patterson in Washington had already begun to have its effect. There were active elements in the cabinet which sought to have him removed. General Scott did not share these fears. He succeeded in mollifying them with some difficulty, suggesting that Charles Sandford be sent to the Valley to waive rank and ask Patterson's permission to fight. The politicians hoped that he would be able to put some spine into the army leadership. In response to the request, Sandford replied that he would be more than happy to rid himself of his anomalous Washington position without troops in exchange for an opportunity to enter combat. The General in Chief issued the necessary orders for Sandford to head into the Valley.[22]

In the meantime, Scott notified Patterson of the departure of some New York troops for the Shenandoah, giving him permission to call up Stone's which had reached Harper's Ferry, Wallace's Indiana regiment at Chambersburg and the regiment at Frederick, Md. Two Wisconsin regiments were also on their way to join him.

If Patterson defeated the enemy, said Scott, he could move toward Alexandria by way of Leesburg but must watch the passes in the Blue Ridge Mountains. Scott then declared himself satisfied with the movements of the Army of the Upper Potomac, a statement which, if broadly twisted, justified inaction at Martinsburg.[23]

Bivouacking at that city, Patterson started the telegraph wire humming. By the time he had rested there four days, there were on route to him: Stone's force of three and one half regiments, Wallace's Regiment, the two Wisconsin regiments, the Second Massachusetts regiment, and General Sandford's four New York regiments.[24] From the position guarding the Williamsport Ford in which he had been left, Doubleday's battery was brought forward with his infantry support. The three guns which made up this artillery unit were of exceptionally heavy calibre,[25] and the horses were new to harness. In climbing the steep southern bank of the ford, the gunners were forced to help the inexperienced horses pull the heavy guns onto Virginia soil before they could march for Martinsburg. But in a short while they reached the army bivouac area to report for duty.[26]

By the eighth day of the month, after lying idle at Martinsburg for five days, Patterson had gathered ten days' rations. He began to feel the necessity of a forward move in spite of the fact that he did not consider his supply situation completely rectified. Although he still wished heartily that he could go to Charlestown and set up a convenient supply depot at Harper's Ferry, he knew that McDowell must be, if not actually advancing on the enemy, at least prepared to set out at any moment. It was up to the Army of the Upper Potomac to hold Johnston. Subconsciously, he continued in the false belief that his was the main effort for the Union. If he were lured into a trap, he could be cut off by forces from Manassas Junction and massacred by the united Rebel armies. To him, the enemy was superior in number; their retreat was nothing more or less than a trap.[27]

Yet he had to advance. As distasteful as it must have been he wrote out an order that day. for an advance to take place the next morning.[28]

That night the first of the reinforcements arrived. Stone's troops from Harper's Ferry were followed by two of Sandford's New York regiments, which had covered the distance from Washington to Martinsburg by way of Williamsport in two days.[29] Patterson, in spite of the evident exhaustion of his latest arrivals, felt that he had to move forward to fulfill his part of the plan which Scott was coordinating; but Fitz-John Porter clearly and forcefully stood out against such a move. With aid from several of the generals he succeeded in getting the movement delayed. In his mind, Patterson knew that he was obligated to move to support Mc-Dowell according to orders; but in his heart, he was most reluctant to step into the jaws of a trap. The following morning, after yielding to pressure for a delay in order to allow the recently arrived regiments to rest, he called a council of war in response to further opposition. In doing this he succumbed to his desires, allowing necessity to be replaced by personal predilection.[30]

Just as he had earlier done, Patterson allowed himself to be misled as to enemy strength. On the fourth of July, the day after he had entered Martinsburg, he wrote Scott that the enemy must include some 15,000 to 18,-000 men, twenty-two guns, and 650 cavalry.[31] A few days later, he reported Rebel reinforcements which raised his opposition to 26,000 men supported by twenty-four guns, many of which were large and rifled.[32] There were many people who sought to report other information to Patterson or who felt strongly that the enemy was probably at least 2,000 men inferior to the Army of the Upper Potomac—which numbered 14,000 to 17,000 before Stone's arrival. In addition, many of the Confederates were reported as raw militia.[33] A private citizen of notable position in the Valley, named D. H. Strother, joined the army the same day that Patterson called the council of war. From personal observation, he reported to Porter and Newton that the Confederates were only 15,000 strong, of which many were sick. Rebel impressments had stirred the spirit of desertion which would reduce them even further in numbers. In a most brusque manner, Strother's information was rejected as untrue,[34] probably never reaching Patterson.

Herein lies another of the main reasons Patterson constantly overestimated his foe. Combined with his tendency to accept reports of Rebel superiority was a physical obstruction which managed to keep out much of the proper information. Few people could get past the army staff which had turned away Strother, and no one managed to get past McMullen's Rangers, the Philadelphia Cavalry Troop. Captain McMullen, the company commander, had a reputation in Philadelphia of being a highly disrespectful bully. He and his men, as Patterson's escort, *knew* that the enemy far outnumbered the Union forces in the Valley, so they did not let any trifling tales to the contrary bother the General.[35]

On the afternoon of July 9, therefore, Robert Patterson, Commander of the Army of the Upper Potomac, which was cooperating in an over-all plan to capture Manassas Junction as a preliminary to an advance on the Rappahannock River, fell into the ignominious position of having his subordinates tell him, in a council of war, what should take place. How he could expect them to make proper judgments when they lacked the over-all information of their own forces, the enemy's forces, the actions necessitated by orders and plans in the capital, he never pondered. There was an old axiom that councils of war never fought. In this small Virginia town, it was reaffirmed.[36]

When all the officers had gathered, he gave vent to the fears which had pressed on his mind in ever-increasing intensity as he drove farther into Virginia and closer to the enemy. It was a curious fact that the nearer the main body of the Confederate Valley army was, the larger it grew in size.

"This force," Patterson began, "was collected originally to retake Harper's Ferry. That evacuated, it was directed to remain so long as Johnston remained in force in this vicinity. Threatening, as he was, to move to the aid of a force attacking Washington and annoying the frontier of Maryland, the army was directed to cross the Potomac and offer battle. If accepted, so soon as Johnston was defeated to return and approach Washington."

Briefly, he had outlined what were the over-all plans and purposes of the army. Now to the great misgivings which plagued him:

"The enemy retires," he continued. "For what? Is it weakness or a trap?

"Can we continue to advance and pursue if he retires?
If so, how far?

"When shall we retire? Our volunteer force will soon
dwindle before us, and we may be left without aid. If
our men go home without a regular battle, a good fight,
they will go home discontented and will not reenlist and
will sour the minds of others.

"We have a long line to defend liable at any moment
to be cut off from our base and depots and to a blow on
our flank. Our forces must not be defeated nor checked
in battle or meet with reverses. 'Twould be fatal to our
cause. A force threatens Washington. If we abandon our
present position, Johnston will be available to aid. The
command has been largely reinforced to enable us to
clear the Valley to Winchester, to defeat the enemy if
he accepts battle, and to be in position to aid General
McDowell or to move upon Washington, Richmond, or
elsewhere as the General in Chief may direct.

"General Sandford with two rifle guns and three regiments[37] will be up tomorrow. Our force will then be as
large as it will ever be.[38] Under the prospect of losing a
large part of our force in a few days by expiration of
service," he concluded, "what shall be done?"[39]

According to custom, established in order that no officer be overawed by his superiors' opinions, the answers
began with the juniors in rank.[40]

Colonel Grossman, the army quartermaster, spoke
first in regard to his field of authority. He thought nine
hundred wagons would be enough. At that moment
there were operational some five hundred with two hundred more expected shortly. Following him, out of turn,
was Captain Beckwith,[41] the commissary officer, who

felt that subsistence was a question of wagons. One day's march would force the army to live off the country, which he felt could not be done. In view of Confederate ability to move 12,000 men round trip by rail between Manassas and the Valley in one day, the topographical engineer, Captain Simpson, felt the army should combine with the Washington forces. The last of the staff members, Captain Newton, the army's engineer, said the present position was abominable. The supply lines could be cut at any time. The proper course was to march the army to Harper's Ferry, Charlestown, or Shepherdstown to flank Johnston.

The brigade commanders except Negley all wanted to pull back to Charlestown as did General Keim. Negley was for following Newton's advice about a better position from which to flank Johnston, and General Cadwalader merely expressed opposition to any move forward.[42]

All these opinions were valid and the advice logical —if each of the officers were to speak of his own area of authority. It was true that Patterson was in a relatively bad position with less supply facilities than he needed, but the mission he had to accomplish was integrally related with the success of McDowell's attack from the capital. To pull back would release Johnston to move to Washington—just as Patterson had pointed out before asking the opinions of his officers. Unfortunately, since none of them were in Patterson's position, none could see the necessity of remaining at Martinsburg and advancing on Winchester.

When it was all finished, Patterson offered no answer for their questions but continued to temporize, deciding

to await General Sandford's arrival. At daybreak the
next day, Sandford pulled in with the Fifth and Twelfth
New York Regiments and reported to Patterson at once.
He delivered orders from Scott, with his own personal
urging for an aggressive forward movement.

All the newly arrived troops were then made into
two brigades with a battery each, under Colonels
Schwalder and Stone,[43] with General Sandford as the
division commander of the whole. In a few days, however, Schwalder was forced to resign because of ill
health[44] and Dan Butterfield was elevated to lead his brigade. Patterson now numbered around 20,000 men with
several batteries; and it seemed likely, as he had stated,
that he would not grow much stronger.[45]

During the delay at Martinsburg, there were other
problems which had to be taken care of in addition to
the responsibilities of movement. Colonel Clark of the
Nineteenth New York Infantry had earned the enmity
of his regimental officers by his drive and impartiality
in whipping the unit into line. With those irregularities
which often characterize good officers, the Colonel rode
a huge horse and wore a red shirt when he led raids; but
his courage and aggressiveness were not enough to save
him at the moment. When his subordinates reported him
incompetent, Patterson ordered him relieved and ar-
rested, delaying the handling of the matter until later
when he had more free time. Good officers were not to
be wasted, and it was unfortunate that this matter was
handled thus.[46]

The men, too, provided difficulties, sometimes humorous. A few of them had hidden a huge whiskey jug
in one of the wagons, imbibing away the vicissitudes of

military life during their free time until an officer discovered the fact. Finding the location of the jug, he
"captured" it in their presence and bracing the men
down, poured its contents out onto the ground. An
Irishman among the group watched mournfully as it
seeped into the dirt and turning to his buddy said, "Den-
nis, if I'm kilt in the next battle bring me back and bury
me here."[47]

But for Patterson the problems of command did not
let up and Scott did not help the situation. From the tone
of the dispatches now received in Washington from the
Valley, Patterson seemed like a horse with the bit in his
teeth charging hard and fast on the enemy. Yet while
Scott's letters and telegrams constantly stressed the value
of caution, leaving Patterson the proper latitude of decision—as long as he kept the over-all plan in mind—he
pressed for ultimate action. Scott, in his own mind, was
merely the hand which guided the naked sword in its
stroke; but in actuality, if the sword, which was Patterson's army, had ever left its sheath, it was held irres-
olutely and limply by the side. Thus, there arose a
complete misunderstanding between the two men.

After the nugatory response of the council of war,
Patterson's doubts were enhanced by a dispatch from
his old friend in the capital enclosing a note of Johnston's intentions. The enemy was portrayed as drawing
the Army of the Upper Potomac too far south for it to
be able to retreat behind its namesake river, then to defeat it, unite with Wise to beat McClellan, and march
against the capital with the forces about Manassas Junction.[48] Whatever anxiety this may have aroused was all
vitiated by the news received on July 13 of McClellan's

victory over his opponents at Rich Mountain. But for
Patterson: "My determination is not changed by this
news. I would rather lose the chance of accomplishing
something brilliant than, by hazarding this column, to
destroy the fruits of the campaign to the country by defeat. If wrong, let me be instructed."[49] This tied directly
with Scott's views for he had sent the victorious report
in order to allow the man to rejoice and feel confident
in their cause but not to hurry Patterson or change the
plans.[50]

The troops were all anxious for a fight. The glory of
soldiering was in combat not in drilling and marching.
The longer they had to wait the more disconcerted they
felt. The order for an advance was published for a move
on Monday, July 15. This had to be it; the appetite for
conflict which had been whetted at Falling Waters
would soon be satiated, they felt sure. Sunday, the day
before advance, saw solemn religious services as the
army prepared for what lay ahead.[51]

Monday, the fifteenth of July, dawned clear and
warm to find Patterson's army on the march. The main
column of 10,000 pressed down the Valley Pike pre-
ceded by skirmishers which were heavily reinforced on
their center and flanks. Up front with the vanguard
were Tompkins's battery and 400 cavalry. Behind the
main column were the trains while out to the left on
parallel roads was Sandford's division, hoping for chance
to strike the flank of the enemy. The country was ver-
dant and lush, the grain crops ripe, and the farm yards
neatly surrounded by white picket fences; but continual traces of the enemy marred the beauty of the scene.
Deserted bivouacs, overturned wagons, and dead horses

lay scattered indiscriminately over the countryside while the cracking of rifle fire to the front announced constant pressure between opposing cavalry pickets. Tompkins finally succeeded in dispersing his foe with a bold charge about one mile south of Parkesville. As the day wore on, the sun beat down, scorching everything and setting loose huge quantities of dust.[52]

Although officially frowned upon and forbidden, foraging was already becoming an art among the rank and file. In spite of the fact that they had not reached the efficiency Sherman's "bummers" would reach in three years, they managed to fare quite well as one colonel learned on the march. This officer was enraged when he shook his sword at a drummer, ordered him to beat cadence, and heard no sound or word. His face livid, he rode up to the man and towering over him shouted, "Why don't you beat that drum, sir?"

In a low tone the drummer answered, "Colonel, I have got two turkeys inside this drum; and one of 'em is for you."

"Oh," replied the officer loudly, "if you are sick then you can fall to the rear; but why didn't you say so in the first place?"[53]

By afternoon the army had marched the fifteen miles to Bunker Hill where they ran onto the main body of the enemy cavalry. A brief twenty-minute fight ensued in which Patterson's artillery drove them out quickly, the Rebels leaving behind one dead man and five prisoners.[54] The Army of the Upper Potomac moved into bivouac, while its commanding officer rode about the lines inspecting. On the left he found General Sandford and a staff officer engaged in laying out the division area

after pushing the Rebel pickets back across a stream
three miles below. Patterson extended a compliment to
his aggressive subordinate on his pickets and layout adding that the position looked quite comfortable.

"Very comfortable," replied Sandford. "When shall
we move on?"

Patterson hesitated. "I don't know yet when we shall
move on. And if I did, I would not tell my own father."

Sandford smiled, thought such a remark a bit odd,
and said, "General, I am only anxious that we shall get
forward, that the enemy shall not escape us."

"There is no danger of that. I will make a reconnaissance tomorrow and we will arrange to move at a very
early period," stated Patterson taking his leave.[55]

The position about Bunker Hill was, indeed, a comfortable one. There were blackberries in plenty, and
food could be bought or traded in great quantity and
good quality by the men.[56] The town itself was a quiet
little village of three or four mills and several houses surrounded on all sides by the ever-present, ripe wheat-
fields.[57] But the task of Patterson's force was not to
occupy this pleasant spot. Rather, he was to hold Johnston in the Valley while McDowell whipped the Confederates at Manassas Junction.

Scott and Patterson had worked up a code by which
the latter could be notified by telegraph of McDowell's
advance without letting anyone know who might be
tapping the wires. Scott would send, "Let me hear of
you on——." The blank space would be some day of the
week. The day of the week mentioned would be the one
on which McDowell was to attack and on which Patterson would advance and offer battle to the enemy.

If the Confederates retired when he did this, he was determined not to follow, requesting permission to retreat to Charlestown where he could easily reinforce the capital or strike out toward Winchester. Thus, he would cover the attack and still escape with a whole skin to Charlestown. The fixation which this town had in Patterson's mind as a refuge had almost overruled the realization of his part in the concerted plan. Scott telegraphed Patterson on July 12, "Let me hear of you on Tuesday."[58] That was tomorrow, July 16, the day on which McDowell did, in fact, set out. But in Patterson's plan to demonstrate or offer battle on the day Scott signaled, there lay the tacit assumption that McDowell would reach the Confederate main army in one day and fight his battle.

Patterson decided he would have to make a reconnaissance for the advance. Tuesday was a perfect day, except for the red dust which boiled up about everything that moved.[59] Lieutenant Colonel David Birney, commanding the Twenty-third Pennsylvania during the illness of its colonel, was selected to lead a force of infantry, cavalry, and artillery toward Winchester.[60] The force moved down the pike until it ran onto a body of cavalry. Some quick fire dispersed the Confederate horsemen and allowed the column to continue onward until its progress was impeded by fallen trees and fence rail barricades. As his instructions were merely to make the enemy think the army was coming, Birney decided that he had fulfilled this task. To proceed beyond was to endanger his men, so he returned to Bunker Hill and reported to Patterson, who telegraphed the gist of the matter to Scott. The barricades, he felt, indicated "no confidence in the large force now said to be at Winchester."[61]

During the day, however, the lack of "confidence" seemed to be more Patterson's than his adversary's. Deserters were coming into the area fairly numerously. One exceptionally talkative citizen of the Bunker Hill area arrived from the Confederate army. From his testimony, Captain Simpson made a map of the supposedly strong Winchester defenses, signed it, and turned it over to Patterson. A young boy of thirteen or fourteen, whose father owned a Bunker Hill store which had been protected by Yankee sentinels, said he knew that this man and his brother were both shiftless and lazy, while a major on Patterson's staff stated openly that he felt sure the man was lying about the great numbers of Rebel troops and fortifications which he described. But the information acquired from him was accepted as true.[62]

Two brothers who had deserted the enemy had come in earlier with an entirely different story. Sickness and desertion, according to them, were depleting the strength of Johnston's few regiments daily. D. H. Strother, the civilian who had joined the column at Martinsburg pointed up that this information fit perfectly with what he had personally seen. The Confederates could not get such a force, they could not supply it if they did, and they would never have retreated so far if they had. A heated argument broke out over the veracity of this report but all to no avail.[63]

It appeared that there were measles, dysentery, and typhoid in the Confederate army confronting Patterson; but this did not dissuade him from his firm belief that he was now confronted by a 42,000-man army with over sixty guns of which several were thirty-two pounders pulled by twenty-eight horses each. Winchester itself was defended by fortifications on high ground all about the city. Logs, barrels filled with earth, and barricades of earth were fronted by deep trenches which communicated with the inside by tunnels. All artillery was artificially masked by evergreen thickets.[64]

The instantaneous acceptance of one deserter's report and the equally hurried rejection of its opposite proves that there was little effort to do other than believe what most fit with current desires. The consequent weakening of Patterson's nerve was overwhelming, but he realized that he must continue. He informed Birney that he expected to hear of a battle by McDowell that day and after that the Army of the Upper Potomac would attack.

An order was prepared for an advance upon Winchester the following morning, and word spread through the bivouac that tomorrow would be the day. The army was anxious to fight.[65]

When Sandford heard of this, he was overjoyed. He was certain that he could cut Johnston's line of retreat in three hours by driving down from the Bunker Hill left flank, crossing the Opequon Creek, and pressing in behind Winchester. Colonel Morell had already been sent out with forty men to clear the road past Winchester and repair it for artillery. The bridge over the Opequon was placed under the guard of two or three hundred men so it would be safe for instant use. Sandford's division had a full ammunition supply and a day's cooked rations in their haversacks. He had decided to move himself to force the issue if Patterson failed.[66]

In the meantime, Patterson rode through the camp
of his regiments checking them and asking small questions here and there. When he reached the Nineteenth
New York he said he expected to engage the enemy next
day and asked if they would support him. A vociferous
"Yes" was followed by three thunderous cheers. "I can
trust that regiment," he said as he rode off. "A soldier
who cheers well fights well."[67] But news of the proposed
action unfortunately set Fitz-John Porter working before it was actually published in an order. Patterson's
adjutant was distinctly against such a move, for he was
certain that the enemy were too strong to be budged. The
whole army would surely march right into the grave or
Richmond prisons. As soon as he could find his commander, he argued against an advance, asking Patterson
to talk to Abercrombie and Thomas.

"No, sir, for I know they will attempt to dissuade me
from it," answered the old Pennsylvanian standing
firmly for what he knew had to be done. Porter persisted
and finally persuaded him to discuss the best way to accomplish the task with them. They were summoned and
told what was to happen on the morrow; the order itself
was all written and ready to be issued. In half an hour,
they had dissuaded Patterson from his "determination."[68]

Why did the commander of the army allow his subordinates to turn aside his plan? Thoughts such as these
may have crossed his mind: McDowell advanced today
and should carry the Junction tomorrow. Johnston,
now at Winchester, could not march to his railhead at
Strasburg and ride to Manassas Junction in time. General Scott had approved the move to Charlestown once

the Valley part of the plan had been completed. His reconnaissance yesterday had struck the enemy; it would certainly suffice as a demonstration. The enemy was superior in numbers, position, and supply; and his officers, with the exception of Sandford, were anxious to retreat. It would, therefore, be perfectly justifiable to head for Charlestown instead of advancing on Winchester. From there the army could outflank Johnston by marching down the Shenandoah or reinforce Washington by crossing the Blue Ridge and passing through Leesburg. The fact remains and must be constantly kept in mind, lest it be obscured by irrelevant facts, that the task of the Army of the Upper Potomac was—first, last, and always during the month of July—to keep Johnston in the Valley. By moving from Bunker Hill to Charlestown, Patterson enlarged the distance between his army and Johnston's from thirteen to more than twenty miles.

At midnight a three-page order went out for the army to march toward Charlestown, not to Winchester, in three hours. In order to avoid arousing the anger of the men by avoiding a fight, they were told that the advance was on Wizard's Cliff to turn south and cut off the Rebels.

The rising sun lit tall columns of smoke marking the location of Winchester, as if from the destruction of buildings or bridges.[69] One of Patterson's colonels had spent the night lying outside under a tree anxiously awaiting battle the next day and had thought he heard the sound of trains moving on the Manassas Gap Railroad. The light rattle—that would be the empties— seemed to be coming; the heavy rattle—the full trains— were apparently leaving. But when he reported this to headquarters next morning it was cavalierly rejected and the plan for withdrawal executed.[70]

While Sandford held fast on the left and guarded the roads by which the Confederates might attack, the other two divisions passed behind him toward Charlestown. At Smithfield, one brigade feinted toward Winchester while the main column continued rearward, but Rebel cavalry was close on the flank keeping the entire movement under constant watch and reporting to Johnston. Sandford attempted to cut them off with the Twelfth New York and a battery of artillery, but they escaped by taking down fences and heading cross-country back to their army.

At the ruin of an old Episcopal church, the main column halted while feelers were sent out and detachments ordered around Charlestown which was supposedly defended by Virginia militia. There was no resistance whatever. The army continued its way into the town with drums playing and flags flying in marked display. But the sight which greeted them here was a far cry from the victorious entry into Martinsburg. All houses were tightly shuttered. The streets were empty except for a few children and Negroes who stared curiously. After the Rebel flag atop a storehouse had been replaced by the Stars and Stripes, the troops were posted; and Patterson set up his headquarters in the house of a Mr. Hunter, lately United States Senator from the sovereign state of Virginia, now a member of the Confederate States of America government. Inhabitants, reassured of their safety began to appear slowly, quietly, on the streets.[71]

After midnight of that day, when General Patterson

and most of his staff had retired, a special messenger accompanied by one of General Patterson's aides arrived with a dispatch at the Hunter House. Major Russell, sitting alone on the porch, received it. He took the note to Fitz-John Porter, who opened and read it. The adjutant rose, showed it to Captain Newton and discussed it briefly with him, then asked Russell to take it to General Patterson and wake him up. Russell, who had just joined the staff, was reluctant to disturb his commanding officer's sleep, feeling also that it was a matter of great importance and that it would be better if Porter delivered the message. But the adjutant was adamant. "You better take it," he affirmed.

"I will do so." Taking the dispatch the major climbed to Patterson's room and rousing him from his sleep, presented the note.

> Headquarters of the Army
> July 17, 1861 — 9:30 p.m.
> Major General Patterson, U. S. Forces,
> Harper's Ferry.
>
> I have nothing official from you since Sunday July 14, but I am glad to learn from the Philadelphia papers that you have advanced. Do not let the enemy amuse and delay you with a small force in front whilst he reinforces the junction with his main body. McDowell's first day's work has driven the enemy beyond Fairfax Court-House. The Junction will probably be taken tomorrow.
>
> Winfield Scott.[72]

After he had read it a second time, Patterson looked up and asked Russell if he had read it. The major replied

affirmatively. The dispatch itself was a clear indication
of the misunderstanding between Scott and Patterson.
The old General in Chief had no idea that his Valley
commander was at Charlestown; in fact, he expected
him to be marching on Winchester. Patterson realized
this only too well. McDowell was a day late already as
far as the old Pennsylvanian was concerned. The advance was Tuesday, July 16; and the battle should have
been fought at the same time that the Army of the Upper Potomac pulled away to Charlestown. But, unfortunately, such was not the case. What should be done
now? Johnston may even have escaped already; he
surely knew from his cavalry that the Union forces were
no longer pressing him and that he could turn all his
energies to reaching Manassas. When Patterson asked
the major what he thought of it, Russell answered with a
reminder that he was new to the staff. Fitz-John Porter
was the man to ask.

"I desire your opinion, sir," demanded the white-
haired, old general.

"I will give you my opinion honestly and without
hesitation. I look upon that dispatch as a positive order
from General Scott to attack Johnston wherever you can
find him. And if you do not do it I think you will be a
ruined man. It will be impossible to meet the public sentiment of the country, if you fail to carry out this order.
And in the event of a misfortune in front of Washington
the whole blame will be laid to your charge.

"Do you think so, sir?"

"That is my honest conviction!"

"I will advance tomorrow, but how can we make a
forced march with our trains?" queried Patterson.

"Sir," replied Russell dramatically, "if you cannot send them across the river into Maryland, we can make a bonfire of them." There was a pause and the major continued, "General, have you positively made up your mind to this advance?"

"I have."

"Then I hope you will allow no one to influence you tomorrow in relation to it," said Russell as he excused himself.

By nine o'clock the next morning, Patterson had assembled all his officers and revealed his determination. "Gentlemen, I have sent for you not for the purpose of consulting you as to the propriety of the movement I intend to make, but to ask the best mode of making it." Here was action and affirmation at last. As soon as the plans were made, the troops were drawn up on their parade grounds.[73] Because many of the three-month regiments had served their term, they would be discharged if Patterson could not persuade them to stay. Beginning with his son's regiment, he delivered an impassioned speech requesting it to stay. Success was limited as he moved from unit to unit. Many of the men were wearing pants patched with pieces of their tent flaps and their shoes were literally falling off their feet. At many regiments he was greeted with cheers followed by cries of "Shoes and pants." None of the army had been paid as yet. In spite of all the privations which the men had borne physically, they would have remained if they had faced an enemy. But the continual promises of a battle on the "next day" had all been unsubstantiated, and the appetite whetted at Falling Waters had died a very hungry death on the road from Bunker Hill to Charlestown. Besides, while haranguing his troops, Patterson merely appealed to their patriotic senses, asking them to stay ten days more. There was no promise of the battle which he had finally determined to fight; but even if he had mentioned such an eventuality, it seems more than likely that few of the troops would have stayed. The great enthusiasm for soldiering had lasted all the way to Bunker Hill but no farther. Now that there seemed no chance that they would ever have a fight, the troops began to think of their own physical comfort which had been neglected for so long.[74]

It was obvious that Patterson could not fight a battle with the army left after discharges; but he telegraphed the situation to Scott anyway with the question, "Shall I attack?" Scott was now beginning to get some true idea of the situation as it was. He had, he replied, expected a victory or at least the delaying of Johnston because Patterson must be the equal if not the superior of his opponent. "Has he not stolen a march and sent reinforcements to Manassas Junction?" Patterson indignantly replied that Johnston had stolen no march but rather had been reinforced. According to the Pennsylvanian, he had done more than Scott had asked—in the face of vastly superior forces.[75]

Patterson sent Major Russell to Washington on July 18 to inform Scott of the reasons why Winchester was not attacked while he prepared his army to march to Harper's Ferry. On July 21, the day that McDowell struck across Bull Run, the Army of the Upper Potomac was on its way to the Ferry.[76] The day before, Patterson had written that Johnston had left with all of his force for Manassas except 5,000 militia and 1,500 sick. Gen-

eral Orders, No. 46, relieving him from his command
at the end of his term of enlistment, July 27, did not
reach him until he read it in the newspapers on the
twenty-third.[77]

In the meantime, Major Russell arrived in Washington on Saturday, the day before McDowell hit Beauregard. The conversation which took place illustrates
perfectly the misunderstanding which characterized the
relations between Scott and Patterson. Calling upon
Scott in his private quarters, Russell presented the sketch
of the Winchester fortification made by Captain Simpson and explained the motives for the movement from
Bunker Hill to Charlestown. The old man was only too
obviously annoyed.

"Why did not General Patterson advance?" he asked.

"Sir," replied Russell, "General Patterson directed me
to say to you that he understood your orders to him
were to make demonstrations. To hold Johnston, not
to drive him."

Scott spun about in his chair and snapped fiercely,
"I will sacrifice my commission if my dispatches will
bear any such interpretation."[78]

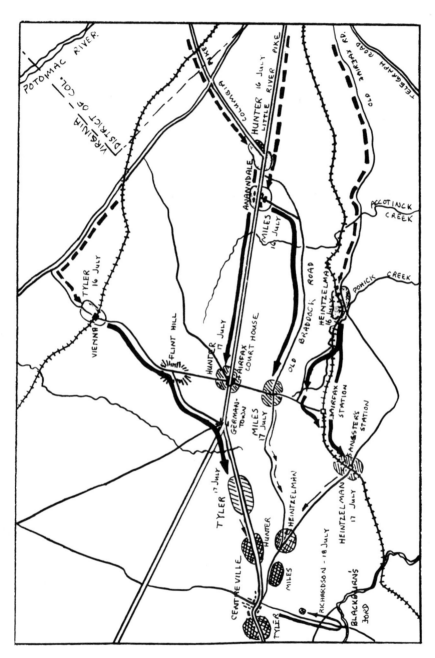

McDOWELL'S ADVANCE TO CENTREVILLE
Bivouac areas as of evening of the date given by each
July 16, 18, 1861

Chapter VI

McDOWELL ADVANCES
TO BATTLE

IT WAS TUESDAY, July 16; from high in the sky, the sun beat down with exceptionally intense heat. While General McDowell's columns advanced on four parallel tracks, he was engaged in last minute details which should have been done by his staff but which he was forced to do himself because of his lack of staff officers.[1] The country ahead of him was typical of all northeastern Virginia, for as one proceeded west from the capital the terrain was uneven and rough. Heavily timbered ridge-lines ran fairly close together in a north-south direction. The main roads crossed these geographical obstacles and the many small creeks and streams which cut through the valleys between the ridges. The terrain itself was interspersed with clearings and small farms, none of which were very profitable. It was a difficult existence which any farmer led in this country because the ground was so unsuited to agricultural pursuits and the impenetrable forests made other occupations impossible.[2]

The sixteenth was used to march the divisions to their jump-off positions in order to be ready to advance upon the known enemy works along the line of Fairfax Court House—Sangster's. The distance each division had to march was in the neighborhood of five miles, so none would be fatigued, for McDowell fully expected to have a battle about the Fairfax line before he could continue with his plan to drop by the left flank. The only stipulation for marching was that the various positions be reached by nightfall.[3] Nightfall found Tyler at Vienna, where a portion of his division spent a most uncomfortable time in close proximity to a foul-smelling swamp.[4] Hunter's division set out at 2 o'clock in the afternoon and after a short march along the Columbia River Turnpike, reached its bivouac area, which was just short of the Little River Turnpike. One of his brigades, Burnside, had been assembled that day for the very first time.[5] Just in front of Hunter camped the brigades forming Dixon Miles's division which marched along the Little River Pike to its junction with the Old Braddock Road.[6] On the left flank, Colonel S. P. Heintzelman had been given permission to push his division to Accotinck Creek or beyond to the Pohick if he could. Held up initially by the late arrival of these instructions, the old colonel was then delayed by a heavy rifle gun which had been attached to his division but not yet arrived. It was 5 o'clock before the artillery piece joined up, with worn-out horses; and McDowell, who had appeared a few minutes before, was anxious that the advance begin. There were no available horses to replace those that were worn out; the cannon was left behind along with a requisition for six fresh horses from the Alexandria sup-

DAVID HUNTER

DIXON MILES

ply depot. "Grim old Heintzelman" was determined to reach Pohick Creek before camping so he pushed on across the Accotinck with the head of his division.[7] The creek itself was only twenty yards wide and knee-deep, but the two leading brigades crossed it on two parallel logs, so that each took two hours to pass over the water. But when the last brigade reached the banks, its young commander, Oliver O. Howard, was shocked at the delay. In his mind flashed the picture of his old military instructor at West Point whose rule in regard to river crossing was, "Do not imperil the success of the campaign from fear of wetting the soldiers' feet." He boldly forded the stream and rapidly closed up on the units ahead.[8] Nightfall had long since passed by the time the division reached its bivouac area along the Pohick, but Heintzelman had proven his fortitude and aggressiveness in spite of slow river crossing and worse roads.

Young Howard, too, had proven his military instincts. Only thirty years old, he was the youngest of the brigade commanders in McDowell's army, having graduated fourth in his class at West Point just seven years before the war. Howard is one of the best and most typical examples of the type of officer found during the early months of the war in regiments which had had no previous militia status prior to the war and thus no officer core. A math instructor at West Point when war broke out, he offered his services at once to the governor of his home state, Maine. In a short time he received a note from the Speaker of the Maine House of Representatives[9] asking, "Will you, if elected, accept the colonelcy of the Kennebec Regiment?" Here before Howard was the problem confronting all West Pointers at

the time, especially those on active duty. Through experience, they fully realized the responsibilities consequent from such a command. They were used to
seeing wizened captains and white-haired field officers.
Should they accept such rapid advancement without experience? The answer usually assumed was positive, for
civilians and militia officers were doing it. Howard went
to his superior officer, Lieutenant Colonel Reynolds,
Commandant of Cadets, to discuss the matter.

"Why, what is the matter?" asked Reynolds smiling
as he noticed the obvious agitation of his subordinate.

"Oh, I've had the tender or what amounts to it of a
Maine regiment. What answer would you give, Colonel?"

"You'll accept, of course, Howard," was the reply,
and the commandant began to turn down the leaves of
a book for Howard to study while speaking of a colonel's duties. "Surely, you know the drill and parades;
and it will not take you long to get well into harness."

With this affirmation, the new colonel set out for
Maine where he was introduced by the governor to the
regiment he had never seen. He had been elected merely
on the recommendation of men, not in the regiment,
who were in a position to speak authoritatively of his
military talent. Thus, rather than elect one of its own
men, the regiment had sought a personally unknown
soldier merely for the benefit of his military experience.
Now before them stood a tall, spare young man whose
pale skin attested his recent illness. Beneath his high fore-
head were earnest, piercing eyes. A deeply religious
nature, instead of hindering his military virtues, bolstered
his gallantry and courage. A short while after reaching

Washington, he had received command of a brigade which was eventually placed in Heintzelman's division.[10]

It was not until around 3:00 a.m.[11] the next morning that the Eleventh Massachusetts finally reached the division area to join its brigade. When it had found the thirty-two pounder mired at the Accotinck, the regiment had manhandled the massive gun across and all the way to the bivouac area. Heintzelman decided that morning that the horses which he had sent to this gun could not be spared from his artillery ammunition wagons and that his heavier cannon slowed the advance too much. When his division set out the next day, he left the big gun and two twenty-pounders behind under an infantry guard from the Fourth Maine Regiment, and by 5:00 a.m. his brigades were on the road for Sangster's Station.[12]

Pohick Creek, however, unlike the Accotinck was too deep and swift to ford though only twenty-five feet wide. Several hours were wasted while the entire division crossed single file on one tree in spite of the fact that pioneers and engineers were there and could have remedied the situation.[13] The roads over which the division marched were narrow and rutted, without any surfacing. Heavy forests of scrubby pines and larger oak trees bore right down to the edge of road, with a few dilapidated farms dotting the way. To impede the advance, the Confederates had felled trees across the narrow road which had to be cleared away. The axmen, fifty soldiers from the First Minnesota and the Fifth Massachusetts with their rifles slung across their backs, moved behind the skirmishers chopping away the obstructions.[14]

Heintzelman, in the meantime, sent constant orders
for the column to hurry its advance; but Franklin, commanding the leading brigade, said he could not move
any faster. When at last they reached Elzy's Fork to
Sangster's Station and Fairfax Court House, the pickets
surprised an enemy outpost which escaped westward.
The-division commander hastened forward, arriving at
11:00 a.m. He divided his force to flank and cut off
any enemy engaged with the remainder of the Army at
Fairfax; Franklin turned north toward the Court House
while Willcox continued on to Sangster's and three companies of Zouaves went to Barne's Mill to capture eighty
Rebels reportedly posted there. When Howard came up
he was posted at Elzy's as a reserve for either wing. The
artillery pieces which had been left behind with a guard
of Maine troops arrived shortly after—drawn all the way
by brute force.[15]

The Zouaves soon returned with a report that the
eleven soldiers and two cavalrymen who had been at the
mill had left earlier in the morning, and in short while
Willcox sent a note reporting his occupation of Fairfax
Station and the retreat of 1,000 Confederates toward
Sangster's Station up the railroad, the other 1,000 heading for the Court House. Heintzelman forwarded this
note to Franklin with orders to push on toward the Court
House while he marched with Howard to join Willcox
at Sangster's. On the way he passed through Fairfax Station where there were numerous signs of hasty retreat.
The much-vaunted trenches were small and poorly made
being only big enough for about 800 men. Clouds of
smoke were rising from partially destroyed supplies and
two bridges were still smouldering. A small amount of

supplies had been captured intact, but the remainder was thoroughly useless. It was five o'clock when Howard's brigade accompanied by Heintzelman finally rejoined Willcox at Sangster's Station.[16]

In the meantime, Franklin proceeded unopposed up the road to the Court House. The enemy fled precipitately, leaving a sergeant, a corporal, and nine men captive plus two bivouac areas which had been so hastily evacuated that fires were still lit and one regimental flag had been left behind. Here, as at the Station, the Confederates had set fire to the bridges they passed in retreat. As soon as his troops made contact with Colonel Miles on the Old Braddock Road, Franklin returned to Fairfax Station and reported to his superior.[17]

Heintzelman had now reached the destination set up for him in the general orders for the march. Establishing his headquarters in the county poorhouse, he ate a sparse dinner and decided that he should await further orders from McDowell before he advanced again, because the plans for the movement to the left across the Occoquan had not been delineated in detail.[18]

Miles, in the meantime, had not gotten as early a start as "grim old Heintzelman"; he set out at half past eight down the Old Braddock Road. With Davies's brigade in the lead, the command proceeded westward at a slow pace, for the Confederates had felled trees across this road, placing a few pickets at each one. Resistance was negligible, the few Rebels firing and then pulling back; but the little spurts of flame from behind the logs, trees, and brush did not make for rapid passing of the obstacles. Davies pressed constantly with his four companies of skirmishers,[19] until he reached the main body of the enemy. Deploying the Sixteenth New York right and the Eighteenth New York left, he swept forward and drove the enemy westward with little difficulty, shortly capturing a prepared position of log and earth barricades which had been secretly abandoned. When he had reached a point about half a mile south of the Court House, Miles halted his division and bivouacked.[20]

While Miles was suffering his four casualties on the Old Braddock Road, Burnside's brigade led Hunter's division along the Little River Turnpike directly toward the enemy works about Fairfax Court House. Although the same obstructions blocked the pike, there were no defenders to resist the advance so that the head of the column pressed forward fairly rapidly. At one place the road passed through a deep cut, and the Confederates had felled a huge tree in such a way as to place its branches down in the cut, its mighty trunk pointing skyward. Burnside led the brigade off the road over the ridge bypassing and negating the rebel effort. When the column had drawn close enough to attack the works about the Court House, the colonel gave his men a few appropriate words on duty and honor then led them gallantly against the emplacements—which were deserted. The advancing brigade was greeted by a newsman and two Rhode Island skirmishers who had entered the town while the pioneers cleared away the last obstructions from the road for the brigade to advance. As the troops cheered, the band struck up the Star Spangled Banner; and the Rebel ensign over the Court House itself was replaced with the flag of the Union to notify Tyler to the north that friends were in occupation. The town itself was deserted, for all the inhabitants had departed some days before. Some of the troops, unfortunately, began to plunder the deserted buildings on the assumption that anything which belongs to a Rebel—i.e., any Virginian —should be viewed as spoils of war.[21]

On the northern flank, Tyler started down the road to Germantown from his bivouac around Vienna at half past five. McDowell had intended him to cut the line of retreat of the Confederates occupying the Fairfax Court House position; but although his march was unopposed and less obstructed than that of the other divisions, Tyler failed to cover the few miles to Germantown before noon. By that time the Rebels had long since evacuated. As the division marched through the village it was confronted with a scene which foretold in a small way the ravages due to come in the war. Flames raged among many of the buildings while the townspeople ran frantically about trying to save at least a portion of their belongings. By four in the afternoon, Tyler had reached a position on the pike just short of Centreville where he received an order to halt and await further orders.[22]

As this day, Wednesday, July 17, had been the first whole day of active marching, it had served to point up the weaknesses of the Army of North-Eastern Virginia. The weather was intensely hot and the roads, few of which were surfaced, very dusty. That the men had not yet been broken into march discipline was sadly evident.[23] Water was drunk whenever it suited the fancy. Many were soon without any; and others who had water were always ready to empty out the tepid, hot contents of their canteens if they could get fresh water. Thus at every pond or creek there was a general breakdown while rank and file, in spite of their officers' demands,

sought to replenish or refresh their supply. Berries, too,
were the order of the day. The countryside abounded
with them, and the soldiers were only too happy to fall
out and feast for a few moments.[24] Needless to say, such
antics slowed the march materially. But there was another factor which should be taken into account and
which aggravated the situation out of all proportion.

The advance of the columns was slow and erratic.[25]
The constant but irregular stopping and starting caused
many of the troops to break ranks when, despite their
greenness, they should not have done so in such a flagrant
manner. The lack of progress was, of course, due in part
to Confederate obstruction, ignorance of proper water
crossing methods, and enemy resistance; but greater perhaps than all of these were two other factors: the memory which Schenck's rebuff at Vienna in June had
produced and the lack of effective cavalry.

The great fear after Schenck's debacle was the
"masked battery," one which could not be seen until,
sometimes even while, it was firing. The Vienna affair
had had little infantry contact; the loss was caused by
hidden artillery alone. The password, then, was "caution." No one should advance upon a position without
having first ascertained its characteristics and defenses.
McDowell himself had considered it not "pardonable in
any commander" in his general orders for the advance:
"To come upon a battery or breastwork without a
knowledge of its position."[26]

Thus all commanders of leading brigades were in no
hurry to move ahead blindly. They deployed their
leading regiments at the slightest provocation, halting
the column behind them; and when, as Heintzelman did

throughout the day, the division commander figuratively kicked the tail of his leading unit to make it hurry, he met with outright refusal.

In the era of the Civil War, the eyes and ears of an army were cavalry. The campaign against Manassas was the precursor of a long period of Confederate supremacy in the mounted arm which was characterized by distinct Union deficiencies both qualitatively and quantitatively. Not until 1863 could the blue-coated horsemen hope to meet the Confederates on even terms and not until a year later would they turn the balance in their own favor. In July, 1861, then, the trained regular cavalry was almost entirely on the frontier. The Army of North-Eastern Virginia had little cavalry and made less use of it. Unable to scout very far ahead without it, the advancing divisions were forced to rely on caution rather than prior knowledge. The battalion of regular cavalry was attached to a brigade, which happened, as a matter of fact, to be in the rear of its division.

These two factors, then, the inability to see ahead and the fear of what could not be seen, caused much of the delay in the advance of the divisions and much of the straggling from ranks.

But the army itself already revealed a resourcefulness common to the ordinary soldier and his officers. Many of the regiments were without tents, but this did not keep the men from learning quickly the art of building shelters from indigenous materials.[27] Much of the rations which had been issued had, to all intents and purposes, been rendered useless by the inability of the small trains to bring up the large cooking kettles.[28] Such was not the case in actuality. In fact, the fertile minds of the troops helped find much more to eat than had been issued. Just as Patterson's troops learned the art of foraging almost at once, so did McDowell's. By the evening of the second day the bills of fare had begun to be bolstered with fresh beef, milk, pork, honey and many other items. In some cases the tacit approval of the officers was given while in others it was refused most vehemently, but the practice continued. Numerous adventures with honey bees served to enliven the advance. McDowell had long since issued his order against foraging and fortified it with threats of dire penalties for pillaging, establishing official rejection of the practice—but all to no avail.[29]

The army commander had fully expected to fight a sizeable battle at Fairfax Court House, but the enemy had constantly pulled back before him and were now in the Manassas-Bull Run Creek area. The positions of the troops were such that further coordinated advance along parallel routes was impossible. The right wing and right center were all concentrated on the Little River Pike between Fairfax Court House and Centreville with the left center, Miles, a short distance to the flank. The army was in the position of having just thrown a mighty punch only to find the face before its fist disappear. The consequent loss of balance, when added to the fatiguing conditions of the march, made any further advance impossible. Whether or not McDowell intended to pursue was no longer revelant.[30] The fact was that he could not, so he halted his troops for the night and began to plan the next day's operations, which would begin the shift past the left flank.

First on the docket would be to ascertain definitely

the location of his divisions. Marching on four separate roads with a green army was a difficult task at best, made harder by the inadequacy of the commanding general's staff. With too few personnel, he had lost track of Tyler until that division was seen on the skyline crossing Flint Hill;[31] and he had yet to learn of Heintzelman's whereabouts.

Around nine in the evening, Tyler was called to headquarters and ordered to take Centreville the next day, July 18, with the aid of two howitzers which would be attached to his division for the purpose.[32] Early the next morning, McDowell sent a note to Heintzelman scrawled in pencil asking where the division was, and would he report his progress to headquarters more often?[33] When this had been done, he sent a note to General Tyler concerning the capture of Centreville, then set out for the left flank to find Heintzelman and study the roads for the movement to cut off Manassas. On the way he passed his chief engineer, Major Barnard, whom he asked to accompany him to the left. McDowell, couching his question in terms of preference, failed to explain the purpose of his trip, leaving Barnard with the impression that he was merely going to find Heintzelman. The major declined to go because he wished to catch up with and accompany Tyler's advance through Centreville.[34] McDowell, therefore, set out to make the reconnaissance without his chief engineer officer. By eleven he had found the position of his leftmost division at Sangster's Station and met its commander. The terrain about this area proved to be unsuitable for aggressive operations. The few roads were indescribably bad, capable of bearing neither large bodies of troops nor artillery. Any crossing of this region would be necessarily slow and vulnerable. The Warrenton Pike which bore off the Little River Turnpike and passed through Centreville would have to be the main route of advance and the movement south of Manassas foregone. The pike itself was an excellent road, as Virginia roads went, and the surrounding area was much less impenetrable. While McDowell and Heintzelman discussed these matters they heard distant firing from the direction of Tyler's advance. The young army commander hastily took his leave and started at once to Centreville, ordering all the troops forward to that place.[35]

At 7:00 a.m. while McDowell was still pondering the location of his left flank, Tyler had set out, as prearranged, for Centreville.[36] While on the march, he received McDowell's note from Major Wadsworth, a volunteer aide on the army staff:

> Hdqrs. Department Northeastern Virginia,
> Between Germantown and Centreville, July 18,
> 1861—8:15 A.M.
> General: I have information which leads me to believe you will find no force at Centreville, and will meet with no resistance in getting there.
> Observe well the roads to Bull Run and to Warrenton. Do not bring on an engagement, but keep up the impression that we are moving on Manassas.
> I go to Heintzelman's to arrange about the plan we have talked over.
> > Irvin McDowell,
> > Brigadier-General.[37]

The major, in delivering McDowell's note, was very diligent in pointing up the responsibility which Tyler had for the movement and the desires of the commanding general not to provoke an engagement because of the necessity for gathering information while undisturbed on the left.[38] Tyler received the order and filed it away in his mind. Just as McDowell had said, Centreville proved to be absolutely undefended when the leading brigade, under Colonel Richardson, arrived around 9:00.[39] Centreville itself was a small country village at the crossroads of the Warrenton Pike and a more insignificant north-south road, situated atop one of the long ridges characteristic of the area. The few houses were constructed almost entirely of stone, which abounded, and were mostly on the western side of the ridge crest and north-south road.[40]

Tyler reported the occupation to McDowell; and while he waited for orders, he sent out a cavalry unit to bring in some respectable local civilians still in the area. Richardson was sent on beyond the town to find water as there was none in Centreville itself. In half an hour the cavalrymen returned with half a dozen citizens who were thoroughly questioned. The Rebels had apparently divided, part retreating across the Stone Bridge toward Gainesville while the larger force moved back across Blackburn's Ford. Tyler continued to wait; but by half past ten, he had been in Centreville an hour and a half without receiving orders. He determined to make some sort of reconnaissance himself, setting out for Richardson's brigade which had found water in an abandoned enemy camp and was now resting there.[41]

In his mind the division commander was certain that

a bold push would reach Manassas Junction. The Rebels
had been falling back for two days; there was no reason
why they should stop now. A bold front would force
them to continue their retreat, and the Junction could
be occupied without great effort. The man who accomplished such a feat would surely receive the laurels of the
day from both his superiors and his country.[42] None of
these factors escaped Tyler's mind as he reached the
abandoned Rebel camp and sought out Richardson.

The two commanders set out at once for Blackburn's
Ford[43] with four companies of infantry and one company of cavalry[44] accompanied by Major Barnard. They
had proceeded some distance and were about to give
up when word came back from the forward elements
that the ford was in sight. Tyler hurried forward and
was greeted with a gratifying sight. Before him stretched
a broad open field unmarred by a single tree and stretch-
ing down to the stream where the bank was covered
with heavy clumps of trees and underbrush. Confederate artillery and a few skirmishers in houses could be
seen but no troops. Keeping his reconnaissance force
under cover, Tyler called up the whole of Richardson's
brigade and Ayres's battery of artillery, both of which
soon arrived.

In a short time the guns were emplaced and firing, but
no visible movement on the far side of the stream evi-
denced any enemy in large numbers. The skirmishers
by this time had entered the trees on the far side of the
open field and firing had broken out. While Benjamin's
two twenty-pounder guns banged away, Richardson
sent three more companies forward to help his forward
units and went to Tyler to see if he could not take all

four regiments of his brigade into action. Barnard and Captain James B. Fry, McDowell's adjutant general, who had just arrived, sent an aide to remind Tyler of the order not to bring on an engagement;[45] but Tyler was determined to cross if he could. He granted Richardson's request, telling him to go down and scour out the woods by the stream while he called up Sherman's brigade to help.

Leading the Twelfth New York in column of companies down a ravine where it was out of fire, Richardson deployed it on the left of the guns. He spoke to it a few moments saying he thought it was good and would do well, then told the colonel in command to charge the woods to his front and clear them out.[46] He went to the right of the battery to deploy the remaining three regiments of his brigade while Ayres brought two guns right in close to the tree line and opened fire. Sudden heavy volleys at this artillery fire proved that the Confederates held the creek line in force. Moving everywhere among his three right regiments, Richardson succeeded in steadying them under fire by his example. In fact, the Third Michigan grew so casual as to take time out amid a hail of artillery shells to eat blackberries. The Twelfth New York on the left, however, did not fare as well. No cavalry was placed in the trees on its flank, which was consequently left unprotected. The Confederates struck this regiment frontally and on its uncovered left, rolling it up and smashing it to pieces. Only two companies held out and were retreating in order when Richardson, who by this time had crossed over to check the left, found the men in full flight.[47]

"What are you running for?" he shouted. "There is

no enemy here. I cannot see anybody at all. Where is your colonel?" But the fugitives were too frightened to know or care. Supreme effort on Richardson's part managed to rally them for a short while, but they soon broke again. He called up Tyler and asked for permission to charge the enemy with his three good regiments, but the division commander knew he had already succeeded in overreaching his instructions. He refused and ordered the brigade back.[48]

Confederate shells still continued to pass overhead in great volume while Sherman in the rear was anxiously bringing up his brigade. When he saw his men pulling in their heads at the sound of musketry in the distance, he ordered them to be cool and not duck so constantly. Just then a large artillery shell crashed through the trees a few feet overhead. As he raised himself from his position flat along his horse's neck, a smile creased his stony face. "Well, boys, you may dodge the big ones."

Once extricated, Tyler redeployed Richardson—at a safe distance from the ford—and placed Sherman on his left.[49] McDowell arrived in a short time to be greeted by his two staff officers, Barnard and Fry, with complaints of Tyler's negligence. The commander ordered a report of the affair made and then tried to forget it but he was rankled nevertheless.[50]

Making his combat debut with the army at Blackburn's Ford was a Vermonter, one Israel B. Richardson, who had graduated with low standing in the West Point Class of 1841. Combat had been his previously in Florida and Mexico where he proved his courage and audacity. The sobriquet "Fighting Dick" was attached to his name in the latter place and never left him. If ever a

nickname was well deserved, it was this; for his intrepid-
ity and disregard for his own life under fire were common knowledge. In 1855 he had resigned his commission as a captain and taken up residence as a farmer in
Michigan. At the outbreak of war, he organized and led
as its colonel a Michigan regiment which was sent to
Washington. When brigade leaders were sought during
the early organization of the army, it was only natural
that forty-five-year-old "Fighting Dick," with his massive frame and unpretentious mannerisms, should have a
brigade.[51]

As a result of Tyler's action, McDowell's entire army
had concentrated at Centreville by the evening of the
eighteenth. It was just as well because he was now
decidedly against moving to his left; yet it was still inconceivable that he should assault a prepared line of
Confederate positions, as Bull Run seemed to be, when
he could outflank it. The left flank was out of the question, Tyler had seen to that. Perhaps the right flank
would serve better for this purpose. That evening he announced these ideas to his staff.[52]

Supplies which had been sidetracked and delayed arrived that night and the next morning, removing a great
burden from McDowell's mind because the army had
eaten the last of its provisions that day.[53] Practically,
the men could already live off the country and even
Heintzelman had begun to gather cattle from nearby
farms when he thought the trains would not be up in
time;[54] but theoretically, it was still bad for the troops
to use any other sustenance than that issued. The Orange
and Alexandria Railroad had proven to be so thoroughly
damaged that the wagons which had been readied as a

precaution were used. Although the railroad would have
been faster, it was in reality a blessing that the track was
unusable because, once the decision to go left had been
reversed and the army concentrated around Centreville,
the line of track lay over five miles to the south on the
open flank. By noon of the nineteenth, the army was
well supplied for the next two or three days at least.[55]

During the night of the eighteenth a thunder shower
cooled away some of the intense heat which had made
the three days of advance almost unbearable, but the
next day broke with a promise of more high temper-
atures.[56] While those supplies which had not been given
out the previous evening were distributed, McDowell
set about gathering terrain information to see if he could
not use his right wing to outflank the Confederates.

The Stone Bridge and the ford below were too important for the Confederates to have left undefended.
There was good reason to believe that several thousand
men and four guns protected by an extensive abatis
guarded the bridge, which was itself mined.[57] It was also
fairly certain that the Sudley Springs Ford, a few miles
up the Run, was fordable for men and vehicles and only
lightly picketed. In addition, another ford midway between the Sudley Ford and the Stone Bridge was reported as useable. Rumors reported that both these
crossings could be reached by way of a road just beyond
Cub Run which roughly paralleled Bull Run. By turning off through farms thereabouts, both fords could be
reached. To ascertain the validity of this information,
Barnard, Captain Woodbury of the Engineers, Governor Sprague of Rhode Island who was serving as a
volunteer aide, and a company of cavalry set out up

Cub Run Valley. After proceeding some distance they turned left across country soon striking a road which apparently went to the fords. The small column continued up the road until they struck enemy patrols.

Barnard felt certain that this route was the one to the fords; but he also felt that, if his reconnaissance continued any farther, it would warn the enemy of the plan. Rather than do that he accepted the assumption that the fords could be reached from this road and returned to Centreville. However, just to be sure, he accepted Captain Woodbury's proposal to return that night with a few Michigan woodsmen from Sherman's brigade to make a thorough investigation under cover of darkness.

That night two groups set out to reconnoiter; Captain Woodbury with two other engineer officers to the Sudley's Ford, and Captain Whipple and Lieutenant Prime to the area between the Stone Bridge and Blackburn's Ford. But strong enemy pickets held the east bank of the Run and both groups were forced to return without accomplishing their purpose.[58]

McDowell was therefore left with the knowledge that a way to the fords did exist; but exactly where it was, no one could say. The lack of adequate road maps made it necessary for him to draw up his plan without definite information.

While these two reconnaissances were being rebuffed, the troops in their bivouac areas could hear the whistle of trains and the clatter of cars far off in the distance toward Manassas Junction. The Confederates were apparently bringing up reinforcements to face the Army of North-Eastern Virginia. And down among the trees along the banks of Bull Run, the rattle of musketry occasionally pinpointed by flashes told of the uneasiness among the pickets on both sides. The night air was otherwise quiet except for the lowing of one or two cows which had not been foraged out of existence.[59]

Once again the sun rose to beat down with intensity on the army clustered about Centreville. It was Saturday, July 20; and all the crowds from Washington began early to pour through the camp, satisfying their curiosity and bound in no way by regulations. With them they brought picnic baskets and liquor in order that they might enjoy their excursion into the realm of the military. Mixed in with this heterogeneous crowd were numerous important officials like Simon Cameron, the able politician but incompetent Secretary of War. When he approached McDowell at army headquarters, apprehension marked his face distinctly. But the youthful commander was full of confidence, some of which he imparted to all who came in contact with him.[60]

At one point, McDowell and Senator Wilson were engaged in conversation when one of the brigade leaders from Hunter's division, Ambrose Burnside, burst in saying he would not advance and fight if it were his choice.

The Senator stared at him as if he were a coward while his superior patiently replied, "If I do not fight them tomorrow, I cannot do it in six months."

"Better wait that time than hazard a battle now," affirmed Burnside;[61] but McDowell was right. If he waited, the terms of his three-month troops would expire leaving few trained volunteers to take their place. If the period necessary for reorganization were not actually six months, it would certainly last at least the rest of the summer.[62] Already the terms of several regiments had expired. Burnside's old First Rhode Island had reached the end of its service that very day but volunteered to stay until no longer needed.[63] Some, however, were not so willing. Both the Fourth Pennsylvania Infantry and a battery of artillery attached to the Eighth New York were due to be released the next day. In spite of McDowell's flattering request for them to remain a day or two more, both units refused and were allowed to pass to the rear the next day.[64]

McDowell, of course, realized that the Rebel trains were active and that reinforcements were being brought up, but he had expected this. The General in Chief had firmly stated on numerous occasions that Patterson would detain Johnston, the major enemy force besides Beauregard, in the Valley. McDowell assumed that this would be done and that the army he would meet would be substantially Beauregard's, with as many troops as could be spared from Richmond and elsewhere.[65]

He now had all the information from Barnard and the other two parties. It would be difficult, if not impossible, to learn more, so he set about drawing up his plan of attack. The same type of plan used on July sixteenth would be employed: the troops would march to assembly areas at six o'clock that evening; they would camp for the night in these places and be ready to jump off fresh early the next morning just that much nearer the battlefield. Several officers were opposed to this. Burnside said that two marches would fatigue his men, who had the farthest to go. Sherman, too, was against the two marches for reasons which he did not bother to state. In deference to his subordinates, then, McDowell altered his plan and the six o'clock march was canceled.[66]

That night the officers in command of brigades and
divisions gathered at army headquarters to be told of the
detailed plan which McDowell had developed during
the day. Sherman arrived early and used this opportunity to write a letter to his wife while he awaited the
arrival of the rest.[67] As the officers arrived, they con-
versed among themselves and with others, for there were
numerous civilians, politicians, and at least one regimental commander there at the time. Willis A. Gorman,
Colonel of the First Minnesota, was sure that Johnston
was up. He was definitely against any attack until the
ground could be more thoroughly examined by reconnaissance, but his opinion mattered little. In fact, no
opinions at all were asked as the plans were discussed;
the meeting was not a council of war, it was a briefing
session.[68]

Tyler, still flamboyant despite his fiasco two days
before, asked, "General, what force do we have to fight
tomorrow?"

"You know as well as I do," was the reply.

"General, we have got the whole of Joe Johnston's
army in our front and we must fight the two armies."
He began to speak of the trains he had heard all afternoon and the night before, but McDowell was already
well aware of it. He merely ignored this outburst, proceeding with the discussion of his plans.[69] Both Mc-
Dowell and Scott had been opposed to the campaign
now in execution, but they had been overruled by their
political superiors in the capital. Whatever the merits or
faults of opening the war with this movement, Mc-
Dowell could not have turned away from battle now if it
were his fondest wish. Too many factors outside the

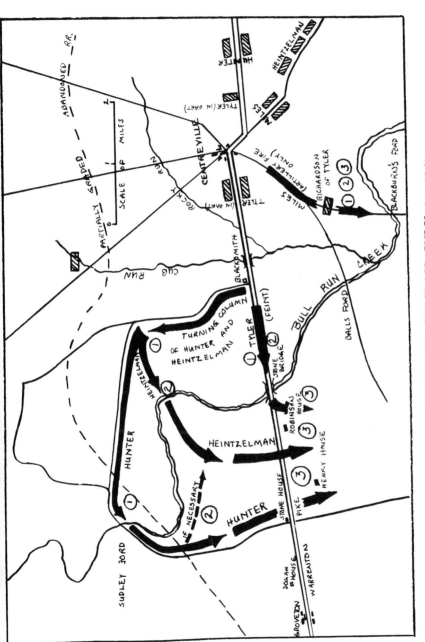

McDOWELL'S PLAN FOR SUNDAY, JULY 21, 1861
Each circled number represents the heads of the columns at
simultaneous times

purely military sphere were integrally related to what was now transpiring in northeastern Virginia and the Shenandoah Valley. It was not possible to judge movements on military expedience alone.

Because there was no flooring in the headquarters tent, McDowell was forced to spread his map on the dirt while he explained in detail what was to happen the following morning.[70]

The enemy was obviously prepared to defend the Stone Bridge, which was one of the most important means of access to the Confederate position on the west bank of Bull Run. If this position could be turned and the defenders cleared away by outflanking, the remainder of the army could cross to help drive the Confederates from Manassas Junction.[71]

Tyler, camped about Centreville itself, would set out at 2:00 a.m. the following morning with three brigades: Schenck, Sherman, and Keyes. He would proceed along the pike to the Stone Bridge and demonstrate against the fortifications there. It was believed that the bridge had been mined in order that the Confederates, if driven from it, could destroy it before it became a means of access to the west bank. For this eventuality a trestle bridge would be ready with the engineers, to be installed at the earliest possible moment in order to facilitate the crossing of artillery and troops when the defenders were driven away.

Hunter, who was camped on the pike behind Centreville, would follow Tyler, setting out at the same time. Just beyond Cub Run he would turn north up the road that ran parallel to Bull Run to the Sudley Springs Ford where he would have no difficulty in crossing, from either the enemy or the terrain. Once over, he would swing south and drive in the exposed flank of any defenders along the Run.

Behind him and starting half an hour later would be the division led by "grim old Heintzelman." Camped on the road leading south from Centreville to the Old Braddock Road and Sangster's Station, he would have to pass through Miles to get to Centreville and follow Hunter. Once on the road up to Sudley's, he would turn off to the ford between Sudley's and the Stone Bridge. If Heintzelman's crossing was contested, Hunter would outflank the defenders, allowing him to cross. Now, perpendicular to the Run and moving in a direction parallel to it on the west bank, would be two divisions which could easily uncover the Stone Bridge area for Tyler and his trestle structure. By slipping to their right in a westerly direction, Hunter and Heintzelman would make room on the line for a third division, presenting a broad front to drive the Rebels from their creek-line defenses completely.

Miles's division, with the brigade of Richardson attached, would be in reserve around Centreville. Demonstrations might be made with artillery around Blackburn's Ford; but McDowell, remembering the last trouble there, was especially explicit about the character of action to be taken.

There were many fords below Blackburn's and it would be quite possible for the Confederates to cross by one of them, turn north, and strike the exposed flank and rear of the army just at the crucial moment when the Union turning column was in transit. It was for this reason that the reinforced division of Miles was left at

Centreville. The plan itself was excellent in its conception. Designed to achieve unopposed stream crossings
by way of the ever increasing flanking column, it would
place many troops on the battle field in fresh condition
as the main force of the enemy grew closer. Heintzelman
would march half as far as Hunter and Tyler; just the
short distance to the Stone Bridge, with a time to rest
before crossing.

The main fault of the plan lay in its deception. Mc-
Dowell assumed from the repulse at Blackburn's Ford
on July 18 that the main enemy force was gathered
about that crossing. Perhaps it was because of Tyler's
brief affair that he was afraid to risk his left wing in any
active operations there. It is certain from the order of
march for the next day that such an idea was on his
mind, yet to make the main demonstration at Stone
Bridge was not wise.[72] Such a major demonstration of
troops and artillery on the Stone Bridge would turn the
Confederate concentration away from Blackburn's into
the direction of the turning column. It was, therefore,
conceivable that they could muster reinforcements
enough to resist Hunter and Heintzelman while pre-
venting Tyler from crossing Bull Run to add the needed
fresh punch. If the main feint were executed by Miles's
division, rather than mere artillery bombardment as
prescribed, the attention of the Southerners would remain fixed upon the Federal left wing while the right
wing gained irresistible strength. Thus the most baleful
effect of the repulse at Blackburn's Ford was not on the
morale of the troops; it was on the readiness of the army
commander to shut it from his mind completely as if it
were a bad dream.

A second weakness in the plan was, unfortunately, intrinsic in any offensive which McDowell could design. He had to cross a defended stream with one wing while the other remained behind. This, in effect, divided his army in half while the Southerners were free to remain entirely on one bank. In addition, the Army of North-Eastern Virginia would have exterior lines about an obtuse angle which would make the reinforcing of one wing from the other costly in time and effort.

All things considered, however, the plan was a good one in its conception. All that remained was to execute it as designed and then trust to the ultimate ruler of battle, Lady Luck.

When the meeting broke up around eleven o'clock,[73] the officers left headquarters for their bivouac areas. The night was cool and beautiful; the moon shone full through the still air, casting long shadows. As the men left McDowell's tent, pitched at the foot of a long, sloping hill east of Centreville, the only sounds audible were the occasional shouts of a soldier in the distance and the intermittent lowing of cattle.[74]

Richardson had said to Tyler at the council, "It is impossible, General, to move an army of regular troops under two hours; and you will take at least that time to move volunteers. And if reveille is not beaten before two o'clock in the morning, you cannot get into action at daylight. If you beat reveille at twelve with volunteer troops, you may get into action at daylight but not before. That is the best you can do."[75] Many of the other brigade and divisional leaders must have pondered this as they returned to their camps. Surely it crossed Mc-Dowell's mind as he retired to try to sleep off the uncomfortable feeling of a badly upset stomach.[76] He must have hoped that neither the stomach nor a late start would plague him next day.

Chapter VII

McDOWELL SPENDS
A HOT SUNDAY

A COOL BREEZE brushed Centreville as the moon
sank in the west.[1] It was not daylight when the
columns set out on the Warrenton Pike. Carlisle's battery of artillery had been ready to march since 2:00
a.m., but Tyler was experiencing just what Richardson
had prophesied the night before. His troops were difficult to organize and get on the road at such an early hour
so it was a half hour or more before his brigades began
the short march to the Stone Bridge.[2] With Schenck's
brigade in the lead followed by Carlisle's battery of
regulars and Lieutenant Haines's massive thirty-pounder
gun,[3] Tyler advanced slowly, constantly patrolling and
probing forward with his skirmishers. Lack of cavalry
closed the eyes of the army to all beyond the sight of
the leading column; and the consequent fear of being
ambushed, which resulted from this inability, aggravated
the slowness of the advance.[4]

In a short while Cub Run came in sight. The ford had
been obstructed by the Southerners with trees, and the
rickety little bridge did not look strong enough to bear

143

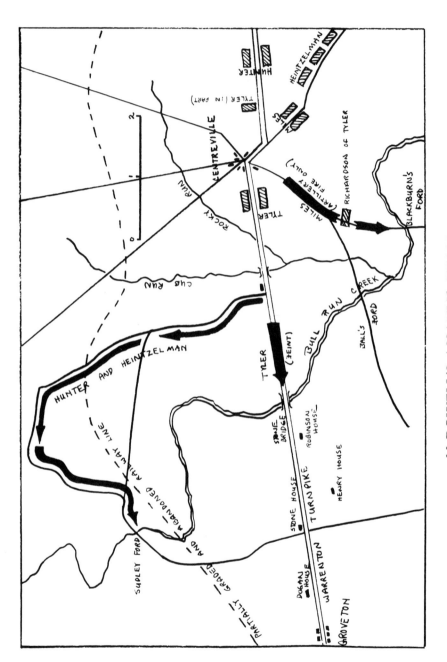

McDOWELL'S ASSAULT, PHASE I
Sunday, July 21

the immense weight of the thirty-pounder. With trepidation the officers watched the huge Parrott gun roll slowly onto the planking. It stuck. Time passed as they struggled to clear it away. Perhaps the bridge would collapse. For a while it certainly looked that way, but at last, after mighty efforts, the wheels rolled onto the road across and rumbled on toward Bull Run.

The march was then quietly resumed. In the meantime, Keyes's brigade, which was in the division rear behind Sherman was ordered off the road. Tyler then rode back to see that his order was carried out because he realized that the pike must be cleared as far as the road to Sudley's Ford so the turning column could set out for its objective as rapidly as possible.[5]

When Tyler's two remaining brigades reached the proximity of the Stone Bridge, they halted behind a ridgeline. Schenck swung down to the left, Sherman strung his regiments out to the right of the pike, and the two then advanced to the crest of the ridge, from which Bull Run was clearly visible.[6] Carlisle brought his battery into position between the two brigades where he could have a clear field of fire across the open ground all the way down to and across the stream.[7] By half-past six the division was in position with its artillery almost emplaced. Lieutenant Haines, in the pike behind the infantry, was ordered to fire the signal with his Parrott gun to notify McDowell that Tyler was set.[8] Three tremendous booms told the army that its leading division was ready to begin the battle.[9]

Major William F. Barry, McDowell's staff officer in charge of artillery arrived around half-past eight while Hunter and Heintzelman were en route to Sudley's

Ford, and suggested that Carlisle open fire on the
Southern abatis at the western end of the bridge. In a
short while shells began to fall about the obstruction and
the brush huts of the defenders with good effect, but no
enemy batteries were seen, and there was no return fire.
One section of two guns, under Lieutenant Wilson was
sent down to the Run to cover the artificial bridge site
while the remainder maintained a more or less continuous fire on the far bank. The two guns close to the
Run received a heavy counterbattery fire as soon as they
opened up. Fighting hard to keep their position in front
of Schenck's brigade, gun crews were forced to expend
their entire ammunition supply. When this happened,
there was no recourse but to withdraw, which was
rapidly done as enemy batteries began to come to life.[10]

Over on the right, Sherman spent the early hours
quietly waiting. At one point one of his men pointed to
a flag flying in the trees across the stream and called out,
"Colonel, there's a flag, a flag of truce."

Another of the men saved Sherman the trouble of
answering. "No, it is no flag of truce, but a flag of de-
fiance!" The Colonel paid little attention to this; he had
other things on his mind. About half an hour after the
artillery to his left opened fire, he was down near the
Run with his pickets when he noticed two mounted
Confederates, one of which was an officer, descending
the ridge on the far side toward the banks. They drove
their horses right into the stream and up the east bank.
The officer waved his gun shouting, "You damned black
abolitionists, come on!" and several other vituperations
of unrecorded but imaginable ilk. Yankee pickets
opened fire on the two men but with no effect other

FAIRFAX COURT HOUSE

CENTREVILLE, VIRGINIA

than to send them back to their own side. Bullet-headed
Sherman, however, filed this event in his mind where it
would be easily recalled. Now he knew where he could
cross the creek by other means than the defended Stone
Bridge and the distant ford Heintzelman was to use.[11]

While Tyler moved slowly up the pike, McDowell
was upset about the delay. He still felt sick from the
bad piece of watermelon he had eaten, and the tension
caused by Tyler's dilatory marching did not alleviate
his discomfort.[12] Hunter had been ready to march since
2:00 a.m. and Heintzelman, who was to follow him,
since half-past two; but when they reached Centreville
the road was choked with Tyler's regiments which
seemed to be making no progress.[13] It was 5:30 before
the road to Sudley's was cleared by the last of Tyler's
men and Burnside could lead the flanking column up its
route.[14] As the Second Rhode Island turned right to
begin the movement, McDowell surveyed the proceedings from the blacksmith shop at that crossroads. He was
pleased with what he saw. There was power in those
men and strength in the officers leading them. A little
toughening of the legs, a little discipline, and a little
privation would make them all good soldiers.[15]

By the time Hunter had passed with Heintzelman
following, Tyler had been firing for some time and was
as yet unanswered. McDowell could hear this plainly,
and it worried him. The Confederates might be preparing to assault from Blackburn's Ford while his own
action hung in the balance. To guard against this, he
detained Howard, the rear brigade of Heintzelman's
division, at the crossroads of the pike and the road to
Sudley's in order that it might reinforce Miles on the

left if necessary.[16] When he had done this, he allowed the pride he felt for his army to overflow and he broke the silence which had hung about while the soldiers filed past. "Gentlemen," he said, "that is a big force." With that he mounted his horse and turned its head toward Sudley's Ford.[17]

The route to Sudley's, however, turned out to be one of the many Virginia tracks hardly deserving to be dignified as a road. The Second Rhode Island was constantly engaged in removing trees which the Confederates had felled, while the artillery struggled along as best it could through the ruts and rocks.[18] Progress, slow at the very best, was worsened by the intense heat from the sun which already promised a scorching July Sunday. Numerous civilians in carriages also helped to impede the troops, for they accompanied the column as if on a joy ride—with the sanction of Secretary of War Cameron.[19] At one place Senator Henry Wilson sat by the roadside in his carriage while his attendant passed out sandwiches freely to all who wished them.[20] The farms in this area were like all the rest which the advance had passed, poor and ramshackle with most of the able-bodied men gone. As the brigades passed one old log hovel, an unkempt woman hollered that there were enough Confederates ahead to whip them all and her "old man" was among them so they had better watch out.[21]

Two things happened on the Sudley Road that disrupted the timing and placement of McDowell's plan. Hunter's guide swung the column to the right at a fork in the Sudley Road although both routes reached Sudley's. If they marched up the left road, he said, they would come close to the Run not only tipping the Confederates off to the plan but also subjecting themselves to artillery fire.[22] This meant that the march no longer paralleled the course of the stream but diverged to the right then turned back again after several extra miles had been added to the distance to the ford. The time of arrival at the ford, already delayed by Tyler's slow advance, would be even later. It would become more and more easy for the Confederates to determine what was happening with every added minute, and it would also allow them to mount an offensive of their own around Blackburn's while the Federals were vulnerably strung out over the countryside. The second occurrence which forceably altered McDowell's course of action took place with Heintzelman's division. His guide failed to find any road on which to turn off so the division followed Hunter all the way to Sudley's Ford.[23] Thus the center point of the three-pronged drive across the creek line was removed and it would be up to Hunter to drive all the way down to clear the Stone Bridge area for Tyler himself, with as much aid as Heintzelman could give him by hastening down from the ford at Sudley's. It was obvious that Heintzelman's troops would be tired by such an effort. Not only had they started from a bivouac on the eastern side of Centreville, which meant that of all McDowell's divisions this one would have to march the farthest, but also they would have to move at the double quick to catch up with Hunter once he had deployed on the west side of Bull Run. Men who had been pushed to such physical exertion, especially when they were green, would hardly be effective in combat;[24] even veterans would have been sorely taxed under these circumstances. As a result it was conceivable that sufficient force could be gathered during the time lag, caused by Tyler and the added distance, to meet and stop Hunter before he could clear the Stone Bridge. The elimination of Heintzelman as a middle prong and flanking force would add to the difficulty by making Hunter attack any defenders frontally without the aid of a flanking force. While the Confederates held Bull Run, they could defeat Hunter and Heintzelman in detail then turn their attention to the Yankees left on the east bank.

At last, however, Burnside's Rhode Islanders in the lead broke clear of the trees which had enclosed the road all the way from the blacksmith shop on the Pike. Ahead lay a mile of open road to the ford, which was reached at half-past nine. Here on the banks of Bull Run Creek, Burnside called a halt to let his men rest up for the action ahead. Water had been used up early in the intense heat of the day and none was found along the road so the men were allowed to refill their canteens and drink.[25]

While the rest of the column waited, Hunter led forward Burnside's artillery battery and the Second Rhode Island to examine the area beyond the trees down toward Stone Bridge. "We expect a great deal of Rhode Island troops today," he called.

"You shall not be disappointed, sir," replied Colonel John Slocum and turning to his men he shouted, "Now show them what Rhode Island can do!"[26]

After about three-quarters of a mile in the woods, the two units suddenly emerged in the open to be hit almost at once by Rebel infantry and artillery fire. Hunter, who

was leading the troops while Burnside, the brigade commander, prepared the other three regiments, ordered the
battery and regiment up to the crest of a ridge to their
front. "Forward your battery," he cried and Reynolds
set his horses at a gallop up the slope ahead of the infantry. His guns were unlimbered speedily and emplaced. Shortly they began to bang away at the tell-tale
puffs of smoke which indicated active Confederate artillery and at a good-sized clump of trees to the front
which was a group of Southerners.[27] Colonel Slocum
called out to his Second Rhode Island, "By the left flank,
march!" and the regiment swung left crossing a rail
fence into a field to the left of the road amid a hail of
ineffectual but intimidating musketry.[28] Captain Woodbury, talking to Hunter, pointed out that the division
should deploy to the left of the road so as to stay close
enough to the fords to act in conjunction with Heintzelman when he crossed, and Tyler later. Hunter agreed
then went forward to urge the Rhode Islanders to hang
on, for they were outnumbered and hard pressed.[29]

In the meantime, McDowell was moving up the road
from the blacksmith shop to Sudley's as fast as he could
because he had seen, through a break in the trees, great
clouds of dust to the south which indicated that the
Rebels were moving up reinforcements to halt the Union
right wing. It was imperative, he knew, that his flanking
column not be caught on both sides of the stream.
McDowell now reversed his orders to Howard, calling
him up from the position he had occupied at the blacksmith shop to strengthen the turning movement.[30] As
McDowell passed the Second New Hampshire, he called
for its colonel, Gilman Marston, saying, "Tell him to

have his men ready, for we shall soon meet the enemy
in large force." The troops immediately began to dump
their blanket rolls and the pioneers their tools in antici-
pation of combat while McDowell hastened on to the
ford.[31] There he met Burnside whose brigade was yet
only half across, moving slowly and stopping to drink.
"The enemy is moving heavy columns from Manassas,"
he said, urging him to hurry. Hastening the last of his
regiments across the ford, Burnside pushed down the
road to join Hunter on Matthews Hill. En route he met
his division commander being helped to the rear; Hunter
had been trying to urge forward the Second Rhode
Island in a bayonet charge when a shell fragment struck
him in the neck, and he was bleeding profusely all over
his tunic.[32]

"Burnside, I leave the matter in your hands. Slocum
and his regiment went in handsomely and drove the
scoundrels." With that Hunter continued to the rear
trying to staunch the flow of blood, while his subordinate entered the field of combat. The situation had
rapidly degenerated in the half hour that the lead regiment and battery held Matthews Hill alone. Hunter had
been hit. Colonel Slocum crossed a rail fence into a
cornfield to reconnoiter for a charge. As he was recross-
ing the fence and urging his men forward, he was hit
twice, the impact of the bullets driving him over the
rails as he fell. The regimental major was also hors de
combat from a cannon ball which passed through his
horse crushing both his own legs.[33]

Taking quick command, Burnside[34] ordered his next
three regiments into position, the First Rhode Island
relieving the hard-pressed Second. Two boat howitzers

of the Seventy-first New York were added to Reynolds's battery on the left of the road. The line held. A hail of musketry rained down, and the New Hampshire regiment supporting the brigade artillery suffered particularly because its position directly behind the guns made it vulnerable to all Rebel overshots.[35] Marston called his regiment to attention to move them out of the fire, but as they rose up to fall in, the colonel was struck in the shoulder and knocked down. His adjutant bent down to help him up, inadvertently grasping the injured arm. To his dismay, "the air was burdened with choice selections from the old colonel's matchless vocabulary." When he had regained his composure, Marston allowed himself to be helped to the rear, command of the regiment passing to its lieutenant colonel.[36]

With two of four colonels and many of the field officers out of action, Burnside found himself sorely tried in an exposed position while the Confederates fired from the cover of trees. It was none too soon when Porter arrived on the field and began to deploy across the road on the right. As he was superior in rank, he now assumed command of the division. Griffin's artillery battery galloped out to Burnside's left flank to augment the fire of Reynolds's guns and the two howitzers. In a short while Ricketts, too, arrived and went into position next to Griffin.[37] It was not long before the effective fire of these guns silenced the Rebel artillery, but Burnside was not yet out of the fire. His left flank remained shaky even after Porter was deployed. To correct this, Burnside spurred his horse over to Porter and requested one of the battalions of regulars. Porter, who had just learned that he was in command, responded at once by sending George Sykes's regular army battalion back with Burnside. With the aid of these experienced campaigners the flank was stabilized and the division could begin to think of aggressive action. The Confederates by this time were strung out from a farmhouse surrounded by haystacks on the right to a second house on their left. All along their lines the puffs of smoke and spurts of flame gave no indication of any intention to retreat.[38]

This was exactly the situation that McDowell did not want. The Southerners had managed to confront his turning column with enough force to halt its progress before the Stone Bridge was cleared for Tyler. There were now two alternatives of action open to him. He could hope to bring up Heintzelman to enlarge his force and drive the enemy back before they could build up to equal him. Howard was already on the way up to Sudley's to join Heintzelman which would give him three brigades. This was a question of legs, however; and the Southerners had a distinct advantage in that they marched on interior lines while the Northerners marched the long way around the outside. The second alternative was to have Tyler force the bridge in his front or cross by any other means, just so long as he reached the west bank. In effect, if Tyler was able to get across the Run, he would produce the same result Heintzelman would have produced had the guide not missed the turn off to the left. In line with this, McDowell had already sent his aide, Lieutenant Kingsbury back to Tyler as soon as Hunter had been halted, to tell him to press the attack with all vigor.[39] It was now a question of which alternative occurred first and whether either would occur be-

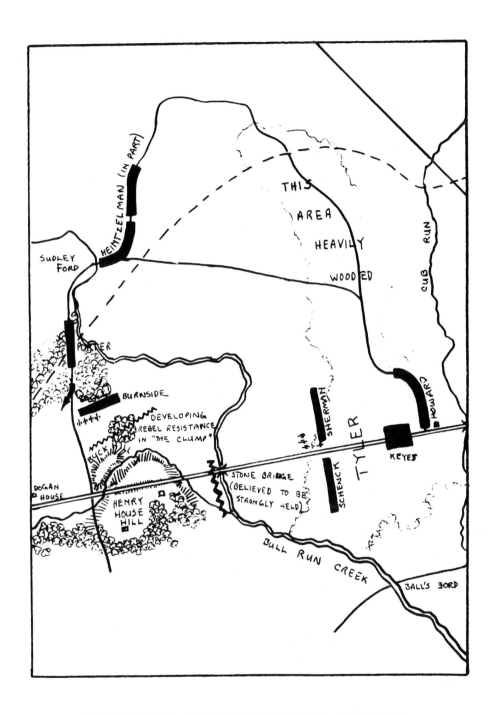

McDOWELL'S ADVANCE BECOMES ENGAGED,
PHASE II

Hunter's Division of Burnside and Porter strike enemy resistance

fore the dust clouds which were rolling northward from
the area around Manassas materialized into Confederates.

Tyler, in the meantime, had been demonstrating about
the Stone Bridge while Hunter was wading through
Sudley's Ford. In order to keep himself well informed
on the situation to the north, he posted himself next to
a tall pine tree and sent one of his aides, Lieutenant
O'Rourke, forty or fifty feet up the trunk with a glass.
When Hunter's first troops emerged from the woods
shortly after ten, they were easily discernible; and when,
an hour later, it became evident that the flanking movement had been stalled, Tyler was aware of it as soon as
anyone else. He began to ponder what should be done.[40]
Three days before, he had been aggressive; and in the
process he had figuratively nearly had his nose shot
away. Should he try again? McDowell had been irate
the last time he over-interpreted his orders in a seemingly
perfect situation. What would he say this time; and, more
important, what would happen if he tried to force a
crossing? He mounted his horse and rode out to Sherman's brigade. The colonel was also aware that Hunter
had reached an impasse because he could hear the firing
of lines which were not drawing closer. Tyler said that
they may have to send a regiment to aid the column if
something did not happen soon. The two men talked
briefly of the situation before the division commander
returned to his tree.[41] It was here that Lieutenant Kingsbury reported to him with orders from General Mc-
Dowell to press the attack quickly.

"What does he mean?" asked Tyler. "Does he mean
that I shall cross the stream?"

"I give you the message exactly as it was given to me."

"I have a great mind to send Sherman across the stream," he thought aloud,[42] and it was not long before thought was transformed into action. Keyes's brigade, which had been placed in the rear after the delay in letting Hunter and Heintzelman have the road, was ordered forward. Sherman must cross Bull Run at once.[43]

Sherman needed no further invitation than that to fight. He instantly remembered the two Rebels who had forded the Run earlier in the day to taunt him. Now he would use their crossing to whip them. With Ayres's battery close behind and Keyes's closing up rapidly, he started toward the stream. A company of skirmishers crossed, then down into the water splashed the rest of the brigade single file. They clambered up the steep west bank and advanced onto the field. Sherman made certain that his colors were well displayed and that his men marched slowly because he had a gray-clad regiment under his command. It would be most disheartening to receive the fire of one's own compatriots. When Ayres reached the Run behind the last regiment, he found the banks were too steep for his horses and guns. As soon as Sherman found this out, he put the artilleryman on his own to handle his pieces as he saw fit.[44]

Porter had just deployed to the west of the road and become engaged when Sherman appeared off to the left and the tip of Heintzelman's column could be seen emerging from the trees back at Sudley's Ford. With these added forces facing them, with the effect of the Union artillery which had only a short time before been augmented by the arrival of Griffin's and Ricketts's batteries, plus a resolute charge by Burnside's brigade supported by Porter, the Confederates gave way desert-

ing their clump of trees. Porter's men carried the stone
farmhouse in front of them overcoming a determined
resistance. Back across the pike the Confederates went
up onto Henry House Hill while Sherman passed behind
Burnside's brigade to turn down the road from Sudley's
toward the enemy.[45]

The first crisis of the day was over. McDowell had a
front of three brigades now to drive down on the Confederates where they had withdrawn below the pike.
Tyler himself followed close behind Sherman with
Keyes's brigade which he soon placed on Burnside's left.
Heintzelman's two leading brigades, Franklin and Willcox, were right behind Sherman on the road leading
south from Sudley's. Howard, the third brigade of that
division, was marching at double quick up the road to
the ford and would soon be across. McDowell rode
along the rear of the line with his staff waving his cap
and shouting, "Victory! Victory! The day is ours."

"Give us a chance at them, General, before they all
run away," called one of Sherman's men stepping
forward.

An old British veteran curtly gave him some sound
advice. "Shut up your damned head. You'll get chances
enough, maybe, before the day is over."[46]

And Tyler on the far left was greeted by McDowell's
adjutant, James B. Fry, standing by a fence shouting
jubilantly, "Victory! Victory! We have done it." They
need only drive the Rebels from Henry House Hill and
the day would belong to the North.[47]

At this point, Burnside realized that his brigade had
been roughly handled and overtaxed because it had
borne the brunt of the fighting for more than an hour.

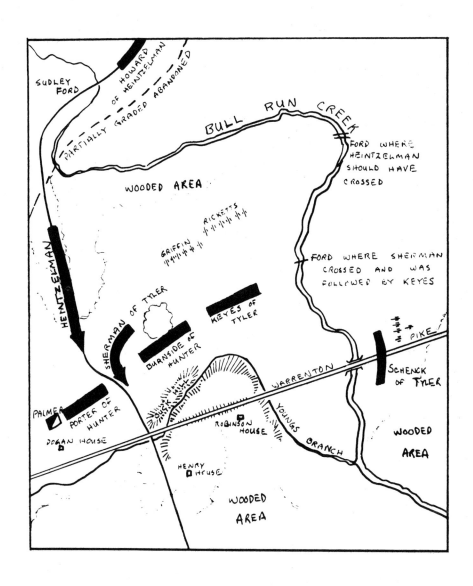

McDOWELL'S ATTACK AT ABOUT 12:30, PHASE III
Tyler's Division is now split into three parts. Heintzelman is
just arriving with his first two brigades with Howard, his third,
on the way.

He decided to withdraw it from the line to give his men
a chance for rest and resupply of ammunition. At his
order the unit halted then marched back up Matthews
Hill where it halted and broke ranks. The troops built
fires to boil coffee talking happily about their victory
and exchanging stories of feats at arms with those of
coincidence. In almost no time the battle itself had progressed southward across Young's Branch, a tiny creek
which emptied into Bull Run below the Stone Bridge,
and up the side of Henry House Hill. Burnside, however, was oblivious to all this, blithely awaiting orders
from superiors who had more to do than follow his
whims.[48]

Porter, too, had been roughly greeted by the Southerners. Two of his regiments were in a high state of
disrepair. Henry Slocum[49] was the second colonel of
that name to be hit that day.[50] His wounding left the
Twenty-seventh New York without a leader, and the
Eighth New York had taken such a pounding that it was
temporarily demoralized.[51] In order to give his men a
chance to rest, Porter allowed Heintzelman's brigades to
pass through and form a line of battle in front of him.
Keyes still held the left flank. Next to him was the
brigade of Sherman advancing with his regiments one
behind the other so that he had a front of only one
regiment. Then came Willcox. To his right was the
brigade of Franklin. Palmer's cavalry battalion pro-
longed Franklin, and on the extreme right was the much
fatigued brigade belonging to Howard. The recuperat-
ing brigade of Porter supported Howard more or less.[52]

If Porter's men had been treated with a heavy hand,
Howard's men had been doubly so handled but in a

different way. They had been retained early in the day at the blacksmith shop by McDowell's order, and it was also McDowell's order sent by Heintzelman which had brought them up the road to Sudley's at double quick time. For almost a mile the brigade ran, shedding packs, blanket rolls, and canteens. When it became obvious that such a killing pace could not be kept up in the broiling sun, the column was slowed to quick time. The aide who guided it followed the only course he knew—the long way round to Sudley's Ford, Howard's men having to run or walk quickly over the whole distance. By the time the regiments reached the ford, many of the men had passed out or fallen by the roadside. The road was strewn with equipment and fallen bodies. As men pressed on into the shallow water, the veins on their heads and necks standing out like whipcords, a staff officer on the far side cried, "You better hurry if you want to have any fun." Down the road they hurried, the signs and sounds of combat growing ever more distinct. Major Fry met them at the edge of the trees with orders to place the brigade out to the right. Nervously they pushed forward, aching all over from the incredible race up the Sudley Road. Now they moved into a hollow, and Howard formed the brigade in two lines of two regiments each just north of the Dogan House.[53]

At this point, there was a general amount of confusion on the battle field because no one seemed to know where his next order would come from or who was to the right and left. Coordination of operations was completely lacking until the brigades were finally got into line, then the situation degenerated again. Burnside had withdrawn without specific authorization or order.

Heintzelman had arrived on the field to find no staff officer or commander to tell him where to go. It was some time before he found McDowell. Even then the placement of his two brigades, Franklin and Willcox, was left to Heintzelman's discretion. He decided that the best place to deploy was on the army right flank in hopes that he could outflank the Rebel left.[54] McDowell himself was preoccupied with the prospect of helping along the Rebel retreat as much as possible. Barry had already brought the Rhode Island battery 500 yards forward; now he was ordered to place two batteries on Henry House Hill in order to give close support to the infantry about the edge of it.[55]

On his own initiative, Griffin had already come forward 200 yards from his first position to a place where he was busily engaged blasting at the Confederates across the pike.[56] It was here that Barry found him when he delivered the order for both his and Ricketts's guns to go forward. Griffin looked out across the valley to Henry House Hill and realized that the spot he was to occupy was the one from which he had shortly before driven a Confederate battery. Surely that was not where he was to go. Why, he could almost spit into the Confederate lines from there, in addition to the fact that he would be a good distance in front of his own troops. Barry assured him that he would have support. With substantial misgivings, Griffin limbered up five of his six guns in preparation for the advance—with a ball lodged immovably in its barrel the sixth gun would hardly be any help, so it was left behind. Followed shortly after by Ricketts's six guns, he started forward.

Yet he could not clear his mind of the doubts he felt in

regard to the advanced position he was to occupy. It was impossible to go forward any more. There was no real support to defend his guns against direct attack. He searched out Barry and told him these things.[57] But Barry was McDowell's artillery staff officer and knew what had to be done. He was not inclined to listen to Griffin very seriously. Besides, the Eleventh New York, the regiment of Fire Zouaves which had belonged to Ellsworth before his death, looked to him like an excellent unit. Barry had seen it march smartly under fire and cross obstacles with the proper procedure which impressed him and caused him to choose it as one of the two to act as battery supports.[58]

When he heard Griffin's complaints, the major said the Zouaves were ready to double quick right behind the batteries. Griffin, however, wanted them to go first and deploy on the hill as a cover while the batteries were unlimbered, then they could assume their post behind. He also was against the position on Henry House Hill. A better place, he felt, would be on Buck Hill about 500 yards north of his present destination. Barry reaffirmed his faith in the Zouaves, adding that the choice of position had been McDowell's, a fact which placed it beyond the authority of both.[59]

Although somewhat reserved, Griffin was the bearer of a cynical disposition and a hot temper both of which often flared up against their provoker.[60] He was nearing that point now as he repeated his convictions about the supporting units Barry had chosen. They would not hold! He was certain.

"Yes, they will. At any rate it is McDowell's order to go there."

"I will go," acquiesced the Captain. "But mark my words, they will not support us." Once again he started his guns southward toward the pike and the hill beyond.[61] The Eleventh Massachusetts broke down a rail fence for Griffin as he trotted toward the ridge. The gunners were confident and cocksure—with good reason. They were regulars, their weapons were excellent, their condition superb, and they had just finished blasting a Rebel battery from the position they were entering.[62]

Ricketts's battery, which was following some distance behind Griffin, became the sudden object of Confederate artillery attention at the same time that they reached the Young's Branch ravine. Ricketts, at the head of his company, heard his lieutenant say, "We cannot pass that ravine."

They had to, Ricketts assured him. Under fire as they were, any countermarch would produce such confusion that they would surely be destroyed. Whip up the horses, then. At a gallop they went down, across and up the far side amid bursting shells. One wheel was smashed on the rough ground. While it was rapidly replaced, the remainder of the cannoneers rushed forward to tear down the fence blocking their advance.[63] In short order the six guns struggled up the Henry House Hill and went into battery. Horses went down. Men were shot while serving the pieces. It seemed to Ricketts as if the fire were coming from the Henry House, which was almost within spitting distance. He turned his guns on the building and cut loose. Shingles, plaster, and wood splinters flew as he thoroughly riddled it before returning to the Confederates in the trees to his front.[64] A few minutes later Griffin arrived. The lieutenant leading his battery had turned left on the way up the hill; and in the time required to rectify the mistake, Ricketts had passed into the lead. With his five guns, he swung in on Ricketts' left; and in a short while there were eleven guns banging away at the Confederates across the ridge.[65] In the trees which rimmed the southern side of the hill, great palls of smoke drifted lazily through the hot air.[66]

Barry arrived with the Eleventh and Fourteenth New York to support the guns in their precarious position.[67] The Fourteenth marched into the woods on the right and the Zouaves deployed behind the guns with the battalion of marines. Franklin's brigade augmented by one regiment from Porter moved out onto the left of the batteries and lay down to protect themselves.[68]

During the time Griffin and Ricketts moved up from their positions on Matthews Hill; and while McDowell was straightening out his line as best he could, there had been a lull of half an hour. At about two o'clock when the guns were finally in position, the supports up, and the brigades deployed in line, the battle resumed in all its intensity. McDowell had thus far succeeded in executing his design. He had four batteries of artillery and seven brigades of infantry on the west bank of Bull Run. He was below the Stone Bridge about to drive the enemy off the last defensible ridge before Manassas Junction. The day was progressing well. He had already decided upon the verdict; and the elation of victory coursed through his veins. It was merely a matter of time.

A peculiar event materially affected the result of the day although divorced from the general action. Keyes's brigade had arrived on the field of combat to assume a position on the left flank of McDowell's line. With it was General Tyler, the division commander. There were two houses atop Henry House Hill, one its namesake and the other farther east and closer to the pike: the Robinson House. When the action resumed around two o'clock, Tyler sent the brigade forward to capture a Confederate battery which was firing destructively on his lines from a position near the latter farmhouse.[69] Up the steep slope at a run went two of Keyes's regiments. After about 100 yards, he ordered them to drop into cover behind a slight rise in the ground and load. They came up again, this time into a hail of fire from Rebel infantry in support of the battery. From positions in the farm buildings themselves, from behind the hedges and fences in the farm yard, Confederate fire poured out. The two regiments captured the positions with great gallantry, but the intensity of the Southern fire made the position untenable, and it was impossible to capture the batteries. Keyes, however, did not want to retreat. Instead, he dropped off to his left and Tyler brought the remainder of the brigade around the base of the hill where they rejoined in a patch of woods.[70] Tyler here lost all grasp of his terrain position, his task relative to the line of battle and his own rank as a division commander. Leading Keyes's brigade, he dropped farther left toward Bull Run, pushing ever southward in the hope that he could find a place to outflank the Confederate batteries. He sent word back to McDowell of his intention before he started, but after that he became engrossed in his own little fight. A Rebel battery deployed to enfilade his brigade but its inaccuracy on the initial rounds allowed the regiments time to escape unscathed. At long last he found a place from which he could strike the Confederates in their flank. It was well over an hour from the time he first attacked the Robinson House; and the unfortunate fact was that, while he played tactical genius with no restrictions other than those of his immediate area, his army had been repulsed.[71] His aide reined in a panting horse and blurted, "The army is in full retreat towards Bull Run!"

Tyler was skeptical. After all, he was about to execute a brilliant maneuver.

"Ride with me to the rear a hundred yards, and I will show you I am right," affirmed the aide.

What Tyler saw amazed him, for the aide had been not only right but also understating the case. Keyes was ordered to withdraw at once and get back across the Run before he was cut off.[72]

To see what caused this disaster, it is necessary to return to Henry House Hill at two o'clock, the time Tyler had taken Keyes off to the left. Griffin and Ricketts had been deployed and supported, the rest of the line had moved into position, McDowell was confident of victory, and the lull in firing was rapidly ending.

At about two, firing resumed with increased pace. Ricketts and Griffin, now together, were pouring their fire through clouds of smoke into the Confederates across the ridge while Union infantry struggled valiantly to seize complete control of the woods to the right of the two batteries. Because of the heavy growth of trees the regiments were broken up and forced to fight individually, or in small groups.[73] The crucial struggle, it was clear, would develop about the two Union batteries near the Henry House and officers on both sides knew it.

To get a better field of fire, Griffin pulled two of his

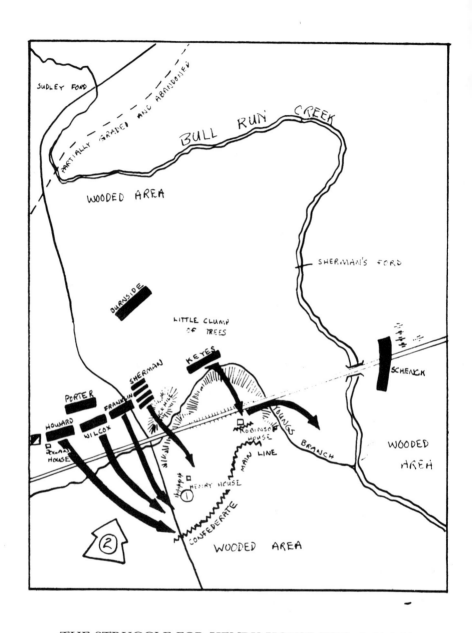

THE STRUGGLE FOR HENRY HOUSE HILL, 2:00-3:30
(1) Represents the final position of Griffin and Ricketts before they were overrun. The contest was resolved: Confederate reinforcements (2) hit McDowell's flank.

guns out of position, marched them around behind Ricketts, and went into battery on the right. Two guns of the Rhode Island battery arrived to unlimber near the two regular batteries.[74] There were now thirteen guns along the ridge line, an excellent concentration of metal. In a short while, however, it became clear that not only would the guns become the focal point of the battle for Henry House Hill and victory but also they were there to stay irrevocably, whether they wanted to leave or not. Confederate rifle fire in almost no time so decimated the horses that there were hardly enough left to pull one caisson let alone two full batteries.[75] Over on the right, Franklin had watched with trepidation as the gallant artillerymen moved into place. He was equally impressed with the spirit of their supporting units particularly the New York Zouave Regiment.

"There goes a gallant regiment," he said, "but it ought to be supported."

Colonel S. C. Lawrence, who had been pacing about his regiment where it lay on the brow of the hill, spoke up. "It can have support, General. The Fifth Massachusetts will go anywhere you order it."

"Move your regiment by the right to their support," was the happily received order; and it started immediately.[76]

At the same time Major Barry, another of the many officers whose attention seemed to gravitate toward this string of guns, left Ricketts's battery where he had been observing and rode to Griffin's two guns on the right.[77] Half an hour had passed since the regulars had opened fire. Their effect was distinctly noticeable through the smoke-wreathed trees across the ridge.

Griffin's alert eyes suddenly picked out a regiment to his right front almost obscured by a fence. It climbed over the rails, dressed its ranks, and waited for its colonel, who shortly stepped out in front. From what Griffin could see, that particular colonel seemed to be exhorting his men to some great feat which might perhaps involve Yankee artillery. They must be Confederates. He was positive. He ordered the section leader to change front and give the Rebels with a taste of canister. The powder was rammed home, then the payload. But at this point one of those unfortunate occurrences happened which sometimes change the obvious course of events. Barry reined in his horse next to Griffin saying, "Captain, don't fire there. Those are your battery support."

"They are Confederates," was the reply. "As certain as the world, they are Confederates."

"I know they are your battery support. It is the regiment taken there by Colonel Wood."[78]

"Very well," replied Griffin and raced to his guns ordering them not to fire at the line of irregularly clad troops. The two muzzles swung again to the front and splattered their canister charges across the field.

The regiment in the meantime faced left, marched fifty yards, faced right, marched forty yards closer to the Union guns then fired a volley. The intense horror which struck everyone at such a disastrous event was redoubled by the effect which it produced. Those horses not dead were slain. Gunners went down like tenpins. Ricketts was knocked from his saddle. There was no chance now to limber up and retreat. The guns had to be defended to the last inch to be saved.[79]

Colonel Lawrence, who had been on the way to reinforce the Zouaves with his Fifth Massachusetts, had
stopped a bullet, which effectively put him out of action
for the remainder of the day. His regiment fell into confusion, and was delayed in reaching the guns.[80]

Just prior to the time when the unidentified regiment
opened fire, Heintzelman, astride his huge, coal-black
horse, rode in among the Zouaves where they sat behind
the artillery line. Intent upon the woods, he did not
notice the regiment scale the fence and march toward
Griffin; but Lieutenant W. W. Averell, Hunter's assistant adjutant general, saw them.

"What troops are those in front of us?" he called to
Heintzelman who was still looking in another direction.
"Here, right in front of the battery," he corrected as he
dropped the reins of his horse across the pommel of his
saddle and picked up his glasses.[81] Heintzelman reined
in his horse with a jerk and looked forward. They must
be Confederates.

He shouted to the Zouaves, "Charge them," and prepared to lead the regiment forward as it leaped to its
feet.[82] Tolstoy propounded in *War and Peace* a neat
little theory that an order is not an order when it is not
obeyed. If such is the case, then here is a perfect example
of his assertion. The Zouaves fired at almost the same
time that the Confederate Regiment[83] cut apart the line
of guns; but instead of charging home with the bayonet,
they began to break. Their disintegration was hastened
on its way by the attack of thirty or forty Rebel horsemen who poured through the regimental ranks firing
their pistols and slashing wildly. Once they had passed
through, the Zouaves fired after them. Three horses went

down with a crash; and when the smoke cleared, there were five empty saddles.[84] The Rebel cavalry was now through the main line of Union troops, in a precarious position. Part of Palmer's regular cavalry battalion swung in on them from the right smashing what formation was left, capturing several Southerners, and effectively scattering the rest. Among the prisoners was Brigadier General George Stewart.[85]

The net effect of this entire action was the disintegration of the Eleventh New York Zouaves as an organized fighting force. Many of them were in the process of proving by their fleetness of foot that a man has great reserves of energy to call upon if events are demanding enough. The majority of the regiment, however, attached itself in small groups to other regiments engaged in trying to retake the guns. Barry and Heintzelman rode in among them, pleading, shouting, and swearing in an effort to hold them together—all to no avail.[86] The marine battalion, too, had fallen apart and disappeared as an organized unit.[87]

The situation devolved into chaos. All eyes were riveted to the spot where Griffin and Ricketts had been. The two Rhode Island guns which had been nearby had miraculously managed to escape[88] the charge of several Confederate regiments which captured the two immobilized regular batteries. Every effort was bent to recapture the lost guns. On the left, Sherman attacked from his position on the Warrenton Pike, but he threw his regiments in one at a time. The ground about the Henry House changed hands several times as his troops struggled up the slope past dead and dying artillery horses and bodies. It was here within a few yards of the building that Secretary of War Cameron's brother was cut down in the hail of small arms fire, leaving his regiment, the Seventy-ninth New York, without a colonel. Officers, in gallantly leading their troops, went down in droves, and it was but a short time before the units began to lose cohesion.[89] Sherman failed to muster sufficient force at any one time to hold what he captured. The only real purpose he served, then, was to produce a fluctuating left wing dangerously in need of support.

Howard, deployed in two lines of two regiments each near the Dogan Farm, was committed for the first time. While Sherman struggled about the Henry House, the first two regiments of Howard's brigade swept up the ridge, through scattered trees, into the fray.

On the run they went passing one of Ricketts's lieutenants, his face covered with blood from a head wound and his horse spouting blood from its wounded nose, bringing off one of the battery caissons. Struggling through thickets and trees at the crest, the two regiments opened fire with a crashing volley while Howard hastened back down to bring up the remainder. In a short time he had three regiments in action with one in reserve, all in the trees off to the right of the fatal artillery position.[90] Down went the color bearer of the Fourth Maine but the colonel, Hiram G. Berry, snatched it up and spurred his wounded horse to the front. Miraculously he remained unhurt despite the many bullet holes which began to appear in his clothes.[91]

Next to Howard went Willcox, into the trees on the western slope of the Henry House Hill, driving the enemy before him and trying to reach a place where his position would make Confederate possession of Griffin's

and Ricketts's batteries untenable.[92] But the brunt of the
fight to hold the ridge and the guns themselves fell to
Franklin's brigade of only three regiments. The Fourth
Pennsylvania, which had demanded its discharge that
morning because of the expiration of its term, had removed one fourth of the brigade's hitting power by its
departure. Two Massachusetts regiments, the Fifth and
Eleventh, had been sent forward while Ricketts and
Griffin were still firing. When they arrived, the holo-
caust was in full eruption. The two units opened fire
while still in column, some men shooting down their own
compatriots ahead of them. In a short while, the intense
fire had so used them up that they began to break up
as the Zouaves had before. "Grim old Heintzelman"
arrived with Willis Gorman's First Minnesota, leading
it into the fray himself. The Southerners were driven
back; the guns retaken. But instead of pulling the artillery
pieces back toward the pike, the regiment began to re-
form and reload its rifles. Those men who tried to tow
the guns out by hand found them so encumbered by
dead horses that they could not move them. Griffin
managed to get three of them going to the rear but a
Rebel counterattack recaptured all eleven. Heintzelman
snatched up the next regiment he could find, the First
Michigan of Willcox's brigade, and threw it forward.
Once again the position was recaptured, and yet again
the Union infantrymen were driven out. The Fourteenth New York, from Andrew Porter's defunct brigade, went forward with Heintzelman in the lead. They
broke and ran at the first fire, white-haired Heintzelman
himself catching a bullet which shattered his arm just
below the elbow. Doctor King rode up and tried to cut

the bullet out while still on his horse but he found it impossible. While Heintzelman fumed and swore from his saddle, he dangled his damaged arm down so the doctor, who had dismounted, could cut the ball out and bandage the wound.

McDowell, by this time, was in Sherman's brigade trying to steady the situation while Heintzelman, with his freshly bandaged arm, and Barry tried desperately to save the guns.[93] The attention of everyone on the field had been drawn to the struggle for control of Henry House Hill and particularly the area about the house itself. All eyes were glued to the surging lines about that place. Sherman, from the left, had angled into the gun position while Willcox and Howard, on the right, drifted left into the trees on the western edge of the ridge to save the two batteries. As a result the Union right flank and rear were forgotten completely in the desperate struggle to the left. It was at this moment, while the struggle about the Henry House hung heavily in the balance, that fresh Confederate reinforcements struck the right flank and rear of the attacking Northerners. No one saw them coming; nothing could stop them when they hit. The preoccupation which encompassed every Yankee in regard to Henry House Hill had so uncovered that wing that no Union brigades were in a position to do more than to save themselves. McDowell sent the regulars from Porter's brigade into the face of the fresh Southerners; and the effect of these seasoned troops blunted the onslaught enough to give the Army of North-Eastern Virginia time to pull back across Bull Run. The men did not race from the field in individual flight but rather in groups moving slowly back to their

camps beyond the stream. Some went by way of the
Sudley's Ford to pick up their blankets and packs; others
forded the stream in various places, moving back across
country toward Centreville.[94]

Major Barry, the unfortunate chief of artillery who
had ordered Griffin not to fire on the unidentified regiment, spurred his horse at a gallop down the slope from
Henry House Hill to escape the onslaught of the victorious Confederates. A mounted officer raced up behind
him shouting, "Halloo, Barry, is that you?"

"Yes," was the reply.

"Where is Griffin?"

"I am afraid he is killed," answered Barry.

"That battery is lost," said the officer stating an all
too obvious fact. "I am afraid we are gone up."

"I am to blame for the loss of that battery," said Barry,
assuming the burden of guilt. "I put Griffin there
myself."[95]

Barry then departed and rode on down the slope until
he came to Young's Branch. There he allowed his much-
jaded horse to halt and water. Suddenly beside him appeared two other officers who reined in their horses to
let them drink, too. It was Griffin and one of his lieutenants. All the bitterness and personal enmity which
Griffin had borne towards Barry long before the battle
welled up inside of him and burst forth in sarcastic
invective.

"Major, do you think the Zouaves will support us?"

"I was mistaken," replied Barry chagrined.

Griffin pressed his attack. "Do you think that was our
support?"

"I was mistaken" repeated the Major.

"Yes, you were mistaken all around," concluded Griffin fiercely and continued on his way back to Centreville.[96]

The army, meanwhile, was having difficulties on the road back. Confederate cavalry drove across the Run south of the Stone Bridge and harassed the retreating soldiers, adding to the disorganization.[97] The straw which broke the camel's back occurred at Cub Run. Rebel artillery from the western bank of Bull Run had been firing for some time on the pike, disrupting the retreat, but now it zeroed in on the ramshackle little bridge across Cub Run just at the moment that a train of wagons was crossing. A direct hit on a vehicle in the middle of the bridge blew off a wheel and overturned it. It was impossible to remove it under the circumstances. Confusion reigned. There was little that could be done. The Cub Run Bridge was blocked; the pike was under artillery fire, clogged with smashed and abandoned wagons, guns, and equipment. Retreat turned to rout and rout, for many, to flight.[98]

What had happened, during the day, to the left wing of the Army of North-Eastern Virginia, under Colonel Dixon S. Miles? The three brigades under his command were entirely separated from the action of the right until the retreat from Henry House Hill. When the right wing set out early that morning, Miles's division, reinforced by Richardson's brigade, was to demonstrate against Blackburn's Ford and protect the army against any assaults from that wing. Richardson, originally in Tyler's division, was on the western side of Centreville in a clear position to advance toward the fords. But the two brigades which originally made up Miles's division,

Davies and Blenker, were bivouacked to the east of the town on the road from Sangster's Station.

When the hour arrived to set out for the positions of the day, Richardson began his unimpeded march down the road to the fords,[99] but the remaining two brigades were forced to wait at Centreville because of the congestion caused by Tyler's slow advance.[100] The division commander had decided that Davies should support Richardson while Blenker remained at Centreville to protect that place.[101] In order to reach Richardson, Davies turned left off the road and pushed through farm fields until he was sufficiently far south to insure that the route would not be blocked by the turning column. He re-entered the road and was moving toward the scene of Tyler's fiasco of July 18, when he passed a road bearing off to the left.

"There is a road that leads around to the enemy's camp direct," his guide stated casually.

"Can they get through that road?" asked Davies.

"Oh, yes, they can," was the reply.

The brigade leader realized immediately that an enemy force which crossed below their left wing and marched up that small road to the Centreville-Blackburn's Ford route would be directly across the only line of retreat for two-thirds of Miles's division. The result of such an action by the Confederates would be ugly indeed, at the very least. Davies halted his brigade, detaching two regiments and two guns to guard against such an eventuality. As soon as this was taken care of he moved on until he found Richardson deployed across the road.[102] In a few moments it was discovered that he ranked Richardson by ten or eleven days,[103] so he

SITE AND RUINS OF STONE BRIDGE

TERRAIN ALONG BULL RUN CREEK

assumed over-all command, sending the remainder of his brigade to the left and posting his artillery near a log barn at Richardson's suggestion.

According to the plan of the previous evening, the artillery opened fire after the signal from Tyler was heard. By ten o'clock, however, the ammunition supply had begun to dwindle rapidly. Davies sent back a request for authorization to cease firing, but Miles denied it. Greene and Hunt continued to fire their guns, though at a much slower rate. If the enemy attacked when there was no artillery ammunition, it would be dangerous and demoralizing to have to fight without artillery support.[104]

During the entire morning, Miles's brigades busily engaged in strengthening their positions with fortifications and obstructions. Log revetments were built, and trees were felled toward the enemy to form an abatis. Blenker built onto the Confederate works about Centreville, improving and enlarging them for his own men.[105] He found himself the heir of six unmanned artillery pieces which had been left behind when their crews demanded recognition of their discharge date that very morning. Among his units, which were predominantly German, were many men who had served as artillerymen in European conflicts. In a short while he had collected enough experienced volunteers from the Eighth and Twenty-ninth New York Infantry Regiments to man these guns for combat.[106]

Miles, in the meantime, rode down toward the Ford to see what was happening there. When he found Davies's two regiments and two guns on the side road, he was instantly annoyed. Without waiting to learn the reason

for this positioning, he hurried forward to find Davies.[107]
A man of violent temper and harsh speech, Miles was
even worse than usual on this particular Sunday. Dysen-
teric diarrhea had plagued him all the way out from
Washington. His doctor had early prescribed opium and
quinine pills to be taken each day, but they seemed to
have no effect on the ailment. Finally, to kill some of the
discomfort and ease the effect of the rest of it, the phy-
sician had authorized the use of brandy on the second
day of the march. In his personal life, Miles was an exceptionally heavy drinker so this remedy was better
received than others; but the fact remained that he felt
quite ill on the day of the battle.[108] When he reached
Davies at the front, therefore, he was not inclined to be
reasonable as he dressed his brigade commander down,
swearing at him profusely. The units at the side road
were called up to be placed in line while Miles turned his
horse to the right to see Richardson. When his superior
had left, Davies quietly sent pioneers back to fell trees
into the side road to obstruct it against the Confederates.[109]

It was almost noon when Miles reached Richardson.
Across the Run, the clouds of dust indicated the Confederates were moving reinforcements northward to
block the flanking movement. Richardson handed Miles
a glass to verify the fact.[110] There did not seem to be
much danger here, and Miles was satisfied with what he
had seen. His tempestuous outburst at Davies had sub-
sided. He returned to Centreville to check Blenker's
position again.[111] He reappeared shortly, at Richardson's
brigade, when the enemy appeared to be falling back
before the right wing of the army.[112] Perhaps it would be

possible to force the ford here and gain some of the laurels of the day for his division. At the council of war the night before, he had expressed his displeasure at being chosen as the army reserve, but orders were orders.[113] There was little he could do then. Now he had a chance.

They had better try to force the Run, he said to Richardson.[114] It was Richardson's brigade which had borne the brunt of Tyler's affair several days previously, and he did not care to be used in such a manner in the exact same spot again. Always outspoken in his relationships with others, whether inferior or superior, Richardson was made more vitriolic because of the dislike he had harbored for Miles over almost a decade. From 1851 to 1853 both men had served in the Third Infantry Regiment at Fort Filmore, New Mexico; Richardson as a captain, Miles as the regimental lieutenant colonel. There they had become embroiled in a personal quarrel which had led to harsh words and strong animosity; but it was saved by the transfer of both, followed by the younger man's resignation in 1855.[115] After almost ten years, the old bitterness began to seep into the two men, especially into Richardson since it was evident from Miles's attitude, behavior, and physical appearance that he had been drinking that day—far beyond the amount specified as a remedy for his ailment.[116]

When Miles told Richardson to force the Run, the latter was in no mood to jeopardize his brigade again, especially under the circumstances surrounding the order.

"Colonel Miles," he said, "I have a positive order for this brigade not to attack at all." He reached into his pocket at the same time, pulled out a piece of paper on which were written the orders for the day, and showed it to the division commander.

"That is positive," replied Miles. Anyway, he could probe the Rebels if nothing else.[117] He ordered both brigades to feel out the enemy down along the Run. Davies sent out several companies from the Thirty-first and Sixteenth New York Regiments; Richardson sent two from the Third Michigan with Brethschneider's Light Infantry Battalion as a support. Down the slope and into the trees they went and were almost immediately greeted by a heavy fire which drove them back. Under the cover of artillery fire from Greene's battery, the Federals regained their jump-off positions unscathed.[118]

Miles then turned his horse back toward Centreville. By the time he reached his headquarters in the town, he was considerably the worse for wear having lost control of most of his faculties. The tide of battle had reversed, and the Union troops were in retreat across Bull Run. On the steps of the house in which he had set up the division headquarters, he met the assistant adjutant general of Heintzelman's division, Chauncy McKeever. McKeever reported the disaster and asked that Blenker's brigade be sent out the pike to block the fugitives and stop the retreat. Miles pushed him away with his hand, saying curtly, "I know all about the fight. You can't give me any information. I have something else to attend to."[119] But in a short time the gravity of the situation waded through the alcohol to his submerged consciousness. He began to act.

Blenker was ordered west on the pike to do what McKeever had requested while Davies and Richardson were called back to Centreville.[120] Richardson started back as soon as he received the order,[121] but Davies did not receive it until it was too late to pull out. The Confederates had crossed the Run on this flank, too, in hopes that they could cut off the retreat of the defeated right wing around Centreville. A good-sized number had pressed up the side road which Davies had blocked by fallen trees after Miles refused to leave the two regiments there. When they reached the fallen trees, the Rebels turned into a valley which led to Davies's left flank. Just as he was turning Hunt's guns toward this force, Davies received the order from Miles to withdraw. If he started back now, there would be organized Confederates breathing down his neck. He waited, carefully arranging his artillery, with his infantry lying down under cover in support. The Southerners moved farther into the valley. He held his fire until their last rank had cleared the cover of the tree line. "FIRE!" The first round scored a direct hit on a horse and rider, sending them flying into the air. The rest of the battery poured in grape and canister, cutting the Confederates apart, disorganizing them, driving them back pell-mell into the trees. With time to spare, Davies started his troops toward Centreville and went to see if Richardson had received the order. To his dismay, he found that he was the only one on the field, his other brigade having passed to the rear while he was fighting. He hurried his men to catch up lest they be caught alone and devoured piecemeal.[122]

Miles had here demonstrated just how intoxicated he really was. The movement of Blenker's brigade, although ineffectual,[123] was good but hardly his own idea. The retreat from Blackburn's Ford was not only contrary to specific orders by McDowell on the previous day,[124] but ill-advised for the very reason that McDowell had cautioned against it—a route was opened up directly into the rear of the Union army at Centreville. If ever the Confederates could interpose across the pike to Washington, it would be all over but the dying. McDowell realized this; surely Miles, in better condition, must have been aware of it. That disaster, worse than had already taken place, did not occur was not because there was no opportunity.

In addition to this, Miles had committed a fundamental error which almost cost him the loss of an entire brigade. In command of the two brigades at Blackburn's Ford was Thomas Davies; yet when the time came to retreat, Miles sent withdrawal orders to both. Thus they retreated independently of each other without the coordination of one leader; and as a result, Richardson marched to the rear to the music of firing which could easily have wiped Davies out with his right flank uncovered as it was. The combination of fortuitous circumstances and Davies's own foresightedness in blocking the road to the lower fords saved the left flank from annihilation in detail.[125]

By pushing his men hard, Davies soon caught up with Richardson. Both men were puzzled by the actions of their division commander and Richardson asked his fellow brigade commander why the retreat had been ordered.

He did not know.

Well, did the enemy attack him from the left?

Yes, but they had been handsomely repulsed. Davies

added that he had no idea what was happening. When they had reached a position three-quarters of a mile from Centreville, an aide from McDowell intercepted them with orders to block the road up from Blackburn's. McDowell was only too well aware of the danger to his rear presented by the lower fords of the Run.[126] The two officers began to deploy their brigades with Richardson stringing his in a ravine across the road and placing his artillery along a ridge crest to the rear. The Third Michigan was placed in close column behind the guns as a reserve.[127]

When he reached Richardson's position, Miles was highly displeased with it. The shadows of late afternoon were beginning to lengthen and blur into those of dusk, but the passage of time had done nothing to sober the division commander. He was worse. First he ordered the position of the Twelfth New York changed; and when someone had done this for him,[128] he rode his big bay horse over to check. Wearing two hats, he presented a ludicrous sight hardly in keeping with the gravity of the moment. Lying behind a fence, the New Yorkers were greeted with this caricature unsteadily riding his horse along their lines, talking monotonously. It was this regiment which had so shamefully broken on July 18, a fact of which Miles was well aware. "You are now where I want you," he said almost incoherently. "Stay there, damn you, and die there."[129]

Next he spied the Third Michigan, lying in close column behind the artillery. He rode up asking for the regimental commander and was informed that it was Colonel Daniel McConnell. He responded by calling out for O'Donnell. The fact that he was corrected made

no impression. He called out again for O'Donnell. The
regimental commander reported to his flushed-faced
superior who ordered him, in thick-tongued speech, to
deploy the unit in line of battle to the front in order that
the ambulances might have some protection. Interspers-
ing his spaces freely with profanity, Miles continued to
talk for a moment then rode away. The regimental officers did not know what to do. The unit had been placed
in the present position by Colonel Richardson, their
brigade commander; but the division commander, who
was obviously drunk, had ordered them elsewhere.
Someone must go see Richardson. In spite of the fact
that he had been sick the entire day, McConnell had
refused to give up his post at the head of his regiment.
Instead of going himself, an added discomfort, he agreed
with his officers that Lieutenant Colonel Stevens should
go.[130]

Stevens set out and met Richardson almost at once.
Why did Colonel Miles order the regiment deployed
into line of battle, Stevens wanted to know. Whose
order should be obeyed?

Richardson replied that the authorization for a move
must come from himself. Why had this move been
ordered?

"I do not know," answered Stevens, "but we have no
confidence in Colonel Miles."

"Why?" demanded Richardson with piercing intensity.

"Because Colonel Miles is drunk!"[131]

This fact had also reached General McDowell, who
had been notified of the confusion of his left wing by
his adjutant. One of Tyler's aides was sent to tell Rich-

ardson to take command of the left wing while Mc-
Dowell himself would head there as soon as possible.[132]
Alexander found Richardson just a few moments after
Stevens had left. When the brigade commander complained of the drunken interference of his superior
officer, he received the news that the command no longer
resided in Miles but in himself. With this information,
Richardson set out to re-alter the "corrections" which
had been made in his dispositions.

First thing to be done must be to correct the position
of the brigade as a whole. Lieutenant Alexander and he
both agreed that the present position was unmanageably
long. The flanks must be drawn back to rest on the
clumps of trees to their rear in order to protect against
cavalry. Major Barry would mass all the artillery he
could find along the ridge crest to their rear.[134] Richardson himself led the Third Michigan in its change of position. A short distance had been covered when Colonel
Miles rode up hardly able to keep his saddle.

"Colonel Richardson, I don't understand this. You
should march that regiment more to the left."

Exercising his new authority, the brigade commander
replied curtly, "Colonel Miles, I will do as I please. I am
in command of these troops."

"I don't understand this, Colonel Richardson."

"Colonel Miles, you are drunk," was the flat reply as
Richardson turned away to take care of the regiment.

"I will put you in arrest," called Miles ineffectually.

But Richardson now knew that such an eventuality
could not happen. "Colonel Miles, you can try that on
if you have a mind to."

Miles fell silent, watching his bold subordinate tend

to the Michigan regiment.[135] He turned his horse back up the ridge to where Barry was posting guns. What was going on here, he demanded in angry tones. Who was moving those guns? Barry said he was. Miles demanded that his arrangements not be interfered with, but Barry also had a mandate from McDowell. He calmly ignored the vehement protests which filled the air about him.[136]

By this time McDowell had sufficiently cleared up the situation along the pike in front of Centreville to personally inspect the Blackburn's Ford front. When he arrived, Miles hastened to him reporting that his troops were being interfered with.

"Colonel Miles, I find you have everything here in great confusion," replied McDowell who had long since reached a verdict for solution of the problem. "You are relieved from the command of your troops." With a sullen salute, Miles moved away to a point where he waited stolidly for half an hour before he left the field. Although the lack of respect was obvious, McDowell allowed it to pass and rode down to see Richardson.[137]

"Great God, Colonel Richardson," he exclaimed, at last able to find out why his flank had been so endangered, "Why didn't you hold onto the position at Blackburn's Ford?"

"Colonel Miles ordered me to retreat to Centreville, and I obeyed the order."

McDowell replied that Richardson should take command of the troops in that area now; and when the Colonel protested the unfitness of his superior for any command, he was greeted by the reply that Miles was relieved.[138]

In a short time the new line was stabilized, and the

mass of artillery to its rear easily broke up a large body
of enemy cavalry approaching from the ford.[139] The
entire army about Centreville began to take some form
once again. It was certain that many regiments would
not meet again as units until the fugitives were sorted
out, but there were more regiments which kept most of
their organization. The brigades of Keyes, Schenck,
Burnside, Richardson, Davies, and Blenker, six of a total
of eleven brigades, were intact except for battle casualties and a few individual deserters. Over half of the army,
then, remained solidly firm about Centreville, not to
mention the entire reserve division of Brigadier General
Theodore Runyon which was being ordered forward in
part.[140] The question remaining before McDowell was
whether or not he should attempt to hold the heights
about the town with his weakened army or march back
to Washington. The consensus of action, however, left
him no choice; many of the organized units had already
started back down the Little River Turnpike to Washington. There is an oft-quoted passage which may well
describe the night of July 21-22 in the life of the Army
of North-Eastern Virginia and the condition of its men:

> The Saturday and Sunday of the battle (20th, 21st) had been
> parch'd and hot to an extreme—the dust, the grime and smoke,
> in layers, sweated in, follow'd by other layers again sweated
> in, absorb'd by those excited souls—their clothes all saturated
> with the clay-powder filling the air—stirr'd up everywhere on
> the dry roads and fields by regiments, swarming wagons, artil-
> lery, &c.—all the men with this coating of muck and sweat and
> rain [in the early hours of July 22 it had begun to rain torrents],
> now recoiling back, pouring over the Long Bridge—a horrible
> march of twenty miles, returning to Washington baffled,
> humiliated, panic-struck. . . .

They drop down anywhere, on the steps of houses, up close by the basements or fences, on the sidewalk, aside on some vacant lot, and deeply sleep. A poor seventeen or eighteen year old boy lies there, on the stoop of a grand house; he sleeps so calmly, so profoundly. Some clutch their muskets firmly even in sleep. Some in squads; comrades, brothers, close together— and on them, as they lay, sulkily drips the rain.[141]

Chapter VIII

THE DEBITS AND CREDITS
OF BATTLE

THE ORIGINS and incipient capabilities of Union company and field grade officers were the best available, but were the qualities in their superior officers as good? Each arm had its own peculiarities of command material. Each produced a different performance evaluation.

For cavalry, the Army of North-Eastern Virginia entered the campaign with one small battalion of regulars, under Major Innis N. Palmer. The men were veteran campaigners, hardened and well drilled. They knew what to do, when to do it, and why it should be done; but they were pitifully deficient in number. They were led by a West Pointer[1] who could be expected to act judiciously under fire or in reconnaissance. But it was inconceivable that skill in leadership could counterbalance the lack of numbers. With a mere 300 men,[2] Palmer would have been unable to perform the duties of a cavalry arm even if he had been called upon for them. Thus, the quality of leadership in the mounted arm was negated by adverse circumstances.

The artillery was another story altogether. Fifty-five guns of all calibres went into battle on Sunday, two of which were the boat howitzers organic to the Seventy-first New York.[3] Disregarding these two guns as being part of an infantry regiment and served by infantrymen, there were, then, eleven batteries of either four or six guns each. All these outfits were regulars except for the six-gun Rhode Island battery under Reynolds and the six-gun battery which belonged to the Eighth New York Infantry. The officers of the regular batteries were West Point graduates ranging up to the Class of 1851,[4] all of whom had been on continuous active duty since the time of their graduation from the academy. Most had seen active combat whether in Mexico, Florida, or on the frontier and all were well instructed in the use of their arm. It has already been pointed out that the better line officers often went into the artillery and that in peacetime the best care was given to that arm. The commanding officers who went into battle along Bull Run at the heads of batteries were highly reliable and experienced. None had undergone any radical change in command status as a result of the officer expansion on May 14, simply because there was no need for higher-ranking officers in the artillery. Thus all the regular officers occupied command positions which they had previously held for some time and were often leading the very same unit which had been theirs in peacetime. Of the two volunteer batteries, the men of the Eighth New York claimed their discharge on the morning of July 21. The guns which had been left behind were served by volunteers who had previous experience as artillerists in European armies.

The homogeneity of command in the artillery arm, when added to the fact that nine of the eleven batteries were long-term, full-time, regular organizations, pointed to a certainty of better than adequate artillery support in the forthcoming battle. In addition, the artillery officer on McDowell's staff, Major William F. Barry, was a subordinate of great promise. In 1838, he had graduated seventeenth in his West Point class, beginning his combat army career in Mexico. Service in Florida brought more action, and by the outbreak of the war he had achieved an estimable reputation. His battery took part in the defense of Fort Pickens during April, May, and June, he himself barely reaching the Army of North-Eastern Virginia in time for the campaign. The march was one day old when he finally joined McDowell to be appointed chief of artillery.[5] For all-round experience and capabilities, therefore, McDowell's artillery commanders were as a group by far the best of the three arms.

Infantry regimental command does not present such a united picture. Many diverse sources were called upon to produce the colonels who set out with McDowell on July 16, but they can generally be broken down into several categories with regard to former military experience: West Point graduates, veterans of Mexico, militia officers, and veterans of foreign armies.

Five of the regimental commanders were United States Military Academy alumni, two of whom had been on continuous duty since their graduation and were on active duty at the fall of the Charleston Harbor defenses in April. Both of these men, George Sykes, the commanding officer of the regular battalion, and Alex-

ander McD. McCook, colonel of the First Ohio, had
seen actual conflict either in Mexico or against Indians.
Thus, they were already battle tested when the campaign began. The remaining three men, Isaac F. Quinby,
colonel of the Thirteenth New York; Henry W.
Slocum, commander of the Twenty-seventh New
York; and Henry Whiting, the colonel at the head of
the Second Vermont, had all resigned their commissions
to enter civilian life although Quinby had been careful
to become a New York militia officer when he quit the
regular army. In spite of the fact that none of these last
three had passed beyond the rank of first lieutenant,
there was no reason to suspect that they would be incapable of handling their units. Indeed, it was taken for
granted that their West Point education had instilled in
them the basic tendencies necessary to command, re-
gardless of the size of the unit; and such an assumption
was quite justifiable when commissions were being given
out in the months prior to McDowell's campaign. Of
the forty-three regiments[6] which set out with the Army
of North-Eastern Virginia, then, five, more than ten per
cent, were under the control of regular or former regular army officers. They could be expected to be well
trained and to behave well under fire if quality of leadership was a large factor in determining the capabilities
of a regiment—as certainly it must be.[7]

A second group of regimental commanders was composed of Mexican War veterans. The ranks held by this
group during the "Rehearsal for Conflict," as the 1846
war has aptly been called, ranged from non-commissioned officer to full colonel;[8] but the important factor
was that they had undergone battle experience in com-

mand positions. They were able to step into command of regiments in 1861 with relatively little difficulty; in some cases many of this group had continued military affiliation in the militia after the Mexican conflict. Thus, to persons in the position to select regimental commanders, this source could be considered highly productive of men who, if not excellent, would be at least dependable.

The choice of officers for any grade of command had to be made—whether by President, cabinet, governor, or electing troops—with one eye on the man and the other eye on his past record. If he had military experience which bore no stigma, he could be considered a valuable candidate. It was not possible to tell with absolute certainty how each one would turn out under the test of fire. The fact that several men of whom lofty hopes were held failed to bring fruition to this hope in no way reflected upon the perspicacity or objectiveness of the chooser.

A man like George Brinton McClellan may be held up as the epitome of this group. To all outward intents and purposes he had everything necessary to make a good field commander; temperamentally he could hardly have been worse. Each man represented a potentiality which might be realized; and in general during this campaign, the higher the potentiality, the higher the rank.[9]

Militia officers formed the third and largest source of regimental leaders under McDowell. Despite the condition of some state militias and the consequent lack of exacting training for the officers, the experience which they gained within these units made them valuable to the government. It has often been said that the task of

a peacetime soldier is to train for an eventuality which
may never come in his lifetime and which he should
never provoke. The militia leaders lived in a situation
where the arts they learned during peacetime might
never be summoned to the test of "blood and iron,"
while they themselves were not in a position which
bound their lives to the military as in the case of a regular army officer. Yet, many of these men were just as
qualified for regimental command as their West Point
counterparts. The mere experience of commanding a
body of troops rendered them valuable as leaders; and
as many of them had been members of their militia units
over a span of years, they had become more and more
imbued with certain military characteristics. It should
not be assumed that they became military minded but
rather that facets of command became second nature to
them. If peacetime militia officers would not produce a
large number of high-ranking commanders, they could
certainly be expected to serve as stable, dependable regimental commanders.[10]

The last group of officers with previous military experience who fought under McDowell as colonels in
command of regiments were foreigners who had served
in European armies before coming to the United States.
The revolutions of 1848 had forced many leaders to
leave their homelands for America because of their
political views. The tendencies toward ethnic enlistment
which produced all-Irish or all-German regiments elevated many of these men to regimental command merely
because of their ethnic origin, but in most cases they
brought with them an experience which exceeded that
of many of their American counterparts. In this way,

Adolph Wilhelm August Friedrich Baron von Stein-
wehr, a Brunswickian noble who had been raised to be
an officer and who had served in the Prussian army,
found himself at the head of the Twenty-ninth New
York, a regiment of Germans which he had recruited.[11]
   Though they might have been considered somewhat
incongruous with the American military system, it was
unavoidably true that these men had experience in actual warfare, a fact not to be overlooked in granting
commissions. Certainly they could be depended upon in
battle, and in the future, they would probably produce
at least several good leaders of higher rank.[12]
   Of the total number of regimental commanders who
set out with McDowell from Washington, less than
twenty per cent and probably closer to ten per cent, had
no previous military experience. This was a small portion considering the conditions governing the build up
of the Army of North-Eastern Virginia. It may be assumed, then, that the leadership at regimental level
could be relied upon when the ultimate test of battle was
presented. While nothing spectacular could be expected,
there need be no fear that, at the crucial moment, a regiment would buckle and give way through faulty direction. If one word were to be used to describe Mc-
Dowell's colonels as they appeared before the battle, it
would best be "dependable."
   The brigade commanders were eleven in number, of
which all but three were graduates of West Point. Robert Schenck was clearly a political appointee but Lewis
Blenker, the other non-regular army man, was as well
qualified to the post he received as anyone. Born in
Hesse Darmstadt, Germany, he had risen from private

to lieutenant in the Bavarian army, an extremely difficult accomplishment considering the stratification of
European armies. Blenker, like many other Germans,
was a "forty-eighter" who had been driven from his
homeland for participation in abortive revolutions; and
when war broke out in the United States, he was a natural choice to lead an ethnic regiment. The four regiments which composed the brigade under his command
were of predominantly, if not of totally, Germanic
origin.[13]

Andrew Porter, the last of the three, was a regular
army officer at the outbreak of war. In 1836, young
Porter, then only sixteen, had entered the military
academy; but a year later he resigned. When war with
Mexico burst upon the scene a decade later, he obtained
a commission as a first lieutenant in the mounted rifles,
winning promotion to captain and brevet to lieutenant
colonel in the course of hostilities. It was at this rank that
the fall of Sumter found him, but the May 14 expansion
of the regular army officer corps promoted him to colonel of the Sixteenth Infantry. Like Sherman, he was
assigned to the Army of North-Eastern Virginia in
command of a brigade until his regiment was recruited.[14]
He could be considered a fully qualified officer.

Of the remaining eight brigade leaders, only Keyes,
Franklin, and Howard were on active duty in April,
1861. The remaining five men had been removed from
regular army life for as much as thirty and as little as
four years, but all eight had seen active combat of one
sort or another whether in Mexico or against hostile
Indians. This was, of course, an important factor in their
qualifications. Experience was worth a thousand class

lessons. The brigade leaders, then, under McDowell were experienced, capable men, chosen more for their capacity than anything else. With the army spread out over the continental United States, many men who would later become noted leaders—or failures—were geographically disqualified from taking part in the campaign; but the factor which is most important in judging the quality of brigade commanders is that they all had definite qualifications for command. That none of them had ever commanded a brigade before was irrelevant; almost no one alive at that time in the United States had actually commanded a brigade in war or in peace. General Scott himself had never led more than 13,000 or 14,000 troops. Choices had to be made on the basis of unrealized potential. With the exception of Robert Schenck, the brigade leadership in the army was the best available.

All more than fifty years of age and considerably older than their commanding officer, the division commanders were highly respected officers with long terms of experience behind them. Of the four only Dan Tyler was not on active duty when the conflict began, but he had earned himself such an esteemed reputation during his service that he was a natural choice for division leadership. There could be little complaint in regard to the selection of these four to command the divisions which composed McDowell's striking force.

In the final analysis, the picture of commanders who set out on the roads to Manassas that sixteenth of July was a good one. The officers were, from company to general grade, the best possible with a very few exceptions; and the criticisms which hindsight has leveled at

these men appear invalid when the situation reveals itself
as it actually was, when the criteria available for choice
become evident, and when the condition of the pre-war
officer corps is considered.

In Patterson's Army of the Upper Potomac, there
existed a peculiar organization which had no Union
counterpart then or later in the war. Composed almost
entirely of Pennsylvania militia regiments and regular
units, the army was officered at the regimental level by
militiamen of that state. There were no West Point men
among its colonels but the percentage of veterans of the
Mexican war was vastly superior to McDowell's. In
addition, there were only one or two men who had not
served in the state militia for a lengthy time. Thus in
spite of the lack of regulars or ex-regulars in command
of the regiments, the colonels brought into battle a considerable amount of combat experience and an almost
universal amount of military experience.

The division commanders reflected the purely Pennsylvania quality of the army in that they were appointed
during the period before the federal government issued
its decree removing the governors' power to appoint
colonels and general officers. Thus Keim and Cadwalader were Andrew Curtin's doing rather than Scott's.
When the May 22 order was issued, it was too late to
remove these men even if such an action were desirable;
and there is no record of any pressure to that effect. By
the first of June, Patterson's army needed complete reorganization along the new lines, but it could not be
done until the three-month terms of its officers expired.

Brigades in the Valley, on the other hand, were divided
equally between West Pointers and militia veterans.

George H. Thomas, John L. Abercrombie, Charles P. Stone, and Dixon S. Miles were academy alumni, while E. C. Williams, George Wynkoop, Daniel Butterfield, James Negley and George Starkweather had served in the armies of their respective states.[15] Only Butterfield, the New Yorker, had not fought in Mexico and was, therefore, the only man lacking combat experience.[16]

Because of its peculiar antecedents, Patterson's army was not officered as well as McDowell's Army of North-Eastern Virginia, but neither can it be said that his command system was lacking. He suffered from the same disadvantages which plagued his Washington counterpart: no cavalry, lack of wagons, and general inefficiency of supply due to the troubles in organization. Both Patterson and McDowell felt that the other had all the available wagons; as a result, both complained that they were restricted in their movements.[17] But the major problem which confronted Patterson and never touched McDowell was his lack of sufficient artillery, a crucial weakness, which was not corrected until long after Patterson himself had left the scene.

It has been said that "the battle is the payoff." How well did the officers measure up to their potential in the actual test of fire? How many had exceeded and how many not reached the expectations held of them before the battle? First and foremost of the men involved was General Winfield Scott. In his principal role as coordinator of two wings in a concerted movement, he had failed, not only because of circumstances but because of his own lack of perception. He did not comprehend the true nature of his subordinate in the Valley until McDowell was already on the march for Manassas. It should have been obvious to him that Patterson was lacking in drive long before the disaster at Bull Run pointed it up. The old General in Chief's dispatches were in several instances unclear or contradictory. Nor was vacillation entirely absent from his actions as he alternately enjoined aggressiveness and caution. What was it that caused him to order the regulars detached from the Valley in the middle of June when Patterson had crossed the Potomac into Virginia? Was Washington really in danger or was Scott showing signs of breaking under the strain? Was he seeing hallucinations? If Washington was in grave danger, why did the regulars arrive after an exhausting race from Williamsport only to find a review in progress and gaiety prevalent?

But there were other failures of which Scott was guilty. The general who had cut himself off from his supply base at Vera Cruz and marched into the Mexican interior allowed himself to forget the imponderables of war which he had so capably handled a decade and a half before. McDowell had fully expected to fight on his second day out, but the enemy did not resist his occupation of Fairfax Court House. Scott, however, not only failed to recognize that this might happen, but also made unjustifiable evaluations of McDowell's advance. "Old Fuss and Feathers" telegraphed Patterson that the battle would be on Tuesday, whereas that was only the day the troops began marching and to make matters worse he telegraphed at the end of that day that the junction would probably be carried on the morrow. Where was the enemy to be during the operation? Or were they merely to stand aside and see if McDowell could possibly march from his position east of the Court

House all the way to Manassas on bad roads and across unmapped, unknown territory some fifteen and more miles as the crow flew, let alone as the routes actually went? Thus, Scott excluded from his calculations and from his orders to Patterson, any of the imponderables which rule all military campaigns. If McDowell had marched out in a vacuum with no opposition and no variables, perhaps he could have fulfilled the expectations of the General in Chief; but he certainly could not if the situation were viewed realistically. Censure must fall upon those massive shoulders, be they ever so aged, for one part of the campaign.

The next officer to consider must be Robert Patterson. In the final judgment, it was his failure to hold Johnston in the Valley which allowed some 9,000 troops to be added to Beauregard's army behind Bull Run, the last of these being the fresh units which hit the naked flank and rear of the Union army on Henry House Hill after Griffin and Ricketts had lost. Patterson's constant prevarication in his reports and dispatches, coupled with minimal amounts of action, sufficed to let the Confederates escape. Although he was misguided by his superior, he himself reciprocated in kind; for Scott was not enabled to notify McDowell of Johnston's departure until July 21—after the Army of North-Eastern Virginia had struck at the reinforced enemy.[18] Although contemporary critics unjustifiably heaped the entirety of blame upon Patterson it would be absurd to claim that he was devoid of it. His conduct during the campaign from its first stages had been far from military. He sought, in his subordinates, confirmation of what he knew to be wrong. He ignored reality. He grasped authority but failed to use it. These and many more weaknesses made his removal from command a necessity. It may be overly harsh to say that he committed an absolute blunder under the circumstances; but whether or not he did, he certainly demonstrated his incapacity to hold high command. The verdict, then, must be that Patterson had risen far above his capabilities; and as a ᵕsult, he committed a series of mistakes which materially aided the Confederate efforts.

Personally, the commander of the Army of the Upper Potomac bore the scorn of his countrymen admirably. In a war waged between officers in newspapers and politics, white-haired old Robert Patterson maintained a manly silence until the war was almost won. Refused a court-martial as "incompatible with the public interest,"[19] he finally published, at the end of 1864, his *Narrative of the Campaign in the Shenandoah*, a work marked by weakly defended assertions and badly copied correspondence and more notable for its lacks than its conclusions. After his misadventures in the early months of the war, however, Patterson never again entered the military lists as a combatant. He lived out the remainder of his extremely lengthy life in great usefulness characterized by an honorable financial wizardry rarely found in reconstruction expansion.[20]

The last of the three principal figures of the campaign was General Irvin McDowell, by far the most unfortunate. It has been said that no commander, no matter how perceptive and well prepared he may be, can hope to win a campaign without luck. If ever a man was lacking in this commodity, it was Irvin McDowell. His plan of advance was excellent; it took into consideration all factors from supply to condition of troops. He expected to fight at Fairfax Court House, which he could not do. He planned to move from his left flank, which he could not do. He devised an excellent plan to flank the enemy behind Bull Run, which was improperly executed. Through all these subversions of his intent he bore up well, dealing flexibly with each in its turn; yet he failed to win the victory his government so coveted. How much, exactly, did he contribute to his own defeat? In comparison with Patterson's easily accomplished fifteen miles of marching a day—when he marched at all—McDowell never covered more than five or six. He did everything in his power to hasten the columns on their way but to no avail. The inexperience of the troops; the rough, wooded nature of the terrain; the dilapidated condition of the roads; and the constant fear of the "masked battery" defeated all attempts to increase speed. In addition to these factors was lack of coordination of the four divisions which made up a green army marching on four separate roads, with an inadequate staff and communications system. The young commander, therefore, is hardly censurable on this account; for in comparison, Patterson marched through open country, unopposed and on one road, the Valley Pike, which was a beautifully paved highway.

The most culpable act that McDowell committed was the delay at Centreville. Every day he allowed to pass brought more and more Confederates to Manassas, and he knew it. Peculiarly enough, he eventually wound up fighting just the number of troops he had estimated he would have to though it is obvious that the arrival on Sunday of the last units from the Valley turned the tide

of battle. But there should be no question about the passing of July 20; it was uselessly wasted. When the reconnaissance ended in failure to reach the fords on Friday
afternoon, McDowell should have drawn upon the
knowledge he had at hand to devise his plan; for there
was absolutely nothing added to his intelligence through
the efforts made that night. The net effect was to force
him to wait another full day, Saturday, July 20, in order
to strike at early dawn. It is impossible to understand
just what prompted McDowell to commit this blunder
but nevertheless, he did it, and the full blame must rest
squarely on him.

His second great error was in not continuing his determination to marshal his forces Saturday evening.
When he set out from the west bank of the Potomac on
Tuesday, he used only the latter half of that day to
march his troops. They moved from their entrenched
positions to what were, in effect, "jump-off" areas.
Without attempting to strike the enemy, the divisions
traversed a short distance easily covered in from one to
three hours, to posts from which they could easily hit
the Confederates at the Court House on the day following. The columns were thereby rested for the attack,
had little distance to march, and were more easily coordinated. Why, then, did McDowell allow himself to be
swayed against this same maneuver on Saturday? The
reason which Burnside adduced against the movement—
that it would tire the infantry more to make two short
marches than a single long one—directly contradicted
experience. McDowell acquiesced, and the result was the
irrevocable delay and mix up about Centreville during
the earliest hours when progress should have been made.

Once again there was no one to blame but the army commander. The decision was his to make, and he made it, however incorrectly.

In the tactical execution of the battle, McDowell was guilty of a serious fault: he allowed himself to be swept up by particular units, directing them himself. The Union army lacked the over-all authority he should have exercised as the coordinator of all units. At some points he reduced himself to a company commander. The major cause of this action was the total inadequacy of McDowell's staff. Not only was it too few in number, but also it was lacking in experience or skill. As a result, many functions which should have been delegated remained McDowell's own, plaguing him and diverting his attention.

There has been much blame placed upon him for sending Ricketts and Griffin to Henry House Hill. Certainly, when the facts are seen, it becomes evident that McDowell was in no way to blame for their loss; the move itself was tactically an excellent and wholly justifiable one. There was, however, one decision made that Sunday which is undefendable under any circumstances: the retention of Howard's brigade at the blacksmith shop. Twenty per cent of the striking power of the flanking column was removed at a stroke, and no advantage was gained in so doing. On the east bank there were six brigades in two divisions, over half the army, to defend against any Confederate assaults. Why should McDowell strengthen the safest wing and weaken the most vulnerable? On a small scale this action is highly reminiscent of the later actions of the Germans, in World War I, who modified the Schlieffen Plan constantly until the actual main thrust had been cut in half.[21]

It is interesting to note that McDowell's original judgment had been right. A movement by the left to cut off the Confederates, if possible, would have forced them to evacuate Manassas or assume the offensive. The movement by the right was not decisive. Once across the Run, the Army of North-Eastern Virginia was still confronted with the necessity of attacking a Rebel force which lay between the Federals and Manassas Junction. The frontal battle which McDowell had sought to avoid thus became a reality.

How well did the division commanders perform in battle and did they bring their potential to fruition? David Hunter was struck down early in the day while rearranging his lone Rhode Island regiment. In the short time that he was on the field, he had already demonstrated the fault that was to plague the entire army all day: he, too, lost over-all vision of his command. When one unit of the division became heavily involved, whether it was a brigade, a regiment, or even a company, his tendency was to hasten to it and bolster it by personal efforts. This left the rest of the command without supervision. Hunter, however, was spared any major blunders because of his wound.

Heintzelman performed best of all four division commanders. He pressed his column hard at every chance, he had been ready on time, his tactical judgment was sound, and his efforts on the field were not too personalized. When the batteries atop Henry House Hill fell, he rode his huge horse into the very teeth of the enemy to encourage his men. Yet in the final analysis, he, too, had failed in perception of the over-all picture. It was his right flank and rear which was so open and unprotected when the fresh Southerners hit, and it was his brigades which swung into the Henry House Hill battle without proper flank cover. Heintzelman's preoccupation with the two batteries accounted for this. Both Hunter and Heintzelman exhibited great personal bravery but varying degrees of success, a characteristic of Union command that day.

Daniel Tyler proved that he had the least capacities for command of all four—even less than Miles. Although he set out on time, his advance was so excruciatingly slow that he threw the finely balanced time table out of kilter by considerably more than an hour. It took him three hours and longer to march the three miles from his bivouac area past the blacksmith shop with only two of his brigades, as Keyes waited beside the road for the turning column to pass in order that the route to Sudley's would be uncovered. Throughout the entire campaign, Tyler had marched enough behind schedule to dislocate his commander's plans. In addition, he had provoked the disastrous Blackburn's Ford affair.

But, it was in the actual battle that he demonstrated his incapacity for high command. When Griffin and Ricketts fell, he had three brigades under his command, but knew the whereabouts of one only. Schenck was somewhere on the east bank of Bull Run and, in fact, he never managed to cross over as he should have. Sherman was somewhere off to the right and rear where he had become the left flank unit when Keyes dropped down to the Run. The single brigade of Tyler's division which he controlled was Keyes's. Not only did Tyler desert two-thirds of his striking force in order to play tactical genius—ineffectually—with the brigade of Keyes, but also he left no particular instructions to guide his subordinates. Neither Sherman nor Schenck could have found him if the need had arisen. Thus, in effect, Keyes's brigade had two commanders while the other two had none to coordinate them or direct their movements in concert with other divisions. Because of Tyler, the strongest and freshest units of the flanking column, those that had no appreciable distance to march and had a long rest when they had completed their advance, were dissipated over a wide area. Tyler was so detached from his other brigades that in his report he naively wrote of the retreat:

> I passed to the rear [from Keyes' brigade] to find General Schenck's brigade, intending, as it was fresh, to have it cover the retreat. I did not find it in the position in which I had left it, and supposed it had moved forward and joined the retreating column. I did not see General Schenck again until near Cub Run. . . .[22]

There can be only one judgment against Tyler: that he had proven himself unworthy of divisional command and that he should be replaced as soon as possible by a more capable person. He was sent west to serve under Pope but in the Corinth campaign his health broke down, aggravated, no doubt, by his age, and he was forced to assume non-combat positions thenceforward. In 1864, death took away his wife, and the shock was so great that he felt compelled to resign his commission to re-enter civilian life. Like Patterson, he also left the army under a certain stigma; for many blamed the Bull Run defeat on him because of his slow march and lack of aggressiveness at the Stone Bridge. Yet once the war ended, he began an old age of scrupulous usefulness.[23]

The most tragic figure to leave the field of defeat was Dixon S. Miles. McDowell refused to censure him for his drunkenness, not even noting it in his report; he merely neglected to mention Miles in any form. As the list of officers cited for bravery and judicious action proceeded down the page, every division and brigade commander was mentioned—with the single exception of the hapless Miles.[24] In the meantime, the allegations to liquor continued, with Richardson devoting a considerable portion of his report to an account of the drunken actions which could easily have wrought disaster.[25] Miles had no recourse but to request a court of inquiry which was granted in early August.[26] By this time, Richardson was fully prepared to attack his commander openly and bitterly in spite of the fact that the illness which caused the original prescription drinking had worsened rather than improved. When Miles, still sick, appeared before the court, Richardson, with counsel, requested permission to act as prosecutor. Protestations by the defense were overruled,[27] and the proceedings began. The testimony clearly indicated that the charge of drunkenness was true. Although he tried vainly to counter the facts, Miles must have known that he was doomed to a court-martial; the facts were too strong against him. Richardson's personal animosity was so great that he had to be cautioned several times about overly aggressive or suggestive questions.[28] On November 6, almost three months to the day from the time the inquiry was granted, a verdict was published as General Orders, No. 42. It had been determined:

1. That Col. I. B. Richardson was justified in applying the term drunkenness to Col. D. S. Miles' condition about 1 o'clock p.m. on the 21st July last.

2. That the evidence is clear that Colonel Miles had been ill for several days before July 21st last—was ill on that day; that the surgeon had prescribed medicines for him, and on the day of the battle had prescribed for him small quantities of brandy.

The court, however, considers his illness as a very slight extenuation of the guilt attached to his condition about 7 p.m. on July 21st last.[29]

In the last paragraph was the real answer to the opinion held by the three officers who composed the court. Miles was thoroughly in the wrong, then, for his conduct. A court-martial should follow by all rights. There must have been a lump in his throat as he awaited the next paragraph, the opinion:

The court is of the opinion that evidence cannot now be found sufficient to convict Colonel Miles of drunkenness before a court-martial; that a proper court could only be organized in this Army with the greatest inconvenience at present, and that it will not be for the interest of the service to convene a court in this case.

The court is therefore of the opinion that no further proceedings in the case are necessary.

He was saved. If ever a reprieve had been granted to a man doomed, it was at this time. The exigencies of McClellen's vast reorganization and expansion had probably done the most to make a full general court-martial impossible. Whatever it was, it had kept Dixon Miles his commission; and he was grateful. Not a drop would he touch again—not as long as he lived. But the army had ways of acknowledging his misdeeds. From July 26

when Richardson had complained to McDowell and the
War Department, Miles had been "on leave of absence
and awaiting orders." As all his comrades in arms rose to
be brigadier and major generals, he remained a forgotten
colonel "on leave." Then in early March of 1862 almost
a year after his debacle, he was given a brigade to guard
the track line of the B. & O. Railroad. It was not combat, but it was a chance. Months passed. It was August.
Union Major General John Pope lost "Stonewall" Jackson somewhere in his rear; and another Bull Run, like the
first except that there were more troops involved, took
place. Soon Lee was in Maryland, and Dixon Miles
found himself suddenly trapped in Harper's Ferry with
Confederates on all three heights around him. After a
series of actions which brought disgrace and dismissal to
many Federal officers, Miles surrendered ignominiously
to the Confederates. An artillery barrage after the capitulation mortally wounded him, saving him from sitting through a court-martial which had to cashier him
even after death. He had not drunk an ounce of liquor
since Bull Run; in fact, it was said that his abstention had
had a deleterious effect on his nerves and decisiveness. It
was under a black cloud of stigma that he left the lists.[30]

The wounding of David Hunter in the early moments of battle illustrates several factors which materially hampered the Union forces on the field. A concerted
attack was a difficult movement at best, and there would
be many veteran units later in the war whose efforts
would not equal those of McDowell's men. To hold a
defensive line was far easier, even more so if the inexperience of the troops is considered. The Confederates lay
under cover behind Bull Run at the outset, and when

the action developed they held a tree line along the
southern edge of Henry House Hill. The Federals, however, were forced to the offensive at all points. In front
of them were concealed enemy riflemen, often marked
only by the small spurts of flame from their muzzles.
Across open ground marched the oncoming Yankees.
There is something horrible about moving, devoid of
cover, against a foe whose presence is only indicated by
the occasional flashes which cut down the men two or
three files over. Will the men on each side run, leaving
you to fight alone? Will you be hit? Or will you be captured? These were the problems which faced all Northerners but most particularly the officers that day. They
had to keep their troops in line and fighting. If the soldiers
were green, this had to be compensated for by the gallantry of the officers in leading, setting a fearless example, and generally being "all things to all men." Perhaps
this explains the amazingly high officer casualty rate. Six
regimental commanders were killed or wounded in the
six brigades on the field,[31] over a quarter of those in
action. Willcox was the only brigade commander hit,
but of the two division commanders who fought with
the turning column on the field—excluding Tyler, who
was preoccupied as a tactical genius—both Hunter and
Heintzelman, were hit. The former was forced to quit
the field and Heintzelman, who stayed on even after he
was struck, lost an appreciable amount of his energy.

This officer casualty rate had a bad effect on the
Yankee battle efforts. By the time Bull Run was fought,
everyone had learned his place and duties through constant drill and daily life. Using their previous experience,
if they had it, or learning from the bottom up, the offi-

cers were sufficiently proficient at their tasks by that hot Sunday; but when they were called upon to assume the post of the next higher rank, many were at a loss. Porter is an excellent example. Whether or not he knew what to do was immaterial in the final analysis; he did not assume active command of the division after Hunter was gone. In spite of the fact that he was fully aware of his superior's injury and that he was next in command,[32] he allowed Burnside to pull out of the line and remain behind on Matthews Hill. Not only did he neglect his newly incumbent duties to lead the division as a whole, but also he allowed his own brigade to become broken up into many ineffectual parts. Some of his men went to Henry House Hill, some to the far flank and some did not even make it south of Buck Hill near the pike.

In other cases, no one bothered to notify the next in command that he had been promoted via a ball of lead or shell fragment. The confusion which resulted immeasurably depreciated the effective striking power of the unit. A prime requisite for success in any battle is officer efficiency and fluidity, both of which spring automatically from a functioning chain of command; but it seems as if the chain of command was wholly unknown by the Northerners in that first engagement. To make matters worse, this failing was considerably accentuated by the task of taking the offensive.

Another weakness which was revealed through the officers' actions and increased by problems of the offensive was the inability of larger units to move together. Many officers like Tyler and Porter refused to assume their proper command position; many others failed of the desired result even when they tried. "Cump" Sher-

man, the same Sherman who was to lead troops in a fifty-
mile-wide swath through the very vitals of the Southern
hinterland, threw his brigade into battle on Henry
House Hill with a front of one regiment. By thus stack-
ing his regiments one behind the other, he decreased the
effective fighting ability of his brigade to one fourth its
normal capacity. Most of the brigades had been in existence for no appreciable length of time, many for only a
very short period, and some merely since the beginning
of the campaign six days before. The division, of course,
had become functional on July 16—not before. The
result, as might be expected, was considerable inability
to achieve unified action at a higher level than the regiment. Some officers, like Israel B. Richardson or O. O.
Howard, were able to achieve coordination through supreme effort but the failures were far more numerous
than the successes.

In totaling the debits and credits of Bull Run, it must
be allowed that McDowell might, in spite of blunders
and mishaps, have carried the day were it not for a desertion and a failure. Lady Luck was not with him; and as
if she had set a precedent, she never rejoined him after
that hot July Sunday. Her desertion did away with his
chances for success; almost everything which could have
happened to dislocate his plans did happen. The failure
lay directly on his staff. Its lack of size hampered him; its
inexperience complicated his tasks; its incapabilities crip-
pled his attack. Two officers in particular were to blame:
John Barnard, chief engineer, and William Barry, chief
of artillery.

It was Barnard who executed the reconnaissance on
July 19 and who had recommended that still another be

made that night. Both failed to turn up any more than McDowell already knew and although the wasted day of July 20 must be blamed on the army commander, the ineffectuality of the reconnaissances to the Sudley Roads must be blamed on Barnard. The results were only too evident the next day. Heintzelman's guide, one of Barnard's engineers, missed the turn off to the middle crossing where the division was to ford, with the consequent removal of the middle prong from the turning movement. In addition, the circuitous route taken by the head of the column to avoid enemy observation and artillery fire inclined away from the Run to the east while the Run itself bent to the left. The distance and time needed to cover it were both considerably increased, adding to the delay of the already-late flanking column. If Tyler slowed the initial departure, Barnard's poor reconnaissance and his ill-advised engineers, who directed the divisions in the turning movement, ruined any chance of recouping the loss of time.

Barry had been placed in complete charge of the movement of Griffin and Ricketts to Henry House Hill. Up to that time he had done nothing to help the battle; any concentrations of artillery fire had been done purely on the initiative of the battery commanders themselves, who showed a high degree of skill throughout the battle. When the eleven guns had bounced up the steep northern slope to the Henry House yard, Barry seemed to lose interest in all but the effect of their shells on the tree line to his front. The supports were improperly placed. In fact, they placed themselves, and Griffin was forced to order one of the two regiments away from his immediate rear where all the counterbattery overs would hit it.[33]

But the most culpable act of all was the failure to fire on
the Confederate regiment which eventually shot the two
batteries to pieces. Before that critical volley, the position
was secure, the guns safe, and the questionable value of
the supports even immaterial; but that crushing fire was
the first knell of actual Federal defeat. It was entirely
Barry's fault, whatever the circumstances may have
been. The fact that this Confederate regiment broke and
ran right after its volley reveals how effectively they
would have been able to resist canister at 200 yards,
which was what Griffin proposed to give them. Barry,
then, performed as much a disservice to his army as did
his colleague Barnard.

What precedents had been established when the acrid
smoke of battle had blown away and the twisted bodies
had been removed? The picture of several retreating
congressmen, armed to the teeth with pistols, rifles, and
knives, pointed directly at a very real influence which
would often cripple the Union war effort, especially in
the eastern theatres: the government. When congressmen, cabinet members, and President took a hand in
tactical combat, there could be only one result. There
were many times when the Union commanders would
be pressed to act one way when common sense demanded another. The most powerful example of this
governmental interference was the Committee on the
Conduct of the War, a joint attempt of the House and
Senate to secure adequate prosecution of the conflict.
The effect of such a body was antagonistic to all military
virtues. It encouraged subordinates to speak out against
their superiors for any of a number of reasons such as
ambition, personal dislike, or revenge; it sought value

judgments of army commanders from lieutenants and captains; it bred uneasiness and fear among the officers, especially the Democrats; and it forced much of what it concluded, often wrongly, on the government. There would come a time when officers could slander their superiors behind their backs and hope to advance their own claims to high command. "Fighting Joe" Hooker became the living symbol of such truth. He began, in the middle of 1862, to lay the groundwork for his eventual command of the Army of the Potomac, McDowell's embryonic Army of North-Eastern Virginia full grown. By the end of Burnside's fumbling efforts at Fredericksburg, there was such a strong Hooker faction in the government that he succeeded easily to the coveted position in spite of the President's misgivings.

The rapid turnover in the highest ranks became characteristic of Union command as the war continued. Patterson had been replaced at once, McDowell had been left in command of most of the Army of North-Eastern Virginia, but it was no longer an army. It was just the First Corps of a huge new force under the command of George B. McClellan. In a year, McDowell would fall completely by the wayside and shortly after him would come three more leaders of the force whose seed he had planted.[34]

In establishing this precedent of removing a commander after the loss of a battle, the government contributed to many of the defeats that were to come. A military organization composed of volunteers needed time to work itself into a flexible force, but the passage of time and the gaining of coordinated experience was always counteracted by the change of command at the

top level. Each new leader had a new command system:
McClellan his corps and corps groups; Burnside his
grand division; Hooker his reshuffled corps and concentrated cavalry. And each new leader also brought
with him his own staff, new to army command. Bull
Run repeated itself time and again in Union blue; only
the names and the places were different. One of the big-
gest reasons for Meade's victory in July of 1863 was his
inability to alter Hooker's command system in the
slightest because of the imminence of battle. As a result,
the army which had fought in vain at Chancellorsville
saved a nation at Gettysburg; one of the main factors
was its length of existence and battle experience as an
unchanged entity.

The Yankees could look for marked cavalry inferiority for some time to come. Not one volunteer regiment left the west bank of the river with McDowell.
Northerners, particularly easterners, did not ride as
much or as often as their foes in peacetime. And when
mounted units began to arrive, they were comical rather
than warlike. The best cavalrymen in the early war came
from western frontier states to form units like George
A. Custer's Michigan Brigade. True, the regular cavalry
was every bit as good as J. E. B. Stuart's cavalry, but a
few battalions could not hope to match the graycoats
who reached corps size by 1864. The Union produced
many cavalry officers of superior quality, men like Custer, Percy Wyndham, John Buford, and Judson Kilpat-
rick, but their troops were two years in learning the art
of war on horseback. Even then, racing their horses to
position and dismounting, they often fought on foot
with stubby, breech-loading carbines.

Last and perhaps most important of the precedents set at Bull Run was the artillery performance as a preview of things to come. Quality, quantity, and superior officership characterized the guns of the Union armies throughout the war. The finest single artilleryman on both sides made his debut at Bull Run. Henry Hunt saved his army many times; more than the once at Bull Run when his guns beat back the Rebels on the Davies flank. The quality of officers in this branch was far superior to anything the Confederates produced, and many artillerymen even made excellent infantry commanders. Ricketts and Ayres ended the war at the head of divisions and Griffin at the head of a corps, while Hunt became chief of artillery for the Army of the Potomac. Almost all the battery commanders of McDowell's army had distinguished careers and advanced rank ahead of them. At Malvern Hill, at Fredericksburg, and again at Gettysburg, Yankee artillery was the deciding factor in paving the way to victory or halting defeat before it turned to rout.

Bull Run had been fought, and Bull Run had been lost; but in spite of the fact that McDowell's army had many of the weaknesses which characterized later Union armies, especially its descendant, the Army of the Potomac, it carried within its organization the very seeds of victory. Men like Sherman, Hunt, Ricketts, Griffin, Howard, Slocum, Barry, Gorman, and others too numerous to name, would lead the armies of Union to success. Some would die like Israel B. Richardson, who met his fate in a hail of bullets while assaulting the sunken road at Antietam. Some would die like William A. Jackson, in beds, with their bodies weakened and fever-ridden. Some like Griffin would never feel the touch of lead throughout the war; but almost all would go on to lead, and lead well, the New Yorkers, Michigan men, Ohioans, Vermonters, Pennsylvanians; the plain Americans who defeated gray-coated secession in four long, trying years of "blood and iron" mixed with tears.

FOOTNOTES

Chapter 1

1. R. M. Johnston, *Bull Run: Its Strategy and Tactics* (Boston 1913), pp. 2, 3 (cited hereafter as *R. M. Johnston*); Edward G. Everett, "Pennsylvania Raises an Army, 1861," *Western Pennsylvania Historical Magazine,* Summer, 1956, vol. 39, no. 2, p. 83 (cited hereafter as *Pennsylvania Raises an Army*).
2. Comte De Paris, *History of the Civil War in America,* 3 vols. (Philadelphia, 1875), vol. I, p. 19 (cited hereafter as *Paris*).
3. *Paris,* vol. I, p. 18.
4. For detailed discussions of this topic see Walter Goerlitz, *History of the German General Staff* or Harold L. Gordon, *The Reichswehr and the German Republic, 1919-1927.*
5. *Annual Report of the Adjutant General of New York, 1861* (Albany, 1862), p. 23 (cited hereafter as *A, G. Report N. Y.*).
6. Company grade officers are those ranked as second lieutenant, first lieutenant, and captain; field grade as major, lieutenant colonel, and colonel.
7. Oliver O. Howard, *The Autobiography of Oliver Otis Howard,* 2 vols. (New York, 1907), vol. I, p. 106 (cited hereafter as *O. O. Howard*).
8. W. T. Sherman to his brother, May 21, 1861, W. T. Sherman MSS; Heintzelman MS Diary; Charles Winslow Elliott, *Winfield Scott: the Soldier and the Man,* p. 719 (cited hereafter as *Elliott's Scott*).
9. *Pennsylvania Raises an Army,* p. 83; Roy P. Basler, ed. *The Collected Works of Abraham Lincoln,* 9 vols., vol. IV, pp. 331-332, for the complete text of the proclamation (cited hereafter as *Lincoln's Collected Works*). The authority by which the President performed this act was the Militia Act

223

of 1795 which gave the executive permission to call out the state forces in time of national crisis.

10. *Annual Report of the Adjutant General to the Legislature of Minnesota, 1861* (St. Paul, 1862), p. 4 (cited hereafter as *A. G. Report Minn.*)

11. *A. G. Report Minn.*, pp. 3-4.

12. *Annual Report of the Adjutant General of the Commonwealth of Massachusetts, 1861* (Boston, 1861), p. 4ff (cited hereafter as *A. G. Report Mass.*); George H. Gordon, *Brook Farm to Cedar Mountain* (Boston, 1883), p. 2 (cited hereafter as *Gordon*).

13. *A. G. Report Minn.*, p. 3ff.

14. To rival the state of Minnesota the state of Maine had 1,200 men who could answer the call for troops out of 60,000 men on the muster rolls. William E. S. Whitman and Charles H. True, *Maine in the War for the Union* (Lewiston, 1865), p. 3 (cited hereafter as *Maine in the War*).

15. The act that rejuvenated the Pennsylvania system was entitled "An Act for the Better Organization of the Militia of this Commonwealth" and was passed on April 12, two days before Sumter surrendered. *Pennsylvania Archives: Papers of the Governors*, 9 series (Harrisburg, 1902), vol. VIII, p. 420; Samuel P. Bates, *History of the Pennsylvania Volunteers, 1861-1865*, 5 vols. (Harrisburg, 1869), vol. I, p. 4 and 4fn (cited hereafter as *Hist. Penn. Vols.*); *Pennsylvania Raises an Army*, p. 83ff.

16. Walter F. Clowes, *The Detroit Light Guard* (Detroit, 1900), p. 34; *Pennsylvania Raises an Army*, p. 92; "Charlie" to John A. Dahlgren, April 23, 1861, John A. Dahlgren MSS; *A. G. Report Mass.*, p. 6; *A. G. Report N. Y.*, p. 9ff; John Robertson, *Michigan in the War* (Lansing, 1882), p. 23 (cited hereafter as *Mich. in the War*); *Annual Report of the Adjutant General of the State of New Jersey for the Year 1861* (Trenton, 1862), p. 3ff (cited hereafter as *A. G. Report N. J.*); *Annual Report of the Adjutant General of the State of Connecticut for the Year 1861* (Hartford, 1862), p. 5ff (cited hereafter as *A. G. Report Conn.*).

17. *Mich. in the War*, pp. 23-24; *A. G. Report Mass.*, pp. 24, 25; *A. G. Report Minn.*, p. 352; *A. G. Report N. Y.*, pp. 6, 7; *O. O. Howard*, p. 110ff; Martin H. Haynes, *A History of the Second New Hampshire Volunteer Infantry in the War of the Rebellion* (Lakeport, 1896), p. 8 (cited hereafter as *2nd N. H.*). *R. M. Johnston* says (p. 5) that recruiting was like ward politics and that (p. 103) the colonels were bad and their field officers worse because they were elected. This seems to be a popular misconception accepted by all writers who study the first months of the war second hand, but the sources fail to support this generalization which is also accepted by *Paris* (vol. I, p. 174).

18. Henry Greenleaf Pearson, *James S. Wadsworth of Geneseo* (New York, 1913), p. 63 (cited hereafter as *Pearson's Wadsworth*).

19. *Pennsylvania Raises an Army*, p. 84.

20. *Pennsylvania Raises an Army*, p. 97; *A. G. Report N. Y.*, p. 6ff; Samuel P. Bates *Martial Deeds of Pennsylvania* (Philadelphia, 1875), pp. 953-954 (cited hereafter as *Martial Deeds*); *Pennsylvania Archives: Papers of the Governors*, vol. VIII, p. 377. Everett says (*Pennsylvania Raises an Army*, p. 97) that Curtin was reluctant to do it, but Curtin's speech (*Pennsylvania Archives: Papers of the Governors*, series 4, vol. VIII, p. 375ff) and the records of correspondence between him and Patterson would seem to belie this.

21. William Swinton, *Campaigns of the Army of the Potomac* (New York, 1862), p. 24 (cited hereafter as *Swinton*).

22. There would be eight new infantry, one new cavalry, and one new artillery regiments for the regular army.

23. *Lincoln's Collected Works*, vol. IV, pp. 353-354, has the full text.

24. *2nd N. H.*, p. 3; *A. G. Report Minn.*, p. 83; *Maine in the War*, p. 4.

25. The only exception to Presidential appointment of brigade and division officers were the personal aides of the general officer in command of the unit.

26. *Pearson's Wadsworth*, pp. 63-64.
27. The complete text of General Orders, No. 12 is printed in *A. G. Report Mass.*, p. 25ff.
28. *Swinton*, p. 30.
29. *Hist. Penn. Vols.*, vol. I, pp. 3, 4, 5, 13-200; *O. O. Howard*, pp. 106-107, 116; *A. G. Report Mass.*, pp. 24-25; *Mich. in the War*, p. 23; John D. Hicks, "The Organization of the Volunteer Army in 1861 with Special Reference to Minnesota," *Minnesota Historical Bulletin*, no. 5, Feb. 1918, pp. 324-368 (cited hereafter as *Org. Vol. Army Minn.*); Newton Martin Curtis, *From Bull Run to Chancellorsville*, (New York, 1906), p. 18ff (cited hereafter as *Curtis*); Abner Small, *The Road to Richmond* (California, 1939), pp. 8-9 (cited hereafter as *Road to Richmond*); R. I. Holcombe, *History of the First Regiment Minnesota Volunteer Infantry* (Stillwater, 1916), p. 6 (cited hereafter as *1st Minn. Vols.*).
30. *Paris*, vol. I, pp. 177-178; T. Harry Williams, *Lincoln and his Generals* (New York, 1952), p. 11; Ella Lonn, *Foreigners in the Union Army and Navy* (Baton Rouge, 1951), chaps. 5, 6 (cited hereafter as *Lonn*).

Chapter II

1. In actuality the secessionists of Maryland were a vociferous and active minority, but their mere noise made them appear stronger than they were. John G. Nicolay, *The Outbreak of Rebellion* (New York, 1881), chaps. VII and VIII.
2. In 1862 Floyd found himself trapped in Fort Donelson by one Ulysses S. Grant, commander of the Union army which captured that place.
3. R. M. *Johnston*, p. 17; Dumas Malone, ed., *Dictionary of American Biography*, 20 vols., vol. XVI, p. 503ff (cited hereafter as *D.A.B.* with the volume and page numbers). The best biography of Scott is the one cited herein as *Elliott's Scott*, and it has been used throughout for clarity on Scott's over-all views.
4. *D.A.B.*, vol. XIV, p. 306; *Martial Deeds*, pp. 953-954; *El-*

liott's Scott, p. 453; Pennsylvania Military Files for the War of 1812 for Patterson in the National Archives.

5. Patterson's General Staff File in the National Archives.

6. General Orders, No. 3, in *War of the Rebellion, Official Records of the Union and Confederate Armies* (Washington, 1885-1905), vol. II, p. 579 (cited hereafter as *O.R.* All references are to Series I. Where the volume is in one part only the volume and page number follow as above. Where the volume is in more than one part the reference will be to part and page, e.g., *O.R.*, vol. 51, pt. 1, p. 300).

7. *Elliott's Scott*, p. 453; Robert Patterson, *A Narrative of the Campaign in the Valley of the Shenandoah in 1861* (Philadelphia, 1865), p. 26 (cited hereafter as *Narrative*). It has not been judged worthwhile to burden the footnotes with the numerous corrections and refutations necessary for this book. The task has been more than adequately handled, although rather harshly, by the Military Historical Society of Massachusetts in their *Proceedings*, vol. 1, no. 1. The first volume, and hence the paper concerned here, was written in the following manner: rather than publish a series of personal narratives or complaints, the Society sought to examine each phase of the war judiciously through the records to present a balanced series of articles. Thus groups of men undertook to handle the various campaigns so that each article is the result of reflective study from several men.

8. George W. Cullum, *Biographical Register of the Officers and Graduates of the U. S. Military Academy at West Point . . .* (Boston and New York, 1891), 3 vols., 2 supplements (cited hereafter as *Cullum* with the number of the cadet. As all graduates were placed in order of class and class standing then numbered consecutively 1,000 men to a volume, it will be easier to cite merely the cadet number rather than volume and page which differs between editions), 1273.

9. *O.R.* vol. II, p. 579; paper of N. D. in Porter MSS.

10. *O.R.*, vol. II, pp. 580, 582-583, 586.

11. *Martial Deeds*, pp. 953-954.
12. Bernard Montgomery in his book *The Memoirs of Field Marshal the Viscount Montgomery of Alamein*, K. G. stated most aptly (p. 76): "By previous thought, by discussion with his staff, and by keeping in close touch with his subordinates by means of visits, a commander should know what he wants to do and whether he can do it. . . . A conference of subordinates to *collect ideas* (Montgomery's italics) is the resort of a weak commander."
13. In his book, Patterson states that the governor refused the request (*Narrative*, pp. 28-29) but for a refutation of this claim see *Pennsylvania Raises an Army*, p. 94; *Pennsylvania Archives: Papers of the Governors*, series VI, vol. VIII, pp. 375, 378.
14. John Sherman to R. B. Price, April 27, 1861, Jno. Sherman MSS; *Narrative*, pp. 29-30.
15. *O.R.*, vol. II, p. 607. General Orders, No. 12.
16. *Pennsylvania Raises an .Army*, p. 97ff; *Narrative*, p. 30; *Pennsylvania Archives: Papers of the Governors*, series VI, vol. VIII, p. 422.
17. James Grant Wilson and John Fiske, eds., *Appleton's Cyclopedia of American Biography*, 6 vols., 6 supplements, vol. I, p. 443 (cited hereafter as *C.A.B.* with volume and page number; Freeman Cleaves, *Rock of Chickamauga: The Life of General George H. Thomas* (Norman, 1948), p. 68 (cited hereafter as *Cleaves' Thomas*).
18. Listed as William K. Keim in his General Staff File in the National Archives, but a full name of William High Keim is given in *C.A.B.*, vol. III, p. 501.
19. *Hist. Penn. Vols.*, vol. I, p. 4 and F.n. p. 4; *C.A.B.*, vol. III, p. 501; General Staff File of William K. Keim in National Archives; *Narrative*, p. 26.
20. *O.R.*, vol. II, pp. 607. 609.
21. *O.R.*, vol. II, p. 615. There were six at York, six at Philadelphia, two at Chambersburg, six at Lancaster, and probably six at Harrisburg.
22. *O.R.*, vol. II, p. 616. On May 3, the federal government

ordered it reopened to public passengers, *O.R.*, vol. II, pp. 618-619.

23. *O.R.*, vol. II, pp. 619-620.

24. Frémont, for example, was serving in Missouri, a state which not only had to be armed from the beginning but also had to be kept in the Union under the most trying circumstances. There was much ill will between and inside both sides over this area.

25. For an interesting example of early revelation of command weakness in another Union officer, General George B. Mc-Clellan, see Robert Underwood Johnson and Clarence Clough Buel, eds., *Battles and Leaders of the Civil War*, 4 vols. (New York, 1887), vol. I, p. 126ff (cited hereafter *as B. & L.*).

26. *O.R.*, vol. II, pp. 624-625, 626. The date he would set out was Wednesday, May 8.

27. *O.R.*, vol. II, p. 632.

28. *O.R.*, vol. II, p. 599; paper of n.d. in Porter MSS.

29. The fort was Fort Federal Hill. Benjamin Butler, *Butler's Book: Autobiography and Personal Reminiscences* (Boston, 1892), p. 226ff.

30. *O.R.*, vol. II, p. 634ff.

31. *O.R.*, vol. II, p. 640.

32. *O.R.*, vol. II, pp. 642-643.

33. *Cullum*, no. 278, *D.A.B.*, vol. 12, p. 257; William Howard Russell, *My Diary North and South* (New York, 1863), p. 159 (cited hereafter as *W. H. Russell*); *Report of the Joint Committee on the Conduct of the War* (Washington, 1863), pt. 2, p. 37—McDowell (cited hereafter as *C.C.W.* followed by the part and page numbers, then the name of the person testifying. The subsequent total of volumes equaled nine but all references in this work are to the second part of the first group of three).

34. The Army of the Potomac, the descendant of McDowell's army, was not notable for its successful river crossings during its war career as witnessed by Ball's Bluff, Fredericksburg, and Deep Bottom to name three.

35. *O.R.*, vol. II, p. 37ff.
36. Julia Butterfield, ed, *A Biographical Memorial of General David Butterfield* (New York, 1904), p. 14 (cited hereafter as *Butterfield Memorial*).
37. Walter F. Clowes stated (*Detroit Light Guard*, pp. 40-41) that A Company of the First Michigan led the advance across the bridge but all contemporary reports and later narratives (*Butterfield Memorial*, p. 14; *O.R.*, vol. II, p. 40ff; Heintzelman MS Diary, May 25) contradict him.
38. *O.R.*, vol. II, p. 40ff; Walter F. Clowes, *Detroit Light Guard*, pp. 40-41; Heintzelman MS Diary, May 25; *Swinton*, p. 30; *A. G. Report N. Y.*, p. 110; *The Massachusetts Register of 1862 Containing a Record of the Government and Institutions of the State Together with a very complete Account of the Massachusetts Volunteers* (Boston, 1862), pp. 126-127 (cited hereafter as *Massachusetts Register*).
39. *Massachusetts Register*, pp. 126-127. The golden circlet, which Ellsworth wore about his neck and which was inscribed: *non nobis sed pro patria*, was driven into his heart by the shot.
40. *O.R.*, vol. II, pp. 38-39; *Butterfield Memorial*, pp. 40-41; Heintzelman MS Diary, May 25; Robert G. Athearn, *Thomas Francis Meagher: An Irish Revolutionary in America* (Boulder, 1949), p. 91 (cited hereafter as *Meagher*); Edward K. Gould, *Major-General Hiram G. Berry* (Rockland, 1899), p. 91 (cited hereafter as *Gould's Berry*).
41. McDowell testified (*C.C.W.*, p. 37) that Scott ordered Mansfield's commission predated a week to his own; but if this is true—and it is not mentioned in any other contemporary source—Scott failed because both brigadier generalships bear the same date, May 14 (see *Cullum*, 963 and 287).
42. James H. Stine, *History of the Army of the Potomac* (Philadelphia, 1892), p. 6 (cited hereafter as *Stine*), quotes Schuyler Hamilton, Scott's military secretary, who said that McDowell was chosen because Mansfield had been promoted Inspector General over Scott's son-in-law when

Jefferson Davis was Secretary of War. All other sources report to the contrary: Whitelaw Reid, *Ohio in the War*, 2 vols. (New York, 1867), vol I, p. 660 (cited hereafter as *Ohio in the War*); James B. Fry, *McDowell and Tyler in the Campaign of Bull Run* (New York, 1884), p. 8ff (cited hereafter as *McDowell and Tyler*); *C.C.W.*, p. 37—McDowell. The actions of the authorities in Washington bear out the fact conclusively that there was hostility toward McDowell.

43. McDowell has left almost nothing behind in the way of MS collections, nor does he appear in the collections of others. There is, in addition, a dearth of judicious appraisals of his actions. Authors have tended to hurry by him as if to bigger and better things and he is at first overshadowed by Scott, then by McClellan, after which he sinks into oblivion. *O.R.*, vol. II, pp. 653-654; *Ohio in the War*, vol. I, p. 656ff for a particularly good personal study of the man; *C.C.W.*, p. 37—McDowell; *O.R.*, vol. 51, pt. 1, p. 335; General Staff Files for Irvin McDowell in National Archives; *D.A.B.*, vol. XII, p. 29ff; *McDowell and Tyler*, p. 7ff; *Stine*, p. 2ff quotes Schuyler Hamilton verbatim and uselessly as Hamilton's conclusions are rendered all the more invalid by incorrect facts; Herman Haupt, *Reminiscenses of Herman Haupt* (Milwaukee, 1901), pp. 303-304; James Harrison Wilson, *Under the Old Flag*, 2 vols. (New York, 1912), vol. I, p. 66.

44. *O.R.*, vol. II, p. 654.

Chapter III

1. For the plan see Scott to McClellan, *O.R.*, series III, vol. I, pp. 177-178, 250. This is one of the first tacit recognitions by a person in high command of the industrial and productive superiority of the North linked with the inability of the South to be self sufficient or survive without external assistance. For a thorough discussion of the plan see *Elliott's Scott*, p. 721ff.

2. *O.R.*, vol. II, p. 652.

3. *Narrative*, p. 31; *O.R.*, vol. LI, pt. 1, pp. 390, 342.

4. It must be remembered that, in heading up the Shenandoah Valley, one marched in a southerly or south-westerly direction.

5. Almost this exact same plan was propounded by Ethan A. Hitchcock, an officer in Washington, to his diary. He would have Patterson join McClellan to drive up the Valley, so the Confederates would have to evacuate Manassas, Va., to protect their capital. W. A. Croffut, ed., *Fifty Years in Camp and Field* (New York, 1909)—edited diary of Hitchcock. It does not seem unreasonable, therefore, to assume that these motives were also Scott's whether by his own invention or from someone else.

6. *O.R.*, vol. II, p. 657.

7. *O.R.*, vol. II, pp. 660-661.

8. *O.R.*, vol. II, pp. 661, 669.

9. Townshend to Patterson, *O.R.*, vol. II, p. 665.

10. *O.R.*, vol. II, p. 670.

11. *O.R.*, vol. II, p. 671.

12. *O.R.*, vol. II, p. 715, vol. LI, pt. 1, pp. 397-398.

13. Williams says he left Hagerstown for Williamsport but the army could not have been there on June 13 because the end of track was at Hagerstown—as he points out himself—thus, making particularly difficult for Keim to progress beyond Hagerstown by rail. *O.R.*, vol. II, p. 679.

14. *O.R.*, vol. LI, pt. 1, pp. 399-400 and vol. II, p. 679.

15. *O.R.*, vol. II, p. 678; *C.C.W.*, p. 79.

16. Memorandum, June 7, Porter MSS; *O.R.*, vol. II, p. 684. Patterson, in a note of June 14, echoed exactly Porter's comment in the June 7 memorandum that they would not be ready to cross until June 17 or 18.

17. *O.R.*, vol. II, p. 685.

18. Jackson (of later "Stonewall" fame) quit Harper's Ferry completely on June 15 and had begun to do so even earlier in part. At this time the Confederates in the Valley under General Joseph E. Johnston numbered some 6,500 as opposed to 18,000 under Patterson. Frank E. Vandiver,

Mighty Stonewall, pp. 147-148 (cited hereafter as *Mighty Stonewall*).

19. *O.R.*, vol. II, pp. 686, 687-689. On page 96 of *Hist. Penn. Vols.*, vol. I, it is stated as June 25; but the events and chronology such as camping south of Williamsport after a march seem to indicate June 15.

20. *O.R.*, vol. II, p. 687.

21. *O.R.*, vol. II, p. 689.

22. *O.R.*, vol. II, p. 691; *Hist. Penn. Vols.*, vol. I, p. 87.

23. *O.R.*, vol. II, p. 693.

24. For a more detailed account of this action, see George E. Pond, *The Shenandoah Valley in 1864* (New York, 1883).

25. *Elliott's Scott*, pp. 727-728; *W. H. Russell*, p. 148; K. P. Williams *Lincoln Finds a General*, 4 vols., vol. I, p. 72 (cited hereafter as *K. P. Williams*). When the regulars arrived in Washington they found a parade and celebration in progress to greet their weary eyes.

26. One battery was of the regular army; the other was organic to the Rhode Island regiment of infantry.

27. *O.R.*, vol. II, p. 696.

28. *O.R.*, vol. II, p. 699ff.

29. *O.R.*, vol. II, pp. 698-699, 703.

30. Patterson to Jno. Sherman, June 27, John Sherman MSS.

31. *O.R.*, vol. II, p. 709.

32. *Narrative*, p. 39. It also seemed to him as the most advisable plan in later years of retrospect but in dealing with this judgment it should be kept in mind that this was what he did in spite of the fact that it was not the plan as matured.

33. *O.R.*, vol. II, p. 711. Here is another example of Porter and Patterson working together in such close thought relation; for in a letter (Porter to Colonel, June 21, Porter MSS) this exact same plan with the same morale fringe benefit was propounded. It is impossible to tell whose idea it was first, but probability suggests that they developed it jointly.

34. *O.R.*, vol. II, p. 717.

35. Reports of the reconnaissance are in *O.R.*, vol. II, pp. 717, 732-733. The impregnability of Maryland Heights was put

to the acid test in 1862 when McClellan managed to make his way across it without too much difficulty and in the face of stiff opposition. Captain Newton's calculations, therefore, may have been a bit over-hasty but were never asked to bear the test of battle.

36. *O.R.*, vol. II, p. 717.
37. *O.R.*, vol. II, pp. 728, 729-730.
38. Patterson to Jno. Sherman, June 29, Sherman MSS.
39. *Mighty Stonewall*, p. 145. Johnston's army, besides numbering only 6,500 men of all arms, was acutely short of all material, *ibid.*, p. 148.
40. For an account of Floyd's actions see John Hope Franklin, *The Militant South* (Cambridge, 1956).
41. For an excellent example of far-sighted logic see W. T. Sherman MSS of April 1 to May 20.
42. *O.R.*, vol. II, p. 717.
43. *O.R.*, vol. II, p. 725.
44. Patterson to Jno. Sherman, June 24, John Sherman MSS; *Hist. Penn. Vols.*, vol. I, p. 97.
45. *O.R.*, vol. II, p. 727.
46. Actual numbers reported were 5,000 from Falling Waters to Dam No. 4, 4,500 at Shepherdstown, 5,500 at Bunker Hill and twenty to twenty-four guns plus 1,000 cavalry, one of the many examples of poor intelligence.
47. *O.R.*, vol. II, pp. 729, 734; Patterson to Jno. Sherman, June 29, John Sherman MSS. The brigades of Negley and Abercrombie were sent down to verify the report and defend if need arose. No Confederates were found.
48. *O.R.*, vol. II, p. 734.
49. *O.R.*, vol. II, p. 735.

Chapter IV

1. *C.C.W.*, pp. 37-38—McDowell.
2. *C.C.W.*, p. 38—McDowell.
3. *O.R.*, vol. II, pp. 654-655, 659. This was originally intended to apply only to those things which had been destroyed or damaged by proper authority but soon came to mean that

all damage should be so dealt with.

4. *O.R.*, Vol. II, p. 655.
5. *W. H. Russell*, p. 147.
6. *C.C.W.*, p. 38—McDowell.
7. Heintzelman MS Diary, May 25.
8. *D.A.B.*, vol. VIII, pp. 505-506; *Martial Deeds*, p. 608; *Cullum*, 445; *O. O. Howard*, p. 142; *Road to Richmond*, p. 14; Heintzelman MS Diary, May 26-30.
9. *O.R.*, vol. II, p. 654; Heintzelman MS Diary, May 28.
10. *O.R.*, vol. LI, pt. 1, pp. 389-390; Heintzelman MS Diary May 26.
11. This would include the Eighth, Twelfth, Twenty-fifth New York Regiments plus any loose regiments within the vicinity.
12. Heintzelman MS Diary, June 1.
13. *Cullum*, 310; *D.A.B.*, vol. IX, pp. 400-401; R. C. Schenck, "Major-General David Hunter," *Magazine of American History*, vol. XVII, no. 2, February, 1887; David Hunter, *Report of the Military Services of General David Hunter, U.S.A., during the War of the Rebellion Made to the United States War Department* (New York, 1873); Otto Eisenschiml, *Why Lincoln Was Murdered* (Boston, 1937), p. 231.
14. Fry in *B. & L.*, vol. I, p. 174; *O.R.*, vol. II, pp. 59-61. In his MS Diary (June 2) Meigs spoke of this raid as occurring on June 1 but it was dated in the reports (*O.R.*, vol. II, p. 50ff) as May 30.
15. Heintzelman says (MS Diary, June 2) that this was on Sunday, June 2; but the telegram is dated June 3 (*O.R.*, vol. II, p. 662).
16. *O.R.*, vol. II, p. 664.
17. *O.R.*, vol. II, pp. 664, 665.
18. *O.R.*, vol. II, p. 683.
19. Heintzelman MS Diary, June 10.
20. *O.R.*, vol. II, p. 690.
21. *O.R.*, vol. LI, pt. 1, pt. 399 for general orders setting up Schenck's brigade, vol. II, pp. 135, 126.

22. *Ohio in the War*, vol. I, pp. 726-727, 738; D.A.B., vol. XVI, pp. 427-428.
23. Two companies were left at the crossing, two sent to Falls Church, and two strung out along the track from the crossing toward Vienna.
24. *O.R.*, vol. II, pp. 117-118, 126ff.
25. *O.R.*, vol. II, p. 700.
26. Although Camp McDowell was cited in the dispatch as Shooters Hill, the only location on the map of Union emplacements (see *O.R. Atlas*, vol. I, plates 6 & 7) is on School House Hill.
27. *O.R.*, vol. LI, pt. 1, p. 396; *D.A.B.*, vol. XIX, pp. 86-87; ed. Donald G. Mitchell, *Daniel Tyler: A Memorial Volume* (New Haven, 1883), pp. 1-49 (cited hereafter as *Tyler*); *Cullum*, 216; Appointments, Commissions, and Promotions File for Daniel Tyler, National Archives; Erasmus Darwin Keyes, *Fifty Years Observation of Men and Events Civil and Military* (New York, 1884), p. 432 (cited hereafter as *Keyes*).
28. Fry in *B. & L.*, vol. I, p. 174.
29. Established on June 24; *O.R.*, vol. II, p. 718.
30. Heintzelman MS Diary, June 21 and 26.
31. *O.R.*, vol. II, pp. 718-719.
32. *O.R.*, vol. II, p. 665.
33. *Elliott's Scott*, p. 723ff; *Stine*, pp. 8-9; *C.C.W.*, p. 37—McDowell; Edward D. Townshend, *Anecdotes of the Civil War* (New York, 1884), p. 55 (cited hereafter as *Townshend*).
34. *C.C.W.*, pp. 35-36—McDowell.
35. *O.R.*, vol. II, pp. 720-721; *C.C.W.*, p. 22—Richardson and p. 35ff—McDowell; *W. H. Russell*, p. 148.
36. Meigs MS Diary, June 25; *C.C.W.*, p. 36—McDowell.
37. It is clear that on this day McDowell still considered that his advance would be in three columns because of his colloquy with Heintzelman both before and after the cabinet session in which he mentioned three as the number, MS Diary June 29.

38. Memorandum (undated) in Heintzelman MSS, Heintzelman MS Diary, June 29.
39. *Townshend* says (p. 57) that John Charles Frémont was present and was asked in particular by the President if he saw anything wrong with the plan, to which Frémont is purported to have replied no. Although he was in Washington at the time (Alan Nevins, *John C. Frémont, Pathfinder of the West* (New York, 1955), pp. 457-458), he is mentioned only in McDowell's testimony (*C.C.W.*, p. 36) and not even in Tyler's Memorial, but he is accepted as in attendance as McDowell's account is the earliest after the actual event.
40. *Townshend* (p. 57) says the map was spread on a table. Schuyler Hamilton in *Stine*, pp. 9-10, says it was tacked to the wall and that McDowell used a pointer.
41. Memorandum of n.d. in Heintzelman MSS.
42. It is not exactly certain that this was said at the council of war but would appear so from McDowell's testimony (*C.C.W.*, p. 36). For a strange account refuted by all other facts and sources, even those antagonistic to McDowell, see *Stine*, pp. 9-10, quoting Schuyler Hamilton.
43. McDowell testified (*C.C.W.*, p. 36) that Mansfield was the only person to criticize his plan with no specifics given; it may be assumed, since there seems to be no motive for Sandford to prevaricate and since he was speaking of his own actions (*C.C.W.*, pp. 55, 62), that McDowell's memory was merely mixed up as to personalities.
44. *Townshend*, p. 57; Meigs MS Diary, June 29; *C.C.W.*, p. 36ff—McDowell and pp. 55, 62—Sandford and p. 22—Richardson; Heintzelman MS Diary, June 29.
45. Heintzelman MS Diary, June 29.
46. *D.A.B.*, vol. XVII, p. 93ff; W. T. Sherman MSS, April 22 to June 28; *O.R.*, vol. LI, pt. 1, p. 406; *Cullum*, 1022; Lloyd Lewis, *Sherman Fighting Prophet* (New York, 1932), p. 162, for the McDowell incident.
47. *D.A.B.*, vol. VI, pp. 601-602; *Cullum*, 1167; *Martial Deeds*, pp. 734-735.

48. Not to be confused with Fitz-John Porter, who was in the Valley. There was no relation.
49. Heintzelman MS Diary, July 8; *O.R.*, vol. LI, pt. 1, pp. 413-414.
50. Miles was 27/30 in 1824.
51. *C.A.B.*, vol. VI, p. 321; MS Court of Inquiry in the Case of Dixon S. Miles (cited hereafter as MS C. I. Miles with the name of the person testifying, if any); Record of Court-martial regarding the fall of Harper's Ferry in September, 1862, *O.R.*, vol. XIX, pt. 1; *Cullum*, 387; *O.R.*, vol. LI, pt. 1, p. 411.
52. *C.C.W.*, p. 23—Richardson; Heintzelman MS Diary, July 10; *Curtis*, pp. 34-35.
53. *Tyler*, pp. 48-49, with the last sentence changed from indirect to direct discourse. Tyler constantly referred to the Confederate Valley commander as Joe Johnston.
54. In his testimony (*C.C.W.*, p. 40), McDowell did not mention Miles; but as he was to precede Hunter on the Little River Turnpike, he would have to set out at the same time at the latest.
55. General and Special Orders for the Department of North-Eastern Virginia; Archives; Heintzelman MS Diary, July 14 and 15; *C.C.W.*, p. 37ff—McDowell.

Chapter V

1. *Hist. Penn. Vols.*, vol. I, p. 97.
2. *Wis. in the War*, p. 218; *Hist. Penn. Vols.*, vol. I, p. 78; *O.R.*, vol. II, pp. 184, 704; William Henry Locke, *The Story of the Regiment* (Philadelphia, 1868), pp. 21-22 (cited hereafter as *Locke*).
3. *Locke*, pp. 21-22.
4. *Hist. Penn. Vols.*, vol. I, p. 97.
5. *O.R.*, vol. II, p. 160.
6. *Locke*, p. 23; *O.R.*, vol. II, p. 160; James O. Pierce, "The Skirmish at Falling Waters," *Glimpses of the Nation's Struggle: Military Order of the Loyal Legion United States*, 5 Series (St. Paul, 1887-1903), series 2, p. 293 (cited here-

after as *MOLLUS-Pierce*).

7. Patterson said (*O.R.*, vol. II, p. 160) they deployed in the road; Hudson (*ibid.*, p. 184); it is stated as to the left in *Life of David Bell Birney Major-General, U. S. Volunteers* (New York, 1867), p. 22 (cited hereafter as *Birney*); Pierce in *MOLLUS-Pierce*, p. 295, says in the road. It is obviously impossible to tell where they actually were unless the word of Hudson be accepted as fresh and directly attendant to the situation.

8. Companies A, B, and C of the Eleventh Pennsylvania.

9. Jackson was under orders not to hold in the face of a determined attack but to pull back on the main body, *Mighty Stonewall*, p. 150.

10. This encounter is variously referred to as Falling Waters, Hoge's Run, Hoke's Run, and Hainsville. *Locke*, p. 23ff; *O.R.*, vol. II, pp. 160, 180ff; *Birney*, p. 21; *MOLLUS-Pierce*, p. 293ff; *Cleaves' Thomas*, p. 734.

11. This Johnston is not to be confused with Joseph Eggleston Johnston who was Patterson's opponent in the Valley.

12. *Cleaves' Thomas*, p. 134; *D.A.B.*, vol. XVIII, p. 434; *Cullum*, 1028; Daniel H. Strother, "Personal Recollections of the War," *Harpers New Monthly Magazine*, vol. 33, July-Nov., 1866, p. 153 (cited hereafter as *Strother*. Since all citations are from vol. 33, there will only be a page number following).

13. *C.C.W.*, p. 58—Sandford; *Cullum*, 322.

14. *MOLLUS-Pierce*, p. 298.

15. *Birney*, p. 22; *O.R.*, vol. II, p. 157.

16. The units involved were B Company, Tenth Pennsylvania Regiment, and the City Troop Cavalry.

17. *Hist. Penn. Vols.*, vol. I, p. 97.

18. *Locke*, pp. 26-27.

19. *O.R.*, vol. II, p. 157.

20. Henry Hall and James Hall, *Cayuga in the Field* . . . (Auburn, 1873), p. 58 (cited hereafter as *Cayuga*).

21. *O.R.*, vol. II, p. 158; Porter to C. P. Stone, July 4, Porter MSS.

22. On the evening of July 6 the Nineteenth and Twenty-eighth New York set out and were followed next morning by the Fifth and Twelfth New York Regiments, *C.C.W.*, p. 55—Sandford.

23. *O.R.*, vol. II, pp. 158-159; Patterson's MS Orderly Book, Scott to Patterson, July 5 (cited hereafter as MS OB).

24. Notation for July 7, MS OB, which only says *a* Massachusetts regiment but the regimental histories of the Second Massachusetts confirm that it was this regiment in particular.

25. The three gun battery was composed of an eight-inch howitzer, a twenty-four pounder, and a thirty pounder.

26. *Hist. Penn. Vols.*, vol. I, p. 78.

27. *O.R.*, vol. II, pp. 161, 162-163.

28. *O.R.*, vol. II, pp. 161-162.

29. The Fifth and Twelfth New York had crossed the Potomac from Williamsport and then marched in one day what Patterson had taken two to cover, *Locke*, p. 27; *Cayuga*, p. 48ff; *O.R.*, vol. II, p. 162. The times of arrival disagree. *Cayuga* says (p. 49) that the arrival of the first two New York regiments was at 11:00 p.m. while Butterfield testified (*C.C.W.*, p. 207) that they arrived at 3:00 a.m. the next morning, July 9. The statement in *Butterfield Memorial*, p. 25, that they arrived at 5:00 a.m. of July 10 appears to have confused the first two regiments with Sandford and the last two who arrived at that time, *C.C.W.*, pp. 55-56—Sandford.

30. *Narrative*, p. 52; *C.C.W.*, pp. 194-195—Biddle.

31. *O.R.*, vol. II, p. 158.

32. *O.R.*, vol. II, p. 159.

33. *C.C.W.*, p. 165—Birney and pp. 67, 68—Doubleday.

34. *Strother*, p. 152.

35. *C.C.W.*, p. 166—Birney and p. 225—Spates, Stake.

36. Patterson claimed in his testimony (*C.C.W.*, p. 84ff) and later in his book (*Narrative*, pp. 52-53) that Scott had told him to "make good use of your engineers and other experienced staff officers and generals." (Scott to Patterson,

July, *O.R.*, vol. II. That Scott meant this is blatantly denied by his actions during the month of July (*Elliott's Scott*, p. 723ff), and that Patterson really believed it, as he later interpreted it, also seems more than questionable. It is probable that he later came to believe it but only as a subsequent rationalization for his action.

37. Sandford made no reference to any rifle guns in his testimony and stated explicitly, as does every other source, that he had two infantry regiments only (*C.C.W.* pp. 55-56).

38. Patterson had either forgotten or neglected the Massachusetts regiment and Lew Wallace's Indiana regiment when he made this statement.

39. Memorandum of July 9, MS OB which was either read from or copied during delivery. Some of the punctuation has been corrected and updated for clarity.

40. *C.C.W.*, p. 236—Cadwalader.

41. Both the minutes in *O.R.*, vol. II, pp. 163-164 and the memorandum, from which the former was probably taken, in MS OB, place these men in this order in spite of custom.

42. *O.R.*, vol. II, pp. 163-164. According to Cadwalader's testimony (*C.C.W.*, pp. 236-237) he said that, since Johnston only remained in the Valley as long as he wished and could leave it at any time, he should be attacked, then the army could move to Washington and join McDowell. As the notes of the meeting can be considered more impartial than an officer trying the dissociate himself from blame in a highly censured and publicly denounced movement, Cadwalader's testimony may be rejected as untrue.

43. Butterfield got the Fifth, Twelfth, Nineteenth, and Twenty-eighth New York regiments; Stone the Ninth, Seventeenth, Twenty-fifth New York and First New Hampshire Regiments.

44. The date was July 13.

45. *Butterfield Memorial*, p. 25; *C.C.W.*, p. 228—Butterfield and p. 56—Sandford; *Cayuga*, p. 52; John W. Jaques, *Three Years Campaign of the Ninth New York State Militia*

during the Southern Rebellion (New York, 1865), p. 30 (cited hereafter as *9NYSM*). The Second Massachusetts was still on the way. Estimates vary from 18,000 to 20,000 with some as high as 25,000 for Patterson (*C.C.W.*, p. 56– Sandford and p. 225–Stake, Spates). In his *Narrative*, pp. 63-64, Patterson manages to reduce himself to 13,000 men ready for action; but as he started out with that many and had been vigorously reinforced, his argument lacks plausibility. His mathematics were an early forerunner of George B. McClellan, the genius of reduction.

46. *Cayuga*, pp. 55-56. When Banks assumed command of the army after the defeat at Bull Run, he took note of the charges against Clark, which were still hanging in abeyance, by summarily dismissing them for what they were— frivolous and improper. Clark himself was shortly after forced to resign because of ill health (*ibid.*, pp. 80-81).

47. "Some Experiences in Wit, Humor, and Repartee in Army and Navy Life." p. 4, Doubleday MSS.

48. *O.R.*, vol. II, p. 164.

49. *O.R.*, vol. II, p. 165.

50. Townshend? to Porter, July 14, Porter MSS.

51. *Butterfield Memorial*, p. 26; *C.C.W.*, p. 226–Stake and p. 52–Morell and p. 166–Birney.

52. *C.C.W.*, p. 56–Sandford and p. 50–Morell; *Strother* p. 154; Lewis Wallace, *Lew Wallace: An Autobiography*, 2 vols. (New York, 1905), vol. I, p. 318 (cited hereafter as *Wallace*).

53. Doubleday MS Reminiscences, p. 34; *Cayuga*, p. 58.

54. *O.R.*, vol. II, p. 166; *C.C.W.*, p. 56–Sandford; *Strother*, p. 154; *Wallace*, vol. I, p. 318.

55. *C.C.W.*, p. 56–Sandford.

56. *9NYSM*, p. 30.

57. *Cayuga*, p. 58.

58. *O.R.*, vol. II, Scott to Patterson, p. 165, Patterson to Scott pp. 162-163; *C.C.W.*, p. 164–Birney.

59. *Wallace*, vol. I, p. 319; *Strother*, p. 154.

60. According to Birney (*C.C.W.*, p. 163), six companies, two

sections of Rhode Island artillery, and one squadron of cavalry; Sandford only mentions (*ibid.*, p. 56) cavalry and artillery.

61. *O.R.*, vol. II, p. 166; *C.C.W.*, p. 163—Birney.

62. *C.C.W.*, p. 229—Russell.

63. *Strother*, p. 155.

64. *Narrative*, p. 57ff; Memorandums, MS OB. Johnston had not really begun constructing any earthwork until he drew back to Winchester about July 15 (*Mighty Stonewall*, p. 152).

65. *C.C.W.*, p. 164—Birney and p. 226—Stake and p. 56—Sandford.

66. *C.C.W.*, p. 56—Sandford.

67. *Cayuga*, p. 60.

68. Porter to Patterson, July 31, MS OB; *C.C.W.*, p. 191—Price.

69. *C.C.W.*, pp. 57, 60—Sandford and pp. 50, 52—Morell and p. 226—Stake; *Strother*, p. 155; *Butterfield Memorial*, p. 27.

70. *Wallace*, vol. I, pp. 319-320.

71. *Strother*, pp. 155-156; *C.C.W.*, p. 57ff—Sandford; Wilder Dwight, *Life and Letters of Wilder Dwight* (Boston, 1868), p. 52.

72. *O.R.*, vol. II, pp. 167-168; *C.C.W.*, p. 230—Russell. The text is the same in both but the form of the body is different in details. Here is a composite of the two which adheres to the form of other military telegraphic communications of the period.

73. *C.C.W.*, pp. 329-331—Russell.

74. *O.R.*, vol. II, p. 169; *Wallace*, vol. I, pp. 322-323; *Locke*, pp. 33-34; *C.C.W.*, pp. 230-231—Russell and pp. 195-196—Biddle; Alonzo H. Quint, *Record of the Second Massachusetts Infantry, 1861-1865* (Boston, 1867), p. 38.

75. *O.R.*, vol. II, p. 168.

76. *O.R.*, vol. II, p. 170; *Wallace*, vol. I, p. 322; *C.C.W.*, p. 231—Russell.

77. *O.R.*, vol. II, p. 171.

78. *C.C.W.*, p. 232—Russell.

Chapter VI

1. *W. H. Russell,* p. 158.
2. Personal trip of the author; H. M. Blake, *Three Years in the Army of the Potomac* (Boston, 1865), p. 8 (cited hereafter as *Blake*); Major John M. Gould, *History of the First —Tenth—Twenty-ninth Maine Regiment,* (Portland, 1871), p. 57 (cited hereafter as *Gould*); R. I. Holcombe, *History of the First Regiment Minnesota Volunteer Infantry* (Stillwater, 1916), p. 39 (cited hereafter as *Holcombe*).
3. *W. H. Russell,* p. 158; *Holcombe,* p. 40; *O.R.,* vol. II, p. 303ff; John G. Barnard, *The C.S.A. and the Battle of Bull Run* (*A letter to an English Friend*), (New York, 1862), p. 47 (cited hereafter as *Barnard*).
4. *C.C.W.,* p. 19—Richardson; W. T. Sherman to John Sherman, July 19, W. T. Sherman MSS; Captain D. P. Conyngham, *The Irish Brigade and its Campaigns* (New York, 1867), p. 28 (cited hereafter as *Conyngham*).
5. *2nd N. H.,* p. 19; *O.R.,* vol. II, p. 303ff; Augustus Woodbury, *The Second Rhode Island Regiment* (Providence, 1875), p. 28 (cited hereafter as *Woodbury 2 R. I.*).
6. *O.R.,* vol. II, p. 303ff.
7. *O.R.,* vol. II, p. 303ff; Heintzelman MS Diary, July 18.
8. *O. O. Howard,* vol. I, p. 148; *Gould,* p. 57; *Road to Richmond,* p. 18.
9. The Speaker was James G. Blaine.
10. *O. O. Howard,* vol. I, pp. 106-107, 116-118, 141; *Road to Richmond,* pp. 8-9; *D. A. B.,* vol. IX, pp. 279-281; *Cullum,* 1634.
11. *Blake* says (p. 8) 3:45 a.m. while Heintzelman in his MS Diary, July 18, says 3:00.
12. *Gould,* p. 59; *Black,* p. 8; Heintzelman MS Diary, July 18.
13. *Blake,* p. 10.
14. Heintzelman MS Diary, July 18; *Gould,* p. 57; *Holcombe,* p. 40; *Blake,* p. 8; Alfred S. Roe, *The Fifth Massachusetts Volunteer Infantry* (Boston, 1870), p. 65 (cited hereafter as *Roe*).
15. *Gould,* p. 59.

16. *Holcombe*, p. 40; *Roe*, p. 66; Heintzelman MS Diary, July 18; O. S. Barrett, *Reminiscences, Incidents, Battles, Marches, and Camp Life of the old Fourth Michigan Infantry in the War of the Rebellion, 1861-1864* (Detroit, 1888), p. 5 (cited hereafter as *Barrett*).
17. *Gould*, pp. 58-59; *O.R.*, vol. II, pp. 309-310.
18. Heintzelman MS Diary, July 18.
19. Companies A and K of the Eighteenth New York and A and B of the Sixteenth New York, *O.R.*, vol. II, p. 433.
20. *O.R.*, vol. II, pp. 423, 433; *C.C.W.*, p. 177—Miles.
21. *Woodbury 2 R. I.*, pp. 28-29; *2nd N. H.*, p. 20; Benjamin Perley Poore, *The Life and Public Services of Ambrose E. Burnside—Soldier—Citizen—Statesman* (Providence, 1882), p. 109 (cited hereafter as *Poore*); Augustus Woodbury, *Narrative of the Campaign of the First Rhode Island Regiment in the Spring and Summer of 1861* (Providence, 1862), pp. 79-80 (cited hereafter as *Woodbury 1 R. I.*); *Personal Narratives of Events in the War of the Rebellion being Papers Read before the Rhode Island Soldiers and Sailors Historical Society* (Providence, 1878-1890), series 1, p. 17 (cited hereafter as *P.N.R.I.*).
22. *Tyler*, pp. 50-51; D. G. Crotty, *Four Years Campaigning in the Army of the Potomac* (Grand Rapids, 1874), p. 20 (cited hereafter as *Crotty*); W. T. Sherman to John Sherman, July 19, W. T. Sherman MSS.
23. *Holcombe*, p. 38; *Roe*, p. 68; *Blake*, p. 10; *2nd N. H.*, p. 20; *C.C.W.*, p. 39—McDowell.
24. *C.C.W.*, p. 39—McDowell.
25. *Blake*, p. 10; Heintzelman MS Diary, July 18.
26. *O.R.*, vol. II, p. 305.
27. *Roe*, p. 65; *P.N.R.I.* series 1, p. 18; *Woodbury 2 R. I.*, p. 15; Edwin C. Bennett, *Musket and Sword or the Camp March and Firing Line in the Army of the Potomac* (Boston, 1900), (cited hereafter as *Bennett*).
28. R. M. *Johnston*, p. 138.
29. *Barrett*, p. 6; *Blake*, p. 11; *2nd N. H.*, p. 21; *O.R.*, vol. II, pp. 304-305; *Bennett*, p. 38.

30. R. M. Johnston says (p. 123) that McDowell's "early intention had been to push on another four or five miles to Centreville," but he cites no source for this statement, nor does it seem evident that McDowell could actually have intended to reach Centreville that day since he thought he would have to fight at Fairfax Courthouse.

31. *R. M. Johnston*, p. 121.

32. *Tyler*, p. 51; *C.C.W.*, pp. 120-121—Tyler.

33. Original in Heintzelman MSS, Fry to Heintzelman, July 18.

34. *O.R.*, vol. II, pp. 312, 328-329.

35. *O.R.*, vol. II, p. 307; Heintzelman MS Diary, July 19; *C.C.W.*, p. 39—McDowell.

36. *Tyler*, p. 51; *O.R.*, vol. II, pp. 312-313.

37. *O.R.*, vol. II, p. 312.

38. *Pearson's Wadsworth*, p. 69. No source states when this note was received but it is timed after he had set out, and it is noted in his report (*O.R.*, vol. II, pp. 312-313) that he received it before he reached Centreville.

39. *O.R.*, vol. II, p. 313.

40. *Holcombe*, p. 41; *O. O. Howard*, p. 146.

41. *Tyler*, pp. 51-52; *O.R.*, vol. II, p. 313; *C.C.W.*, p. 199—Tyler.

42. *Swinton*, pp. 47-48; *Barnard*, p. 49.

43. In *McDowell and Tyler*, pp. 23, 39, it is pointed out that the actual ford around which most of the action took place was Mitchell's, not Blackburn's. The latter had long since fallen into disuse and while it fell under fire often enough was the center of attraction as noted in the reports. For clarity's sake, the author has refrained from altering the naming of the fords or the action about them. In addition, it should be noted that almost all maps of the area do not properly represent the hooking of Bull Run at that point, which is much more acute than most people realize.

44. In his report (*O.R.*, vol. II, pp. 312-313), Tyler stated that he took only two companies with him; but he gave the above composition in both his memorial (*Tyler*, p. 52) and his testimony (*C.C.W.*, p. 119).

45. Barnard says (*Barnard*, pp. 47-49) that he pressured Tyler for a drive to Manassas but that Tyler merely deployed his brigade and allowed it to be shot up. This does not seem to be consistent with his report submitted a few days after the battle (*O.R.*, vol. II, pp. 328-329) in which he stated that he and Fry twice warned against the push or with his testimony (*C.C.W.*, p. 162) in which he said that he cautioned against advance. Johnston noted (*op. cit.*, p. 136) that there was a good deal of recrimination by Barnard and Fry when McDowell arrived.

46. *Tyler*, pp. 54-55, says Richardson charged without orders, but this is untrue as noted in Richardson's report (*O.R.*, vol. II, p. 313) and testimony (*C.C.W.*, p. 20) and in Tyler's own report which says he sent Richardson down to the Run (*O.R.*, vol. II, p. 311).

47. *O.R.*, vol. II, pp. 310-311, 312-313, 328-330; *Crotty*, pp. 21-22; *Tyler*, p. 51ff; *C.C.W.*, pp. 199, 200, 205—Tyler and pp. 19-20—Richardson; *O. O. Howard*, p. 150.

48. *C.C.W.*, p. 20—Richardson.

49. W. T. Sherman to John Sherman, July 19, W. T. Sherman MSS; William Todd, *The Seventy-ninth Highlanders New York Volunteers in the War of the Rebellion, 1861-1865* (Albany, 1886), p. 25 (cited hereafter as *Todd*).

50. *R. M. Johnston*, p. 136.

51. *D.A.B.*, vol. XV, pp. 570-571; *Cullum*, 1096.

52. *O.R.*, vol. II, p. 330.

53. *O.R.*, vol. II, p. 336ff; *R. M. Johnston*, p. 137ff.

54. Heintzelman MS Diary, July 19.

55. See the reports by the supply train commanders (*O.R.*, vol. II, p. 336ff) and an adequate analysis by Johnston (*op. cit.*, p. 138).

56. Heintzelman MS Diary, July 19.

57. As it turned out the bridge was not so protected nor was it ruined. Tyler could have used it the next day with impunity and it is conceivable that McDowell may have been able to carry it by a lightning frontal assault.

58. *O.R.*, vol. II, pp. 330-331.

59. Sherman mentioned the trains in a letter to his brother on July 19 which means that he heard them during the night of the eighteenth, W. T. Sherman MSS; Warren H. Cudworth, *History of the First Regiment* (Boston, 1866), p. 52 (cited hereafter as *Cudworth*); *Tyler*, p. 56; *C.C.W.*, p. 23 —Richardson and p. 34—Franklin and p. 162—Barnard and p. 207—Tyler.

60. *Holcombe*, pp. 42-43; Fry in *B. & L.*, vol. I, p. 183.

61. *Poore*, p. 110.

62. George B. McClellan managed to escape a major campaign from July 26, 1861 until the spring of 1862 when he followed McDowell.

63. *Poore*, p. 122.

64. *O.R.*, vol. II, p. 745.

65. *O.R.*, vol. II, p. 308; *C.C.W.*, p. 39ff—McDowell.

66. Mark De Wolfe Howe, ed. *Howe Letters of General Sherman* (New York, 1909), p. 202 (cited hereafter as *Howe Letters*); *C.C.W.*, p. 39—McDowell; Heintzelman MS Diary, July 20.

67. Lloyd Lewis, *Sherman*, p. 172.

68. Heintzelman MS Diary, Sept. 1; Wilkinson to Heintzelman, August 15, Heintzelman to Wilkinson, August 13 or September 13, Heintzelman MSS. The last letter though undated would seem to be of September because Heintzelman's arm, badly hit at Bull Run, was still unhealed in August.

69. *C.C.W.*, p. 207—Tyler. A more embellished version is given in *Tyler*, pp. 50-51; but as it was written twenty years later and in self justification, it has been disregarded.

70. *O. O. Howard*, p. 152.

71. For the plan, see *O.R.*, vol. II, p. 317; for the engineer part, see Barnard in *O.R.*, vol. II, p. 330ff; and *C.C.W.*, p. 39ff—McDowell for details.

72. The Confederate forces were actually massed at Blackburn's Ford for Union attack; and when McDowell struck on July 21, they were trying to do the same from Blackburn's.

73. Heintzelman MS Diary, Sept. 1.
74. *C.C.W.*, p. 42—McDowell; J. Cutler Andrews, *The North Reports the War* (Pittsburgh, 1955), pp. 87-88.
75. *C.C.W.*, p. 24—Richardson.
76. *C.C.W.*, p. 42—McDowell.

Chapter VII

1. *Woodbury*, IRI, p. 87.
2. There is some discrepancy in times as to when Tyler started. Carlisle said (*O.R.*, vol. II, p. 362) that the march began at 3:00; Burnham of Keyes's brigade (*A. G. Report Conn.*, p. 12) 2:00; while Tyler in his report (*O.R.*, vol. II, p. 349) and his testimony (*C.C.W.*, p. 200) says 2:30; and he is supported by both Schenck (*O.R.*, vol. II, p. 357) and Sherman (*ibid.*, p. 368). It seems that Tyler managed to overcome the difficulty of getting volunteers on the road at an early hour quite acceptably. The crucial time is not really when Tyler began his march, which he seems to have done on time, but rather, when he cleared the road to the Sudley Ford with his rear brigade. It was in this that he failed; his advance was so incredibly slow that he delayed the flanking column at least an hour, probably two—not because of a late start as historians aver but because of a slow advance.
3. *O.R.*, vol. II, p. 357.
4. *C.C.W.*, p. 201—Tyler.
5. *C.C.W.*, pp. 202-203—Tyler and corroborated by Mc-Dowell in *ibid.*, p. 43.
6. *O.R.*, vol. II, pp. 357-358, 360.
7. *O.R.*, vol. II, pp. 362, 364.
8. Wilson says in *O.R.*, vol. II, p. 362 that Tyler opened up at 5:00 and R. M. Johnston accepted this. Tyler in his report says 6:30 (*O.R.*, vol. II, p. 349) and in his testimony 6:15 (*C.C.W.*, p. 200). McDowell corroborates the former time in *O.R.*, vol. II, p. 318.
9. Van L. Naisawald, "Bull Run: The Artillery and the Infantry," *Civil War History*, vol. III, no. 2, June, 1957, p.

164 (cited hereafter as *Naisawald*).

10. *O.R.*, vol. II, pp. 362-364; *Naisawald*, p. 164.
11. *Home Letters*, p. 206; *O.R.*, vol. II, p. 368; *Todd*, p. 33.
12. Henry E. Clement, *The Bull Run Rout* (Cambridge, 1909), p. 13.
13. *O.R.*, vol. II, pp. 383, 402; *C.C.W.*, p. 30—Heintzelman.
14. *O.R.*, vol. II, pp. 334, 383, 416.
15. Fry in *B. & L.*, vol. I, p. 187; *Woodbury 2 R. I.*, p. 31; *Road to Richmond*, p. 20.
16. *O.R.*, vol. II, pp. 319, 418; *O. O. Howard*, vol. I, p. 153.
17. *Fry in B & L*, vol. I, p. 187.
18. *Woodbury 2 R. I.*, p. 31; *O.R.*, vol. II, p. 334.
19. *Blake*, p. 14; *Woodbury 2 R. I.*, p. 31; Albert G. Riddle, *Recollections of War Times, 1860-1865* (New York, 1895), p. 45.
20. *Bennett*, p. 16.
21. *2nd N. H.*, pp. 23-24.
22. *C.C.W.*, p. 161—Barnard.
23. *O. O. Howard*, p. 153, says McDowell ordered Heintzelman to march all the way to Sudley's Ford but in his report (*O.R.*, vol. II, p. 402) Heintzelman said the guide could not find the turn off road, which fact he again stated in his testimony (*C.C.W.*, p. 30).
24. Even late in the war there were instances of overuse of tired troops. In late 1864, the Second Corps was taken directly from one action and sent across the James River below Petersburg where it was forced to fight again without rest in the battle at Reams's Station. Their physical exhaustion was so great that they could not hold up and for one of the few times in its career, the corps which had smashed Pickett at Gettysburg gave way in utter defeat. Francis A. Walker, *General Hancock* (New York, 1894), p. 297ff.
25. *Woodbury 2 R. I.*, p. 31; *Barnard*, p. 51; *O.R.*, vol. II, pp. 319, 395, 413; *C.C.W.*, p. 161—Barnard.
26. *Woodbury 2 R. I.*, p. 372.
27. *O.R.*, vol. II, pp. 395, 334; *PNRI*, series I, p. 14ff; *Woodbury 2 R. I.*, p. 32.

28. *PNRI*, series II, p. 19.

29. *O.R.*, vol. II, pp. 334-335.

30. *O.R.*, vol. II, p. 319.

31. *2nd N. H.*, p. 24.

32. David Hunter, *Report of Services*, p. 8; *Woodbury 2 R. I.*, pp. 32-33.

33. *O.R.*, vol. II, pp. 395-396; *PNRI*, series II, p. 19; *Poore*, pp. 114-115; *Woodbury 2 R. I.*, pp. 33-34.

34. Ambrose Edward Burnside; born Indiana; graduated 18/38 in West Point Class of 1847; saw small action in Mexico after which in 1853, he resigned the army as a first lieutenant. The inventor of a breech-loading carbine which bears his name, he became involved in railroads until the outbreak of war when the governor of Rhode Island sent for him and asked if he, as an ex-regular army officer, would not lead a regiment of Rhode Island troops bound for Washington. Burnside was only too happy to go. Personally he was honest, gay, and jovial, with a recognized social position in the army. *Cullum*, 1348; *PNRI*, series II, p. 11ff; *Poore*, pp. 93-98.

35. *2nd N. H.*, p. 26; *PNRI*, series I, p. 15ff; *O.R.*, vol. II, pp. 346, 395-396.

36. *2nd N. H.*, p. 29.

37. *O.R.*, vol. II, pp. 383-384, 346.

38. *O.R.*, vol. II, pp. 383-384, 387, 390, 393-394, 319; *Woodbury IRI*, p. 99; *2nd N. H.*, p. 29; *Woodbury 2 R. I.*, p. 35.

39. *O.R.*, vol. II, p. 337; *C.C.W.*, p. 42—McDowell.

40. *Tyler*, p. 60; *O.R.*, vol. II, p. 349.

41. *Home Letters*, p. 206; *O.R.*, vol. II, p. 368.

42. *C.C.W.*, p. 43—McDowell.

43. *O.R.*, vol. II, p. 349. *R. M. Johnston*, p. 193, says Tyler did this on his own initiative. Tyler's report (*O.R.*, vol. II, p. 349) is misleading because it does not mention Lieutenant Kingsbury, and Sherman (*ibid.*, pp. 368-369) observes only through his own eyes which attributed motivation to Tyler without knowing the facts; but when Tyler testified a second time, he corrected a former statement by saying that

he received word from an aide around 11:00 to press the attack (*C.C.W.*, p. 206); and he bears this out in *Tyler*, p. 60.

44. *Home Letters*, p. 206; *O.R.*, vol. II, pp. 369, 372.
45. *2nd N. H.*, p. 30; *O.R.*, vol. II, pp. 384, 388, 396; *Woodbury 2 R. I.*, p. 35; McDowell mistakenly reported that Schenck and Keyes crossed at the brigade road (*O.R.*, vol. II, p. 319).
46. *Todd*, p. 34.
47. *C.C.W.*, p. 201—Tyler.
48. *PNRI*, series II, p. 22; *2nd N. H.*, p. 30; *O.R.*, vol. LI, pt. I, p. 23; *Woodbury 2 R. I.*, p. 35; he did send forward the Second New Hampshire to help Heintzelman, *O.R.*, vol. II, p. 396.
49. Henry Warner Slocum, later a wing commander in Sherman's march through the Carolinas, not to be confused with John S. Slocum, who died of wounds at Bull Run.
50. *O.R.*, vol. II, p. 389. He was struck in the thigh by a ball.
51. *O.R.*, vol. II, pp. 384, 387-388.
52. *O.R.*, vol. II, pp. 319-320, 370. Orlando B. Willcox, born Michigan, graduated 8/38 in the West Point Class of 1848. He served in the late days of the Mexican War and saw active combat against the Seminoles in Florida. As a first lieutenant, he resigned the army in 1857 to become a lawyer and writer. At the outbreak of war, he was offered a regiment of Michigan troops which he readily accepted and soon found himself in Washington where he received a brigade in McDowell's army. *Cullum*, 1338.
53. *O. O. Howard*, vol. I, pp. 157-158; *Road to Richmond*, p. 21; *Gould's Berry*, p. 62; *Holcombe*, p. 44; *MOLLUS-Minnesota*, p. 84; *O.R.*, vol. II, pp. 419, 421.
54. Heintzelman MS Diary, Sept. 1.
55. *O.R.*, vol. II, pp. 346-347.
56. *O.R.*, vol. II, p. 394.
57. *C.C.W.*, pp. 168-169—Griffin.
58. *C.C.W.*, p. 143—Barry.
59. *C.C.W.*, pp. 168-169—Griffin.

60. *Cullum*, 1353.
61. *C.C.W.*, p. 169—Griffin.
62. *Blake*, p. 20. Although it does not specifically mention Griffin, it must have been him because Ricketts testified (*C.C.W.*, p. 243) that he took down his own fence.
63. Although Ricketts did not specify Young's Branch (*C.C.W.*, p. 243) this ravine is the only one bad enough to break a wheel and he next speaks of taking down a fence, probably along the Warrenton Pike, so that he can ascend Henry House Hill.
64. *C.C.W.*, p. 243—Ricketts.
65. *C.C.W.*, p. 169—Griffin.
66. *Blake*, p. 17.
67. Barry testified that he ordered a change in the first position of the guns (*C.C.W.*, p. 144) but neither Griffin nor Ricketts, in neither their reports nor their testimony, verify the fact. Griffin did move two guns to the right while Barry was with Ricketts.
68. *C.C.W.*, p. 144—Barry; *O.R.*, vol. II, pp. 384-485.
69. Johnston has Keyes attacking the van Pelt House but terrain analysis compared with both Tyler's and Keyes's reports show this to be false. *Tyler* (p. 61) says the brigade attacked the Henry House but this is merely a slip of memory over a long period of time.
70. *O.R.*, vol. II, pp. 349, 354; *Tyler*, p. 60.
71. *C.C.W.*, p. 201—Tyler; *O.R.*, vol. II, pp. 350-354; *A. G. Report Conn.*, pp. 12-13.
72. *Tyler*, p. 61.
73. *C.C.W.*, p. 243—Ricketts.
74. *C.C.W.*, p. 169—Griffin; *PNRI*, series I, p. 20ff.
75. *C.C.W.*, p. 243—Ricketts.
76. *Roe*, pp. 71, 81.
77. *C.C.W.*, p. 146—Barry and p. 169—Griffin; *O.R.*, vol. II, p. 347.
78. The name Wood is represented by a blank and is probably the result of a lapse of memory. The only support regiment in that position was Colonel A. M. Wood's Fourteenth

New York.

79. *C.C.W.*, p. 169—Griffin. Barry denied this whole colloquy in *ibid.*, p. 145 but Griffin is supported by Lieutenant Reed in *ibid.*, p. 220.
80. *Roe*, p. 72.
81. *C.C.W.*, p. 216—Averell.
82. *C.C.W.*, p. 30—Heintzelman; Heintzelman MS Diary, September 1.
83. The regiment was the Thirty-third Virginia.
84. *O.R.*, vol. II, pp. 347, 385, 402-403; *C.C.W.*, p. 30—Heintzelman.
85. *O.R.*, vol. II, p. 393.
86. *O.R.*, vol. II, pp. 403, 347; *C.C.W.*, p. 146—Barry; Heintzelman MS Diary, September 5.
87. *O.R.*, vol. II, p. 385.
88. *PNRI*, series I, p. 20ff.
89. *O.R.*, vol. II, p. 370; *Home Letters*, p. 208.
90. *O. O. Howard*, vol. I, pp. 158-159; *O.R.*, vol. II, p. 418.
91. *Gould's Berry*, p. 64.
92. *O.R.*, vol. II, p. 408.
93. *O.R.*, vol. II, pp. 320, 270, 385, 402-403, 406-407; *ibid.*, vol. LI, pt. 1, p. 21ff; *Blake*, p. 20ff; *C.C.W.*, pp. 146-147—Barry.
94. *C.C.W.*, p. 33—Franklin and p. 120—Griffin; *O.R.*, vol. II, pp. 320-321, 385, 390.
95. *C.C.W.*, pp. 1216, 1217—Averell.
96. *C.C.W.*, pp. 165, 175—Griffin.
97. Heintzelman MS Diary, September 5.
98. *O.R.*, vol. II, pp. 404, 320ff.
99. *O.R.*, vol. II, p. 374.
100. *O.R.*, vol. II, pp. 428-429; *C.C.W.*, p. 178—Davies.
101. *O.R.*, vol. II, p. 424.
102. *C.C.W.*, pp. 178-179—Davies; *O.R.*, vol. II, p. 429.
103. Richardson's report says ten days (*O.R.*, vol. II, p. 374) and his testimony (*C.C.W.*, p. 25) eleven.
104. Henry Hunt was to find himself in this position again at Gettysburg, under more disastrous circumstances.
105. *O.R.*, vol. II, pp. 374, 424.

106. *O.R.*, vol. II, p. 427.

107. *C.C.W.*, p. 179—Davies.

108. MS Court of Inquiry in the Case of Dixon S. Miles—G. A. Mendell and Dr. J. J. Woodward (cited hereafter as CIM followed by the name of the witness testifying).

109. *O.R.*, vol. II, p. 429; *C.C.W.*, p. 179—Davies. The order of events is not specifically given but it could hardly have happened in any other way.

110. *C.C.W.*, p. 25—Richardson.

111. *O.R.*, vol. II, p. 424.

112. *O.R.*, vol. II, p. 374, 424; *C.C.W.*, p. 25—Richardson.

113. *C.C.W.*, p. 76—Miles.

114. CIM—Ricketts; *C.C.W.*, p. 25—Ricketts.

115. In testifying to the court of inquiry, Richardson denied that he threatened to harm Miles at the first possible chance, but he made no effort to deny that there was bad blood between the two men. See *Cullum*, 387 and 1096 for the time in Mexico when their periods of assignment overlap which is not mentioned in CIM.

116. Greene, Locke, and Ritchie all verify in CIM actual drinking of liquor by Miles. There are numerous others who reported his drunkenness from the witness stand.

117. *C.C.W.*, p. 25—Richardson.

118. *Curtis*, pp. 40-42: *O.R.*, vol. II, pp. 375, 424-425, 430.

119. CIM—McKeever; *O.R.*, vol. II, p. 425.

120. *O.R.*, vol. II, p. 425.

121. *O.R.*, vol. II, p. 376.

122. *O.R.*, vol. II, p. 430; *C.C.W.*, pp. 179-180—Davies. Thomas A. Davies, born New York, graduated West Point 25/46 in 1829 and resigned in 1831 to be a civil engineer and merchant in New York City. Davies was offered a regiment by its men who had never seen him, merely on the recommendation that he was militarily experienced. *Cullum*, 565; *Curtis*, pp. 19-21.

123. *C.C.W.*, pp. 76-77—Blenker; *O.R.*, vol. II, p. 427.

124. *C.C.W.*, p. 26—Richardson.

125. In his report (*O.R.*, vol. II, p. 425) Miles said he received

word from Davies that he was under attack and could not retreat so the order was cancelled for both brigades. This, however, is not supported by and of Richardson's testimony in CIM or *C.C.W.* or in his report and Davies fails to mention it in his report and his testimony before the Committee.

126. CIM—McDowell; *O.R.*, vol. II, p. 376; *C.C.W.*, p. 25—Richardson.
127. *O.R.*, vol. II, p. 376.
128. Walrath in CIM says an "unidentified Colonel."
129. CIM—Todd and Walrath. There is no account which gives a sequence of events here. The problem is handled in the manner which seems to fit most logically under the circumstances and according to the evidence.
130. *O.R.*, vol. II, p. 376; CIM—McConnell, Stevens, Judd.
131. *C.C.W.*, p. 26—Richardson; CIM—Stevens; *O.R.*, vol. II, p. 376. The conversation above is a synthesis of the three, with emphasis on *O.R.* and CIM, because they are more similar and closer to the event.
132. CIM—Alexander, McDowell.
133. The exact position that McDowell wished Richardson to have is not exactly clear. McDowell seemed to want him to have (CIM) complete independence of Miles as far as his own brigade went, but Alexander told Richardson when he delivered the order (CIM) to take command of the entire divisional force facing Blackburn's Ford and this is what he did. (*O.R.*, vol. II, p. 377; *C.C.W.*, p. 26—Richardson).
134. CIM—Barry; *C.C.W.*, p. 26—Richardson.
135. *C.C.W.*, p. 27—Richardson; CIM—Richardson; *O.R.*, vol. II, p. 377; all these accounts are the same with only the slightest variation; the first mentioned is the one quoted above because it is given in greatest detail. The conversation itself was verified by Walrath and Ritchie in CIM.
136. CIM—Barry.
137. McDowell makes no mention of this in his report (*O.R.*, vol. II, p. 324ff) and he testified in CIM that he did not

relieve Miles, just ignored his presence; but Vincent
(CIM) stated that he definitely was relieved, which fact
Richardson corroborates (*C.C.W.*, p. 26).

138. *C.C.W.*, p. 26—Richardson.
139. *O.R.*, vol. II, p. 377.
140. *O.R.*, vol. II, p. 747.
141. Walt Whitman, *Prose Works* (Philadelphia, 1892), pp.
23, 24.

Chapter VIII

1. *Cullum*, 1309.
2. *B. & L.*, vol. I, p. 194.
3. In his report (*O.R.*, vol. II, pp. 345-346), Barry disqualifies
the six guns attached to the Eighth New York Militia, but
they were served during the day by volunteers after their
crews demanded discharge so the total should not be
Barry's forty-nine, but rather fifty-five.
4. Cullum has sketches of all these men. Lieutenant John Edwards was the youngest of the regular artillery officers in
command of a battery.
5. *Cullum*, 957; *D.A.B.*, vol. I, p. 657.
6. Including the Fourth Pennsylvania which demanded its
discharge that day but not the regular army battalion or
the battalion of marine recruits.
7. See *Cullum*, 1033, 1149, 1172, 1542, 1565; for additional information on Slocum see his biography and for McCook
see *Ohio in the War*, vol. I, p. 807ff for a hostile sketch with
details.
8. J. H. Hobart Ward had been an NCO, and Willis A. Gorman had been Colonel of the Fourth Indiana.
9. *Massachusetts Register*, p. 132; *Woodbury 1RI*, pp. 154-
155; *Holcombe*, pp. 10-11; *New York at Gettysburg*, vol.
III, p. 1356; *Martial Deeds*, pp. 410-411.
10. For examples see: *C.A.B.*, vol. II, pp. 65, 261; *Gould's Berry*,
p. 23ff; *Martial Deeds*, p. 662ff; *Roe*, pp. 319-320; *History
of the Fighting Fourteenth* (n.a., n.p., n.d.), p. 359; *2nd
N. H.*, p. 272ff; Ahearn, *Thomas F. Meagher*, pp. 92-93;

Lonn, p. 201; officers in this category included men like Berry, Corcoran, Terry, Farnham, Marston, Lawrence, Wood.

11. *Lonn*, p. 193ff.

12. *Lonn* sketches all foreign officers who served with the rank of colonel or above in the Union Army, with the exception of Max Einstein.

13. *Lonn*, pp. 188-189.

14. *C.A.B.*, vol. V, p. 72.

15. *Butterfield Memorial*, p. 7ff, points out that he was the lone New Yorker in command of a brigade under Patterson; in fact, the lone non-Pennsylvanian with the exception of regulars like Thomas.

16. Almost all the colonels in Patterson's army are sketched in *Martial Deeds*. For others see *Cayuga*, p. 26; *Butterfield Memorial*, p. 7ff; *New York at Gettysburg*, vol. III, p. 1340.

17. There was an interesting parallel in World War II when the Allies were faced with the problem of landing craft priority to Pacific and European theatres. Both sides felt under-supplied and retarded.

18. *O.R.*, vol. II, p. 746.

19. Details of this are in *Narrative*, p. 1ff, and Patterson's MS OB.

20. *D.A.B.*, vol. XIV, pp. 306-307.

21. See Görlitz, *History of the German General Staff*. The ratio of wing to army was reduced from 7-to-1 to 3-to-1.

22. *O.R.*, vol. II, p. 350.

23. *Tyler*, p. 68ff.

24. *O.R.*, vol. II, pp. 322-323.

25. *O.R.*, vol. II, p. 374ff.

26. Richardson to McDowell, July 26, 1861, MS in CIM; *O.R.*, vol. II, p. 439.

27. Miles to Court, August 13, 1861, MS in CIM.

28. CIM.

29. *O.R.*, vol. II, pp. 438-439 has the full text.

30. *Cullum*, 387, a very terse sketch; Court martial in *O.R.*, vol. XIX, pt. 1, pp. 248-308.

31. The six considered here are Sherman, Howard, Willcox, Franklin, Burnside, and Porter. Keyes, divorced from the action, is not included.

32. *O.R.*, vol. II, p. 384.

33. *C.C.W.*, p. 168ff—Griffin.

34. McClellan, Pope, Burnside were to follow in short order. Technically, Pope led the Army of Virginia, an amalgamation of the scattered forces in the Shenandoah in 1862; but he fought his battle with much of the Army of the Potomac under him.

SELECT CRITICAL BIBLIOGRAPHY

It would be useless to list every source consulted in the preparation of this work. The author has, therefore, taken the liberty of mentioning only those sources which have been of major assistance. In some cases, these may not even appear in the footnotes but their value is not less because of this, for much of the research performed was done for subjects which appear only as a whole, as in the case of the previous careers of regimental commanders. Information has been acquired about the many officers involved through biographies, manuscript collections, archives, memoirs, and campaign histories. Hard-to-find details on a particular man will almost always be set down in his regimental history if he was ever a colonel or a regimental officer. Besides the numerous and often valuable regimental histories, most of the states published in one form or another biographies of all their officers from colonel upwards. These range in length per man from one or two pages to twenty or thirty pages, and at times they are particularly incisive.

Major reliance has been placed on two works. One is the excellent *War of the Rebellion: A Compilation of the Official Records of the Union and Confederate Armies*, 128 vols. (Washington 1885-1905), which has most often been cited in these pages as *O.R.* Almost all the post-action reports may be found herein as well as a good portion of the circulars, general and special orders, and correspondence. The second of the two is the *Report of the Joint Committee on the Conduct of the War*, 3 series of 3 vols. each (Washington, 1863-1865), cited in the footnotes as *C.C.W.* While the testimony was gathered in a most biased, highly prejudicial, and often exasperating way, this does not detract in the slightest from the value of the work. Only vol. II of series I was used so no direct reference was made to the volume or series number other than in the initial reference.

Manuscript Sources

1. Appointments, Commissions, and Promotions Files, National Archives. If there is any record of a man having served as an officer in the service of the federal government, it will be found in the collections, filed by person and dating from about 1863.
2. Manuscript Court of Inquiry in the case of Dixon S. Miles. As far as is ascertainable, this has not been previously consulted. It is filled with excellent material and is amazingly legible considering that it was completely hand written. Located in the National Archives.
3. Ulric Dahlgren MSS, Library of Congress. Especially useful in reflecting the flavor of early recruiting of both officers and enlisted men.
4. Abner Doubleday MSS, New York Historical Society. Handwritten memoirs in the form of anecdotes and incidents. There are also some sixteen volumes of newspaper clippings which reflect almost every published word on one Abner Doubleday, but they are of little use. The memoirs were humorous and helpful.
5. General and Special Orders, Department of North-Eastern Virginia, 1861, National Archives. Most of the information herein may be found in *O.R.*
6. General Staff Files, National Archives. Similar to the A. C. P. Files but for a different period.
7. Samuel Peter Heintzelman MSS, Library of Congress. One of the most voluminous and valuable collections. Although the handwriting in his diary is perhaps the most illegible ever set to paper, the humor and sarcasm contained therein make its deciphering enjoyable and profitable.
8. Montgomery C. Meigs MS Diary, Library of Congress. Useful for details; rivals Heintzelman for bad script.
9. Patterson's MS Orderly Book, Pennsylvania Historical Society. Much of this appears in *O.R.* or his own narrative, but there is a good deal that is useful in the form of memorandums, etc.

10. Pennsylvania Militia Files for the War of 1812 (Patterson), National Archives.
11. Fitz-John Porter MSS, Library of Congress. Useful in many ways but particularly as it reveals the relationship between Porter and Patterson while in the Valley.
12. Winfield Scott MSS, Library of Congress. Almost devoid of information.
13. John Sherman MSS, Library of Congress. Sherman served as a volunteer aide with Patterson in the early weeks of the war and then continued a voluminous correspondence with him afterwards.
14. William Tecumseh Sherman MSS, Library of Congress. An interesting revelation of a personality combined with useful information on officers and officer procurement in particular and in general.

State Participation Accounts

1. Everett, Edward G., "Pennsylvania Raises an Army 1861," *Western Pennsylvania Historical Magazine, Summer*, 1956, vol. 39, No. 2.
2. Hicks, John D., "The Organization of the Volunteer Army in 1861 with Special Reference to Minnesota," *Minnesota Historical Bulletin*, No. 5, February, 1918.
3. Robertson, John, *Michigan in the War*, Lansing, 1882.
4. Whitman, William E. S. and True, Charles H., *Maine in the War for the Union*, Lewiston, 1865.
5. *Annual Report of the Adjutant General of the State of Connecticut for the Year 1861*, Hartford, 1862. All adjutant general reports reflect the condition of preparedness in their own state, the procurement of officers and numerous other factors. Several of them have reports not found in *O.R.*, which were useful.
6. *Annual Report of the Adjutant General of the Commonwealth of Massachusetts*, Boston, 1861.
7. *Annual Report of the Adjutant General to the Legislature*

of Minnesota, St. Paul, 1862.

8. *Annual Report of the Adjutant General of the State of New Jersey for the Year 1861*, Trenton, 1862.

9. *Annual Report of the Adjutant General of New York, 1861*, Albany, 1862.

Collected Source Materials

1. *Pennsylvania Archives: Papers of the Governors*, 9 series, Harrisburg, 1902. Useful in studying the original development of the Army of the Upper Potomac during April and May.

2. Bassler, Roy P., ed., *The Collected Works of Abraham Lincoln*, 9 volumes, New Brunswick, 1953-1955. The most recent and best of the many Lincoln collections.

3. Johnson, Robert Underwood and Buel, Clarence Clough, eds., *Battles and Leaders of the Civil War*, 4 vols, New York, 1887. No student of the period can neglect these first-hand, often vitriolic, always entertaining accounts. The four volumes are a collection of articles almost all by first-hand participants.

Biographical Aids and Collections

1. Bates, Samuel P., *Martial Deeds of Pennsylvania*, Philadelphia, 1875. Excellent for command sketches of Patterson's army and also for Pennsylvanians under McDowell.

2. Clark, Rufus W., *Heroes of Albany*, Albany, 1866.

3. Cullum, George W., *Biographical Register of the Officers and Graduates of the U. S. Military Academy at West Point, N.Y.*, 3 vols. and 2 supplements, Boston, 1891. Unmatched and invaluable. In addition to career records, personal sketches are appended in the cases of notable officers.

4. Lonn, Ella, *Foreigners in the Union Army and Navy*, Baton Rouge, 1951. Detailed, comprehensive and enjoyable.

5. Malone, Dumas, ed., *Dictionary of American Biography*, 20 vols., New York, 1928-1936. The best of several such attempts. Each sketch has a bibliography appended.

6. *The Massachusetts Register, 1862, containing a Record of the Government and Institutions of the State together with a very Complete Account of the Massachusetts Volunteers*, Adams, 1862.

7. *New York State Monuments Commission for the Battle-fields of Gettysburg and Chattanooga*, 3 vols., Albany, 1902. In volume III are some useful sketches of New York officers.

8. Phisterer, Frederick, *New York in the War of the Rebellion*, 5 vols., Albany, 1912. New York officer records.

9. Reid, Whitelaw, *Ohio in the War*, 2 vols., New York, 1867. Contains excellent sketches of Ohio officers, particularly of McDowell.

10. Wilson, James Grant and Fiske, John, *Appleton's Cyclopedia of American Biography*, 6 vols., 6 supplements, New York, 1887-1931. Not as good as *D.A.B.* but sketches several lesser officers not in that series.

General and Special Studies

1. Andrews, J. Cutler, *The North Reports the Civil War*, Pittsburgh, 1955. Best of many studies of the "Bohemian Brigade."

2. Barnard, John G., *The C.S.A. and the Battle of Bull Run (A Letter to an English Friend)*, New York, 1862. Written as an answer to W. H. Russell (see infra.) on the rout at Bull Run. The valuable information contained herein must be sorted out from the hairsplitting and the numerous quotes from reports which are available in *O.R.*

3. Dwight, Theodore, ed., *Papers of the Military Historical Society of Massachusetts*, 10 vols., Boston, 1895. Sound and judicious in the early volumes, where my research was done.

4. Fry, James B., *McDowell and Tyler in the Campaign of*

Bull Run, New York, 1884. Written in reply to Tyler's Memorial volume, this small volume succinctly clears up several moot points.

5. Johnston, R. M., *Bull Run: its Strategy and its Tactics*, Boston, 1913. The standard, though now outdated, work on Bull Run. Overly harsh on McDowell, factually incorrect in many places, and bad in value judgments.

6. Nicolay, John G., *The Outbreak of the Rebellion*, New York, 1881.

7. Paris, Comte de, *History of the Civil War in America*, 3 vols., Philadelphia, 1875. Useful in studying the Union armies from a detached standpoint (the author was a Frenchman who served with the Army of the Potomac and elsewhere).

8. Pierce, James O., "The Skirmish at Falling Waters," *Glimpses of the Nation's Struggle: Military Order of the Loyal Legion of the United States (Minnesota)*, series 2.

9. Stine, J. H., *History of the Army of the Potomac*, Philadelphia, 1892. Originally written as a history of the First Corps which was fairly effectively wiped out at Gettysburg on the first day and was later combined with another corps. McDowell's Army of North-Eastern Virginia later became the First Corps of the Army of the Potomac. Stine has unfortunately assumed the burden of several fruitless crusades, but on the whole his work is good. Beware of quotations.

10. Swinton, William, *Campaigns of the Army of the Potomac*, New York, 1882. Favorable to Scott and McDowell while slashing concerning their subordinates and Lincoln. Valuable insights.

11. Williams, Kenneth P., *Lincoln Finds a General*, 4 vols. The author is one of a series of "debunkers." Somehow he managed to find excellent generalship in John Pope at Second Bull Run, probably the low point in command for the entire history of the American military. Williams glorifies Patterson and deprecates McDowell and Scott.

12. Williams, T. Harry, *Lincoln and his Generals*, New York, 1952. Oversimplification and categorization concerning all

officers; Lincoln is glorified all out of proportion.

Biographies, Autobiographies and Memoirs

1. Athearn, Robert G., *Thomas Francis Meagher: An Irish Revolutionary in America*, Boulder, 1949. An excellent doctoral dissertation.
2. Bennett, Edwin C., *Musket and Sword or the Camp, March, and Firing Line in the Army of the Potomac*, Boston, 1900. Interesting details with particularly good insight in Bull Run problems, for all its brevity.
3. Butler, Benjamin Franklin, *Autobiography and Personal Reminiscences: Butler's Book*, Boston, 1892. Self-laudatory.
4. Butterfield, Julia, ed., *Biographical Memorial of General Daniel Butterfield*, New York, 1904.
5. Cleaves, Freeman, *Rock of Chickamauga: The Life of George H. Thomas*, Norman, 1948.
6. Croffutt, W. A., ed., *Fifty Years in Camp and Field*, New York, 1909. Diary of Ethan Alan Hitchcock.
7. Crotty, D. G., *Four Years Campaigning in the Army of the Potomac*, Grand Rapids, 1874. Generally useless except for details.
8. Curtis, Newton Martin, *From Bull Run to Chancellorsville*, New York, 1906. Good account, well written.
9. Dwight, Wilder, *Life and Letters of Wilder Dwight*, Boston, 1868. These letters are detailed and interesting. Dwight himself was slain in the war.
10. Elliott, Charles Winslow, *Winfield Scott: The Soldier and The Man*, New York, 1937. The best work on Scott available.
11. Gould, Edward K., *Major-General Hiram G. Berry*, Rockland, 1899. Very good study.
12. Haupt, Herman, *Reminiscences of Herman Haupt*, Milwaukee, 1901.
13. Howard, O. O., *Autobiography of Oliver Otis Howard*, 2 vols., New York, 1907. One of the best and most enter-

taining memoirs of the war.

14. Howe, Mark DeWolfe, ed., *Home Letters of General Sherman*, New York, 1909. These letters to his wife and family fill in a large gap in his MS collection which concerns friends and male kin.

15. Hunter, David, *Report of the Military Services of General David Hunter U. S. A. During the War of the Rebellion made to the U. S. War Department*, New York, 1873.

16. Keyes, Erasmus D., *Fifty Years Observation of Men and Events, Civil and Military*, New York, 1884. Unfortunately spends more time discussing others than himself.

17. Lewis, Lloyd, *Sherman, Fighting Prophet*, New York, 1932. Very readable.

18. *Life of Major-General David Bell Birney United States Volunteers*, Philadelphia, 1867.

19. Mitchell, Donald, *Daniel Tyler: A Memorial Volume*, New Haven, 1883. Written by Tyler himself up to the end of Bull Run in reply to G. W. Cullum's request for information (see supra). Much of that contributed by others to complete it after his death is apocryphal and useless; but his own information, while dubious, is revealing. Should be used with one thumb in *O. R.*

20. Patterson, Robert, *A Narrative of the Campaign in the Valley of the Shenandoah in 1861*, Philadelphia, 1865. Quotes out of context, warps meanings, and spends much time arguing about the actual fight at Bull Run in mitigation of himself. Censure of Scott generally valid.

21. Pearson, Henry Greenleaf, *James S. Wadsworth of Geneseo*, New York, 1913. Excellently written and well documented.

22. *Personal Narratives of Events in the War of the Rebellion being Papers Read before the Rhode Island Soldiers and Sailors Historical Society*, Providence, 1878-1890.

23. Poore, Ben. Perley, *The Life and Public Services of Ambrose E. Burnside, Soldier—Citizen—Statesman*, Providence, 1882. Eulogistic with some factual errors in the parts which do not concern Burnside but merely fill out the narrative.

24. Riddle, Albert Gallatin, *Recollections of War Times*, New York, 1895. Illustrative, by example rather than intent, of the debilitating effect of Congress on the war effort in the field.

25. Russell, William Howard ("Bull Run"), *My Diary North and South*, New York, 1863. A peculiar collection of facts and hearsay which should be used with care. Those things for which he damns Yankee newsmen, he commits himself.

26. Slocum, Charles Elihu, *The Life and Services of Major-General Henry Warner Slocum*, Toledo, 1913. Quotes many useful letters.

27. Small, Harold Adams, ed., *Road to Richmond*, California, 1939. Diary of Abner Small; readable, highly amusing, and useful.

28. Strother, Daniel H., "Personal Recollections of the War," *Harper's New Monthly Magazine*, vol. 33, July-November, 1866. Invaluable for the Valley Campaigns of 1861 and 1862 although deprecatory of almost all military leaders.

29. Townshend, E. D., *Anecdotes of the Civil War*, New York, 1884. Useful for personalities and early plans.

30. Wallace, Lewis, *Lew Wallace: an Autobiography*, New York, 1905.

31. Wilson, James Harrison, *Under the Old Flag*, 2 vols., New York, 1912.

Regimental Histories

In using these works, any author should beware the glorifications which pervade almost all of them. If they were taken at face value, no regiment ever broke under fire, each regiment suffered the most casualties of any unit in the war, and they were all composed entirely of officers—no enlisted men.

1. *Address delivered at the unveiling of the Bull Run Memorial at the Seventy-first Regiment Armory*, March 12, 1895, New York, 1895.

2. Barrett, O. S., *Reminiscences, Incidents, Battles, Marches,*

and Camp Life of the Old Fourth Michigan Infantry in the War of the Rebellion 1861-1864, Detroit, 1888.

3. Blake, H. M., *Three Years in the Army of the Potomac*, Boston, 1865.

4. Bryant, Edwin C., *History of the Third Regiment of Wisconsin Veteran Volunteer Infantry*, 1861-1865, Madison, 1891.

5. Clement, E. H., *Bull Run Rout*, Cambridge, 1909.

6. Clowes, Walter F., *The Detroit Light Guard*, Detroit, 1900.

7. Conyngham, Captain D. P., *The Irish Brigade and Its Campaigns*.

8. Cudworth, Warren H., *History of the First Regiment*, Boston, 1866. Massachusetts Infantry.

9. Gordon, George H., *Brook Farm to Cedar Mountain*, Boston, 1883. Self-eulogistic but well done.

10. Gould, Major John M., *History of the First—Tenth—Twenty-ninth Marine Regiment*, Portland, 1871.

11. Hall, Henry and Hall, James, *Cayuga in the Field*, Auburn, 1873. History of the Nineteenth New York Volunteers.

12. Haynes, Martin H., *A History of the Second Regiment New Hampshire Volunteer Infantry in the War of the Rebellion*, Lakeport, 1896.

13. *History of the Fighting Fourteenth* (New York Regiment), n.a., n.p., n.d.

14. Holcombe, R. I., *History of the First Regiment Minnesota Volunteer Infantry*, Stillwater, 1916. One of the better histories about one of the better regiments.

15. Jaques, John W., *Three Years Campaign of the Ninth New York State Militia during the Southern Rebellion*, New York, 1865.

16. Locke, William Henry, *The Story of a Regiment*, Philadelphia, 1868. History of the Eleventh Pennsylvania in the Valley, a three-month unit which re-enlisted *in toto* for three years.

17. Quint, Alonzo H., *Record of the Second Massachusetts Infantry*, Boston, 1867.

18. Roe, Alfred S., *The Fifth Massachusetts Volunteer Infantry*, Boston, 1870.

19. Swinton, William, *History of the Seventh Regiment, National Guard, State of New York, during the War of the Rebellion,* New York, 1870. Detailed account of a regiment which did little in three years of Washington garrison duty.

20. Todd, William, *The Seventy-ninth Highlanders, New York Volunteers, in the War of the Rebellion, 1861-1865,* Albany, 1886. An excellent work.

21. Woodbury, Augustus, *Narrative of the Campaign of the First Rhode Island Regiment in the Spring and Summer of 1861,* Providence, 1862.

22. Woodbury, Augustus, *The Second Rhode Island Regiment,* Providence, 1875. Far more balanced and readable than most regimental histories.

Confederate Sources

As far as Confederate activities have been concerned herein, the author has seen fit to present no more than could be known by the Yankee officers, in order to avoid second guessing. Where the disparity between the actual and accepted has been too great, presentation of the Southern movements has been placed in the footnotes. Main reliance has been placed on Vandiver, Frank, *Mighty Stonewall,* New York, 1957; and Freeman, Douglas S., *Lee's Lieutenants,* 3 vols., New York, 1942-1944.

Some maps have been drawn to represent the hypothetical happenings or plans. Reliance has been placed on the Atlas to accompany *O.R.,* in the main, with aid from Barnard, Nicolay, and Johnston (see supra).

Short Title Index

1. *B. & L.*: Robert Underwood Johnson and Clarence Clough Buel, eds., *Battles and Leaders of the Civil War.*
2. *Barnard*: John G. Barnard, *The C.S.A. and the Battle of Bull Run.*
3. *Barrett*: O. S. Barrett, *Reminiscences, Incidents, Battles, Marches, and Camp Life of the Old Fourth Michigan Infantry in the War of the Rebellion, 1861-1864.*
4. *Blake*: H. M. Blake, *Three Years in the Army of the Potomac.*
5. *Butterfield Memorial*: Julia Butterfield, ed., *A Biographical Memorial of General Daniel Butterfield.*
6. *C.A.B.*: James Grant Wilson and John Fiske, eds., *Appleton's Cyclopedia of American Biography.*
7. *Cayuga*: Henry and James Hall, *Cayuga in the Field.*
8. *C.C.W.*: *Report of the Joint Committee on the Conduct of the War.*
9. *Cleaves' Thomas*: Freeman Cleaves, *Rock of Chickamauga: The Life of George H. Thomas.*
10. *Cudworth*: Warren Cudworth, *History of The First Regiment.*
11. *Cullum*: George W. Cullum, *Biographical Register of the Officers and Graduates of the U. S. Military Academy at West Point, N. Y.*
12. *Curtis*: Newton Martin Curtis, *Bull Run to Chancellorsville.*
13. *D.A.B.*: Dumas Malone, ed., *Dictionary of American Biography.*
14. *Elliott's Scott*: Charles Winslow Elliott, *Winfield Scott: The Soldier and The Man.*
15. *Gordon*: George H. Gordon, *Brook Farm to Cedar Mountain.*
16. *Gould*: Major John M. Gould, *History of The First—Tenth—Twenty-ninth Maine Regiment.*

17. *Gould's Berry*: Edward K. Gould, *Major-General Hiram G. Berry.*
18. *Hist. Penn. Vols.*: Samuel P. Bates, *History of The Pennsylvania Volunteers.*
19. *Home Letters*: Marke de Wolfe Howe, ed., *Home Letters of General Sherman.*
20. *Holcombe*: R. I. Holcombe, *History of The First Regiment Minnesota Volunteer Infantry.*
21. *Keyes*: Erasmus D. Keyes, *Fifty Years Observation of Men and Events Civil and Military.*
22. *Locke*: William Henry Locke, *The Story of a Regiment.*
23. *Lonn*: Ella Lonn, *Foreigners in the Union Army and Navy.*
24. *Maine in the War*: William E. S. Whitman and Charles H. True, *Maine in the War for the Union.*
25. *Martial Deeds*: Samuel P. Bates, *Martial Deeds of Pennsylvania.*
26. *McDowell and Tyler*: James B. Fry, *McDowell and Tyler in the Campaign of Bull Run.*
27. *Mich. in the War*: John Robertson, *Michigan in the War.*
28. *Mighty Stonewall*: Frank E. Vandiver, *Mighty Stonewall.*
29. *MOLLUS-Pierce*: James O. Pierce, "The Skirmish at Falling Waters," *Glimpses of the Nation's Struggle.*
30. *Narrative*: Robert Patterson, *A Narrative of the Campaign in the Valley of the Shenandoah in 1861.*
31. *9NYSM*: John W. Jaques, *Three Years Campaign in the Ninth New York State Militia during The Southern Rebellion.*
32. *Ohio in The War*: Whitelaw Reid, *Ohio in The War.*
33. *O. O. Howard*: O. O. Howard, *Autobiography of Oliver Otis Howard.*
34. *O.R.: War of the Rebellion*: *Official Records of the Union and Confederate Armies.*
35. *Org. Vol. Army Minn.*: John D. Hicks, "The Organization of the Volunteer Army in 1861 with Special Reference to Minnesota," *Minnesota Historical Bulletin.*
36. *Pearson's Wadsworth*: Henry Greenleaf Pearson, *James S. Wadsworth of Geneseo.*

37. *Penn. Raises an Army*: Edward G. Everett, "Pennsylvania Raises an Army, 1861," *Western Pennsylvania Historical Magazine.*
38. *R. M. Johnston*: R. M. Johnston, *Bull Run: Its Strategy and its Tactics.*
39. *Road to Richmond*: Harold Adams Small, ed., *The Road to Richmond.*
40. *2nd N. H.*: Martin H. Haynes, *A History of the Second Regiment New Hampshire Volunteer Infantry in the War of the Rebellion.*
41. *Stine*: James H. Stine, *History of the Army of the Potomac.*
42. *Strother*: D. H. Strother, "Personal Recollections of the War," *Harpers New Monthly Magazine.*
43. *Townshend*: E. D. Townshend, *Anecdotes of the War.*
44. *Tyler*: Donald G. Mitchell, ed., *Biographical Memorial of Daniel Tyler.*
45. *Wallace*: Lew Wallace, *Lew Wallace: An Autobiography.*
46. *W. H. Russell*: William Howard ("Bull Run") Russell, *My Diary North and South.*
47. *Woodbury 1RI*: Augustus Woodbury, *Narrative of the Campaign of the First Rhode Island Regiment in the Spring and Summer of 1861.*
48. *Woodbury 2 R. I.*: Augustus Woodbury, *The Second Rhode Island Regiment.*

INDEX

Abercrombie, John J., 84, 85;
biography, 87; 104, 201
Accotinck Creek, 114, 115,
117
Alexander, Lt., 187
Alexandria, 34, 35, 40, 41, 44,
62, 66, 71, 89, 114
Alexandria-Arlington line, 57,
59
Alleghanies, 40
American Revolution, army
of, 2
Anaconda Plan, 72
Anderson, Robert, surrender
of Sumter, 1, 4
Andrew, Gov., 5
Annandale, 81
Annapolis, 19, 25
Antietam, 221
Arlington, 34, 35, 40, 61, 81
Army of North-Eastern
Virginia, 59, 60, 63, 71, 77,
78, 81; weaknesses of,
121-123; 133, 141, 175, 177,
189, 191, 193, 194, 197, 198,
201, 203, 208, 219
Army of Pennsylvania, 47
Army of the Potomac, 219,
221
Army of the Upper Potomac,
53, 84, 87, 88, 90, 92, 93, 97,
99, 103, 105, 108, 110, 200,
204
Army of the Valley, 45

Artillery, 2; Patterson, 27, 51,
52, 58, 99; Doubleday, 52,
53; 55, 66, 68, 70;
McDowell, 75; 76, 85, 90;
Sandford, 94; 101, 103, 106,
128, 139, 143; Parrott gun,
145; 146; Burnside, 148, 150;
151, 153, 157; Griffin, 162;
164, 165; Henry House Hill,
169, 170, 172, 174, 177;
Centreville, 179, 182, 183,
187, 189; summary, 192, 193,
201; 213, 217; Bull Run
summary, 221
Averell, W. W., 171
Ayres, 128, 129, 157, 221

Ball's Cross Roads, 69
Baltimore, 19, 25, 27, 29, 30,
31, 43, 44
Baltimore & Ohio Railroad, 19,
49, 50, 213
Barnard, John, 125, 128-130,
132, 133, 135; summary,
216-218
Barne's Mill, 118
Barry, William F., 145, 162,
163, 165, 169, 170, 172, 174,
176, 187, 188; biography,
193; summary, 216-218, 221
Beauregard, G. T., 76, 77, 81,
111, 135, 203
Beckwith, Capt., 94
Benjamin, 128

274

INDEX

DATE DUE